MW01097701

Fly Fishing Guide to the Colorado River and Tributaries

Hatches, Fly Patterns, and Guide's Advice

TO - Scott

Bob Dye

STACKPOLE BOOKS

Guilford, Connecticut

Published by Stackpole Books
An imprint of The Rowman & Littlefield Publishing Group, Inc.
4501 Forbes Boulevard, Suite 200, Lanham, Maryland 20706
www.rowman.com

Distributed by
NATIONAL BOOK NETWORK
800-462-6420

Copyright © 2018 by Bob Dye

All rights reserved. No part of this book may be reproduced in any form or by any electronic or mechanical means, including information storage and retrieval systems, without written permission from the publisher, except by a reviewer who may quote passages in a review.

British Library Cataloguing in Publication Information available

Library of Congress Cataloging-in-Publication Data
Names: Dye, Bob (Fly fishing guide), author.
Title: Fly fishing guide to the Colorado River and tributaries hatches, fly patterns, and guide's advice / Bob Dye.
Description: Guilford, Connecticut : Stackpole Books, [2018] | Includes bibliographical references and index.
Identifiers: LCCN 2018003019 (print) | LCCN 2018004094 (ebook) | ISBN 9780811766869 | ISBN 9780811737241 (paperback) | ISBN 9780811766869 (ebook)
Subjects: LCSH: Fly fishing—Colorado River (Colo.-Mexico)—Guidebooks.
Classification: LCC SH456 (ebook) | LCC SH456 .D94 2018 (print) | DDC 799.12/4097925—dc23
LC record available at https://lccn.loc.gov/2018003019

♾™ The paper used in this publication meets the minimum requirements of American National Standard for Information Sciences—Permanence of Paper for Printed Library Materials, ANSI/NISO Z39.48-1992.

Printed in the United States of America

Contents

Acknowledgments

I was fortunate enough to fish the Colorado River as a young kid and have now spent most of my guiding career learning its hidden secrets. Shortly after I started this project, I realized I was going to need a ton of help. Thankfully, quite a few guys and gals make the Colorado River what it is today, from the angler who visits the river on a regular basis to all the hardworking people at Colorado Parks & Wildlife and the Bureau of Land Management. Fortunately for me, a bunch of other guides, fly fishers, and outdoor enthusiasts know the Colorado River intimately, and thanks to their input, this project was possible.

First, I want to extend a sincere thanks to Pat Dorsey and Landon Mayer for all their help in guiding me through this venture. Second, I have fished or guided with a number of ladies and gentleman whose contributions, whether photography, fly patterns, or techniques, have certainly added to my knowledge of the vast sport of fly fishing. These extraordinary people include Jim Cannon, Pat Dorsey, Landon Mayer, Mark Adams, Jonathon Keisling, Jim Neiberger, Deborah Dye, John Barr, Dean Billington, Jay Nichols, Scott Willoughby, Trent Tatum, Eric Aune, Stuart Birdsong, J. J. Randolph, Seth Kapust, Brett Van Rensselaer, Art Van Rensselaer, Adrian Keeler, Bob Dye Senior, Dave Pinkerton, John Perizzolo, Mathew Thomas, Billy Berger, Teri Parvin, Joe Shafer, Jerry Vigil, Steve Parrott, Jeremy Hyatt, Terry and Lori Nicholson, Dick Mill, J Core, Richard Pilatzke, Ryan Hempkins, Sara Barclay, Scott Harkins, Steve Schweitzer, Greg Garcia, Chris Steinbeck, Cody Scott, Dave Dickensheets, Eric Atha, Mike Kruise, Kelli Blue, Casey Blue, and John Gonzales. I also include several fly shops: The Blue Quill Angler, Angler's All, Cutthroat Anglers, Breckenridge Outfitters, and Roaring Fork Anglers.

Lastly, I think most anglers that have made a career of guiding or just enjoy the art of fly fishing had one or two people who influenced them in the sport that they grew to love. I was fortunate enough to have two. My dad, who was a school principal, had the summertime free, which enabled us to spend countless hours on the river. I can remember using worms and Pautzke's Balls O' Fire as a young kid, but always keeping an eye on fly fishers we encountered on the stream. While these encounters definitely sparked my interest, it was not till my dad bought me the first edition of Jack Dennis's fly-tying book that I completely immersed myself in the sport. From there, I experienced a great number of accomplishments and failures as I soon realized how instinctively intelligent trout are.

It was not until my late teen years that I met a fly fisherman who seemed to have all the answers when it came to fooling fish on a regular basis. Jim Neiberger was that guy, and the times he took me fishing, it was always the same scenario: Jim would land 25, and I would land 4 or 5. Nowadays, when I look back, I realize that Jim taught me more about the sport of fly fishing than anybody, and not only was he extremely influential in my fishing career, but he contributed countless hours of photography, flies, and advice to this book project. So for all his hard work and keeping me on life's right path, I am truly thankful.

The Colorado River is one of the West's most formidable trout streams. It encompasses just about every style of trout water there is, from long riffles to deep plunge pools. Anglers could fish it for a year and never cover it all. MARK ADAMS

Introduction

When I was a boy, my father took my brother and me on several outdoor adventures, including numerous elk hunting trips and what seemed like nonstop fishing trips. We felt fortunate to have a father who not only enjoyed fishing and hunting, but who had, as a school principal, most of the summer free. This allowed me to submerse myself for days in Colorado's rivers and small creeks.

I didn't start fly fishing until I was about 10 years old; however, the tools needed were being honed by countless hours of drowning worms and salmon eggs and learning over time that dead-drifting live bait was more effective than dragging those presentations through the water. I vividly remember fishing the Crystal River just outside of Marble, Colorado, on a hot July afternoon. It seemed like every trout in the river was taking insects off the top of the surface, when an old gentleman startled me: "Catching any?" "A few on worms," I replied. As I made my way towards him, he asked if I had ever casted a fly rod. I told him I had a few times in beaver ponds, but never really casted a fly rod in a river. For the next couple hours, he spent time showing me the true nature of the sport, and from that point forward, it was the only thing I could think about.

As the years rolled by, my dad got so tired of me asking "Can we go fishing again?" that he began taking me and a friend from the neighborhood on weekend trips. The funny thing about this was that he would drop us off on a Friday afternoon and come pick us back up on Sunday. Nowadays, if you did that with your kids, you would be arrested. But those trips were definitely the beginning of my figuring out fly fishing and realizing this was something that I wasn't going to forget about as time went on.

As I started fishing different rivers, one always topped my list when it came to fly-fishing opportunities, and that was the Colorado River. Whether it was the scenery or the scent of the sagebrush after a rain, this waterway quickly became stuck in my head for years to come.

The author scoops up a nice brown.

MARK ADAMS

The Colorado River below Windy Gap Reservoir, west of the town of Granby, offers public fishing as well as scenic views. JIM NEIBERGER

From high atop the western side of the Continental Divide, the Colorado River descends through some of the West's most scenic landscapes. While the river extends 1,490 miles to the Gulf of California, it is in the state of Colorado that it is most important to fly fishers. Anglers can take advantage of this extraordinary resource, from fishing a small creek in the high country to floating one of the West's most formidable rivers. Like most rivers, the Colorado is in a state of constant change, but through it all, from years of heavy snowpack to periods of severe drought, it remains one of the state's top fishing destinations.

The Colorado River is without a doubt the lifeblood of the state. From its humble beginnings in Rocky Mountain National Park to the drift-boat-driven sections of the lower river, there is an amazing diversity of water. Some of the West's finest trout streams feed its flow on its journey through the state, including the Fraser River, Troublesome Creek, Williams Fork River, Blue River, Muddy Creek, Piney River, Eagle River, and Roaring Fork River. In addition to the Colorado River, anglers have a lifetime of opportunities to fish these major tributaries, and for the angler that enjoys a more intimate experience, there are important creeks such as Beaver Creek, Reeder Creek, Derby Creek, Deep Creek, Grizzly Creek, No Name Creek, Canyon Creek, and Elk Creek—all of which would take years to cover with a fly rod.

The Colorado River and its tributaries also have some of the finest insect hatches of any river in the country. From its famed Salmonfly hatch from the Two Bridges boat launch all the way to Hot Sulphur Springs to its consistent midge, Blue-Winged

Olive, Pale Morning Dun, Yellow Sally, Red Quill, Trico, and caddis hatches, there is always something hatching along the river system.

To top it off, the Colorado is a year-round fishery. The upper river has six dams along its path, and besides providing year-round fishing in their tailwaters, these reservoirs add much-needed cold water to the river system down below. The lower Colorado, including the Roaring Fork River all the way down to Silt, fishes well throughout the season, but it is an overlooked winter fishery. Even when the water is high or off-color, especially due to runoff in June, you can often find fishable conditions in one of the six tailwaters: Shadow Mountain Reservoir, Granby Reservoir, Willow Creek Reservoir (part of the Big Thompson Water Project and has limited access) Williams Fork Reservoir, Wolford Mountain Reservoir, and Green Mountain Reservoir.

Many people make a living from this great river, and many are responsible for keeping the river healthy. I happen to fall in both of those categories. I have spent over 35 years fishing the entire system, learning its tendencies, weather patterns, insect life, and most importantly, the behavior of its fish. With so many anglers and other outdoor enthusiasts using the river on a daily basis, I decided to write this book and share my knowledge with all the people who enjoy this tremendous river system. Those who use the river are like the tributaries of the river itself: If one part of the system fails, the whole system crashes.

The Colorado River perched above Little Gore Canyon. The Colorado offers a multitude of outdoor recreational activities. BOB DYE

FISH SPECIES

Trout inhabit the Colorado River from Rocky Mountain National Park (RMNP) all the way down to Silt. Due to the variety of water conditions throughout this long stretch, different species predominate. Generally speaking, the Colorado is a big freestone river, but several reservoirs alter the fish habitat, especially in the river's upper reaches. The stretch between RMNP and Hot Sulphur Springs has the greatest diversity of trout species: Brookies, browns, rainbows, Colorado River cutthroat, and cutbows inhabit most of the river here, but kokanee salmon and an occasional lake trout can be caught below Shadow Mountain.

From Windy Gap down toward State Bridge (Middle Park), whirling disease decimated rainbow trout populations and basically turned the river into a brown trout fishery. While the browns have flourished under these conditions, rainbows have recently started taking a stronger stand in this section of river.

Moving downstream, the section between Kremmling and State Bridge is mostly made up of browns and rainbows, with browns still composing most of the biomass. Below Gore Canyon marks the first point where mountain whitefish can be found. Whitefish are truly one of Colorado's native fish, the other being the greenback cutthroat. Don't be surprised to hook up with an occasional Colorado River cutthroat; while this species was once more prevalent, anglers still have a shot at one of these elusive fish.

While mountain whitefish cruise the rest of the river's passage through Silt, the section between State Bridge and Dotsero primarily consists of brown trout. The reason for this is the high water temperatures during the summer. If Colorado has a below-average snowpack year, these temperatures can rise to 75°F. Browns have

This rainbow fell for a size 16 Prince Nymph. This fly should be in every angler's fly box when fishing the Colorado River and its tributaries. BOB DYE

a much higher tolerance for warmer water than rainbows, but expect to catch a few rainbows along this stretch.

With the addition of the Eagle and Roaring Fork Rivers, the Colorado's rainbow populations become more prevalent, and some sizable rainbows can be caught in the stretches between Dotsero and Silt. From Glenwood Springs downstream, some unfamiliar fish can turn up at the end of your line, including pikeminnows, humpback chubs, razorback suckers, and squawfish. All of these fish have an endangered species designation and should be released back into the water immediately.

The Colorado River has several issues facing its overall health, and one of the most glaring is water demand. With the Front Range growing at a fast rate, the demand for water is ever increasing. Much of the Colorado River is diverted from the Western Slope over the Continental Divide and onto the eastern slope via the Big Thompson Water Project. Trout are a sensitive species and require cold, clean, oxygenated water. If water levels drop below historic flows and remain there for prolonged periods, water temperatures climb and the oxygen in the water dissolves. This puts a lot of stress on trout populations, not to mention the increase in the mortality rate of caught-and-released fish. Furthermore, without flushable flows, silt builds up between the rocks and boulders in the river and begins to take a toll on the aquatic life that lives in the substrate on the river bottom. Less water, more silt, and less aquatic life equals lower fish populations. So while a couple of drought years can make an impact on a river, many years of low-water conditions can spell disaster.

All is not lost, however. The Colorado River in Colorado remains a top fishery, and while it shares many of the issues that face western rivers, there are many things anglers and outdoor enthusiasts can do to ensure the Colorado and all trout streams maintain a healthy balance. One of the largest organizations committed to conserving, protecting, and enhancing coldwater fisheries is Trout Unlimited. Contact your local chapter and learn how you can get involved in protecting your favorite fishery

Rainbow Trout

Rainbows were historically the predominant trout species in the upper sections of the Colorado from Hot Sulphur Springs to Kremmling until being decimated by whirling disease in the 1980s. Despite several attempts in the 1990s by the Colorado Division of Wildlife to restore rainbow trout populations to the Colorado River, the light was beginning to dim.

In 2002 there was a glimmer of hope when a German researcher studying the effects of the whirling disease parasite across Europe found a strain of rainbow trout to be resistant. He named it Hofer after his family's hatchery. The Hofer-crossed strain is now working its magic in the upper reaches of the Colorado River. The idea is to get these fish to naturally reproduce to lessen the amount of stocking needed to restore rainbows to the upper Colorado.

Due to the continuing efforts of Colorado Parks & Wildlife (CPW), Hofer rainbow trout are starting to rebound in this section. Most of the fish are in the 10- to 12-inch range, but several 16- to 19-inch rainbows were caught during the 2015 season.

From Kremmling to Dotsero, you will mostly catch brown trout, though you do have a chance to catch rainbows in the 14- to 16-inch range in the slower deep pools

Rainbow trout like this one may not be as plentiful on certain sections of the river as they once were, but due to the continuing efforts of Colorado Parks & Wildlife, their numbers are beginning to rebound. BOB DYE

This wild rainbow is starting to shed its parr marks. The Colorado's rainbow population has dwindled over the years partly due to the whirling disease that affected the river in the late 1980s. JIM NEIBERGER

during cold months and the fastest, most oxygenated riffled water during hot weather. When aquatic insect hatches come off the river, these rainbows always seem to be the first in the feeding lane off of gravel shelves and mid-seam currents. From State Bridge to Dotsero, however, I have on occasion found pockets of numerous bows. It seems that one week you find them in one stretch of river, and the next week they are in another. Constantly changing water flows and changing water temperatures keep these fish, which average 12 to 15 inches, on the move for the most favorable conditions. Look for these trout to hang around the numerous tributary creeks that feed the Colorado River in this section of water.

The stretch of river between Dotsero and Silt has the largest rainbow trout population. Several main tributaries, such as the Eagle River, Roaring Fork River, and Grizzly Creek, help keep this section of river in the prime temperature zone for rainbows. Fish average between 12 and 16 inches, but the river grows several rainbows over the 20-inch mark. This piece of water has several deep stretches to it, and with its numerous shelves and drop-offs, it is prime rainbow habitat. It can be one of the best dry-fly sections along the entire river, especially during the months of March and April when midges, Blue-Winged Olives, and caddis start to appear on the water.

Brown Trout

Since the introduction of whirling disease in the late 1980s, brown trout have taken over the river system. Browns have a much higher tolerance for high water temperatures, low-water conditions, and even slightly polluted waterways. With many of the rivers in the West falling victim to urban development, it is easy to see why brown trout predominate.

Browns have done well in the river system over the last 15 years or so and now make up most of the biomass in the river's upper reaches. While many anglers are under the belief that browns are native to Colorado, this is not quite true. In fact, they were introduced in the eastern United States in 1883 and did not arrive in Colorado until the mid-1890s.

Browns are one of my favorite fish species to chase on a daily basis. They can be sipping Blue-Winged Olive emergers one minute, and be slamming a streamer the

Brown trout have thrived in most of Colorado's fisheries since their introduction in the late 1800s and are now one of the most sought-after game fish in the West. BOB DYE

Buck browns like this one can make a day fishing the Colorado River a rewarding one.
MARK ADAMS

next. When browns reach a certain size, they are not eating small midge patterns; rather, they have changed their feeding habits to prey on other fish. This elusive trout has thrived in the river system, and with their yearly spawning rituals, have produced year classes of fish ranging from 4 to 24 inches. From March through October, you can bring a different year class of fish to the net each day. One day it seems all the 16- to 19-inch fish are feeding, and then you don't see those fish for a week and a different year class takes their place. In 2014 CPW electroshocked a 17-pound brown near the Pumphouse Recreation Site. Though uncommon, these brutes are in the river.

Mountain Whitefish

Mountain whitefish are indigenous to some of the West's finest trout rivers. The Colorado River is home to these underappreciated fish from Rifle all the way up to Gore Canyon, near Kremmling. The mountain whitefish can also be found in some of the Colorado River's main tributaries and smaller creeks, such as the Roaring Fork River, lower Eagle River, Canyon Creek, Grizzly Creek, and Deep Creek. They prefer cold, clean water and generally seek out the deepest parts of the river.

Mountain whitefish range in size from 6 to 20 inches, with the most common being around the 16-inch mark, but several top the scales at over 5 pounds. They will compete with trout for food, but their presence is usually the sign of a healthy trout river. Over the years I've heard anglers refer to them as "trash fish," but they were here long before nonnative species were introduced. They have saved my day more times than not and are a good fighting fish.

Whitefish are found in great numbers in the Colorado River and some of its tributaries. While some anglers consider them trash fish, they are indigenous to several western rivers and can keep the rod bent on tough trout days. JIM NEIBERGER

Colorado River Cutthroat Trout

Colorado River cutthroat trout can be found in the river's upper reaches from Rocky Mountain National Park through Silt, Colorado. While their numbers have declined due to unstable water flows, mining, climate change, and degradation, they still have a way of finding the end of your line from time to time. In the 2015 guide season, I could count on both hands how many were landed, but you will still catch them on occasion. Generally speaking, they can be found in the same type of water as browns and rainbows—it's just a matter of how lucky you are on a given day. These vividly colored trout average between 12 and 16 inches.

Colorado River cutthroat trout are not as plentiful as the river's other species, but a few can be found throughout the river system. HECKY HECKENDORF

Kokanee salmon are a formidable sport fish found in certain sections of the upper Colorado River. One of the best places to catch them is the section between Shadow Mountain Reservoir and Granby Reservoir. JIM NEIBERGER

Kokanee Salmon

Kokanee salmon migrate out of the reservoirs and into the streams that feed them during early fall. These hard-fighting fish have over 50 years of residency thanks to Colorado Parks & Wildlife and are established in over 25 locations. While most of the Colorado River is not known for kokanee salmon runs, the section of stream between Shadow Mountain Reservoir and Granby Reservoir is at times one of the best places to find these fish. They will start showing up in the river in September; however, fishing is prohibited October 1 through December 31 for spawning salmon. CPW uses this time to milk the salmon for future stockings.

When the kokanees show up in the river, it's not the pattern of the fly but rather its color that matters most. I've usually found purple, blue, and pink San Juan Worms work the best. Some of these kokanees can reach 4 or 5 pounds, but 1-pounders seem to be the most common. Other areas of interest for kokanee salmon along the Colorado River corridor include Wolford Mountain Reservoir, Williams Fork Reservoir, and Green Mountain Reservoir.

Seasons of the Colorado

The Colorado River is a big waterway, and weather, tributaries, and reservoir levels all play a huge part in how different sections are fishing. For the best results, anglers need to do a little homework before trekking out. Checking water flow data or contacting local fly shops can mean the difference between a good day on the water and a day struggling with tough fishing conditions.

The Colorado is constantly changing from day to day, and what worked one day may not work the next. Since the river is controlled by six reservoirs upstream, water temperatures play a vital role in what insect hatches are available to the trout. Pumphouse, for example, has two reservoirs above it, and when generous amounts of water are sent downstream, it can affect the fishing, sometimes for the best and sometimes not. As water temperatures change throughout the season, so does the insect life that inhabits the river. Timing is everything when targeting the river's fish. For example, if the river was running at 1,300 cfs on a day in July when Pale Morning Duns were hatching and the fish were eating emergers and a day later it's

Colorado's changing weather can be about as up and down as the river itself. Wearing layers is a smart choice when fishing the river, especially during spring and fall months. JIM NEIBERGER

running at 2,000 cfs, larger attractor flies are probably going to be the ticket. Fly fishing is a lot like the river flows themselves—they both have their highs and lows.

In the prime times of summer, many rivers receive a ton of angling pressure, and the Colorado is no different. If you show up at your favorite stretch of water and there are anglers standing in your favorite holes, try locating fish in the nonobvious lies. For example, during the summer, fish are spread out over the entire river. Try fishing the fastest part of the riffles, or pick off a few of the trout that are hugging the banks in that stretch. Oftentimes a bowling ball–size rock in the middle of fast water is enough to hold a fish or two. These areas tend to get overlooked. Another example is to change the times you are on the water. Anglers often show up at 9 a.m. and have had enough by 4 p.m. or so, but some of the best fishing happens in the evening hours. While I enjoy fishing throughout the year, some of my best days are in the wintertime. Although insect hatches are at their lowest point, so are the number of anglers.

SPRING

March

Average flow in cfs: upper, 81–183; middle, 537–737; lower, 1,480–1,910

Even though the lower river (Dotsero to Silt) has been fishing well through the winter, lengthening days warm the water, and March brings the first signs of insect hatches. On the lower river you will encounter incredible midge hatches and by the middle of March, Blue-Winged Olives. Around St. Patrick's Day the sections between Kremmling and State Bridge and State Bridge to Dotsero shed their ice pack (in a normal snowpack year) and fishing can be outstanding for trout that have not seen a fly for about three months.

I have usually found Saint Patrick's Day to be the beginning of the fishing season in the middle river. Trout that have been docile through the winter are eager to put on the feed bag with the

John Gonzales fights the elements and this respectable brown on an early spring day near Radium. The weather in Colorado is unpredictable, but being prepared can make for a great day on the water. BOB DYE

Much of the Colorado begins to freeze up by December and is unfishable till the longer days of spring begin to unlock the river. Most years mid-March marks the beginning of the fishing season on these sections of water. BOB DYE

warming water temperatures. Rainbows are definitely on the move in an effort to find spawning grounds, and the browns and whitefish are becoming more energetic due to the increase in aquatic insects. Midge fishing can be good near the Kemp-Breeze units off US Highway 40 just below Parshall. Though midge larvae and pupae are the main game, you should plan on encountering rising fish as well, especially in the upper stretches around Parshall.

On the lower river, rising fish are more hit-and-miss due to fluctuating water temperatures "I have seen blanket hatches this time of year in March," explains Billy Berger, guide for the Mountain Angler fly shop in Breckenridge. The little bugs will start coming off the water around 9 a.m. I usually start fishing the slow water in the morning and, as the hatch progresses, move up along shelves and slower riffles. In addition to midges, worm (annelids) and free-living caddis patterns also work well.

Though much of the upper river is locked in ice, the stretch of water downstream of the Williams Fork confluence and the lower river from Glenwood Springs to Silt can provide good midge fishing. In March the Kemp-Breeze units downstream from the town of Parshall start to have good midge fishing, even though this area is extremely cold during the winter. The tailwaters that feed the Colorado—the Williams Fork, Shadow Mountain, Granby, and Green Mountain Reservoirs—are also good places to start.

Checking flows on these tailwaters is a must: Without significant flows, they can fish slow in the spring. For example, if the Williams Fork has a flow of 20 cfs, and sometimes it does, it probably is going to be a tough day. Look for flows in early spring to be in the 60 to 100 cfs range for optimal fishing conditions. Shadow

Midges are prevalent in the river system 365 days a year and make up 90 percent of the trout's diet during the winter and early spring months. Carrying a variety of colors and sizes will ensure you match the hatch when it presents itself on the water. JAY NICHOLS

Mountain and Granby rely on generous flows to move fish into the tailwater sections below them. Again, if flows are in the 20 to 40 cfs range, there is probably not going to be the number of fish found at 200 cfs or higher. Green Mountain Reservoir typically has flows between 100 and 200 cfs through the winter and early spring prior to runoff. This can be a good cold-weather option.

Though the water below the Williams Fork to the Kemp-Breeze units fishes well in the winter, it really comes alive in March and April. Look for mega midge hatches to begin about the third week of March and last well into April. This can be the first really great dry-fly fishing of the year. The first Blue-Winged Olives can hatch as early as the first week April and can become a daily event through the entire month.

The best midge fishing occurs in sections of river with longer wide riffles followed by long slicks and slower pools. Silt that has been trapped in the slower water provides nutrient-rich midge habitat, and the hatches along this stretch can be prolific. On the lower river this is evident around the Pumphouse-Radium areas. Holes such as Crescent Moon, Beaver Run, and Miller Time all provide excellent midge fishing. Look for areas coming out of a riffle into the slower glass-like water. Trout either will be taking the larvae or emergers coming down the current or will be picking these insects off in the calm water while they are trying to reach the surface.

As March transitions into April on the lower river, some of the best caddis hatches can occur anywhere along the river. Look for these insects (Brachycentridae) to become active about the second week of April starting around Silt, and if conditions are right and water temps hold around 50 degrees, look for the caddis hatch to progress upriver through the entire month. Worm patterns also become very important spring selections.

April

Average flow in cfs: upper, 190–352; middle, 748–1,160; lower, 1,940–3,650

As the middle of April approaches, Blue-Winged Olives (*Baetis*) begin to appear and on the right day can come off in impressive numbers. The Colorado River still has its best BWO hatches in the upper reaches around Parshall, but the hatches between Pumphouse and State Bridge are nothing to sneeze at. On the middle river, April brings hatches of BWOs and good fishing at the Sunset lease, Kemp-Breeze units, Lone Buck lease, Paul Gilbert lease, Byers Canyon, and Pioneer Park in Hot Sulphur Springs.

As soon as the first BWOs start to hatch, I generally run a midge/egg combo with or without a third fly—a size 22 Post Foam Emerger to emulate emerging midges and *Baetis*. While the water is still cold, it warms enough to get these fish functioning again, particularly between 10 a.m. and 3 p.m. Granted, they normally will not be in the faster parts of a riffle, but pay attention to the water that drops off of shelves. Trout will congregate in these areas in an effort to feed heavily on the insects filtering into their feeding lies. Fish that missed your presentation in the first part of the run will be more than likely to hit your emerging pattern before it exits the hole.

Often towards the end of April, warmer temperatures that hold in the mid-50s or low 60s for several days will cause the river to rise from a normal 400 to 600

Landon Mayer holds a quality brown that was taken on a size 22 Landon Tube Midge during the month of April in the Kemp-Breeze units. These midge patterns are extremely effective when trout are taking midge emergers. BOB DYE

Springtime conditions can vary wildly, as John Gonzales of Littleton can attest. This trout was hooked in a mid-seam current just above the bridge in Radium on a size 22 Stalcup's Baetis Nymph. BOB DYE

cfs to 700 or higher. While the water turns off-color, it turns many anglers away as well. However, the rising water dislodges lots of food, and the trout can really put on the feed bags. During this period it is time to stop thinking about what's hatching and dig out the "big flies"—hello 3X. Anglers that are not scared by a little dirty water start licking their chops. Stoneflies, aquatic worms, and cased caddis become the food source during these pre-runoff surges of water. Patterns should include Pat's Rubber Legs, Pine Squirrel Leeches, San Juan Worms, large Hare's Ears, and multiple big, ugly beaded patterns. The trout typically will not be holding in the fast water; they will be just outside the faster current, letting the water bring the dislodged food to them. Finding the softer edges along runs is the key.

Eventually another round of cold weather brings stability to the river, and the fish resume normal feeding habits. The Pumphouse to State Bridge stretch is great walk-wade water from mid-March through April. While higher water is on the way and accessing the river from a drift boat will become more efficient, take advantage of these early months' low-water conditions.

Though March and April can offer outstanding fishing, weather has to be taken into account anywhere along the Colorado River. Over the years I have had plenty of 50- and 60-degree days during the spring, but heavy snowfall and windy conditions are to be expected. After all, March and April are generally the wettest months on record for the Colorado high country.

Rainbow Spawn

During the 1980s the Colorado River had good populations of rainbow trout, especially from Hot Sulphur Springs down to Kremmling and Glenwood Springs down to Silt. The river's middle stretches never really boasted huge numbers because of water temperatures during the late summer months. Since the introduction of whirling disease, some of these populations have declined dramatically. Some of the historic spawning grounds these trout once used disappeared when the genetic strains died out. But now with Colorado Parks & Wildlife's continual stocking of disease-resistant rainbow trout, these fish are finding their own spawning grounds and hopefully passing them to new generations of fish.

Mature rainbow trout will use the same spawning gravel as brown trout, but at different times of the year. Browns spawn in the fall, and rainbows spawn in early spring, usually mid-March through mid-May. During these months great care must be taken while fishing the river. Spawning beds are extremely fragile, and with all the trouble the rainbow population has had over the years, it is extremely important to give these fish a fighting chance to repopulate the river. Make it a point while out on the water not to walk through spawning beds. ■

Rainbow trout have endured many hardships throughout the years, including low-water conditions and whirling disease. With the help of Trout Unlimited and Colorado Parks & Wildlife, these fish remain in the river for all anglers to enjoy. JIM NEIBERGER

May

Average flow in cfs: upper, 370–973; middle, 1,180–2,390; lower, 3,790–10,200

As May approaches, look for slight discoloration of the water on the river's upper reaches, and in a normal water year, dirty water in the river's lower stretches. This does not mean, however, that the Colorado River will not fish well. May can offer outstanding fishing opportunities, particularly in the sections between Hot Sulphur Springs and Kremmling, and if everything falls into place, the stretch between Kremmling and State Bridge. The early part of May brings good caddis hatches to the river's upper regions on days when the air temperatures climb into the upper 60s.

Giant stonefly nymphs (*Pteronarcys*) begin to get active with the warming water temperatures. I usually try to hit State Bridge to Hot Sulphur Springs during early May because in a high-snowpack year, the water is too high and dirty to fish the stonefly hatch effectively when it finally rolls around the first week of June.

May can be hit-and-miss on the Colorado. Some of the river's largest hatches happen this time of year, but certain water conditions can make for tough sledding. I rely on the USGS water graph this time of year. Flows that are stable between 700 and 800 cfs for the first two weeks of May usually mean pack your vehicle and go fishing. Flows that spike upwards from the norm usually mean muddy water. Fishing the Colorado below Gore Canyon this time of year, anglers rarely see clear water, but fishing when there's just a couple of inches of water clarity can spell disaster.

Pontoon boats can sometimes be a safer way to navigate the river during the high flows of runoff. Checking flows during May, June, and July is a must when floating the Colorado River.

JIM NEIBERGER

When this happens, I usually find myself driving toward the Parshall area in search of better water conditions. But on days when there is 1 to 2 feet of clarity, it can be some of the best fishing this time of year.

Brachycentrus caddis hatches in May can be spectacular if you can find good water conditions. Caddis begin to come on strong about the first week of May—when the water temperatures hit 50 to 55—with intermittent hatches all the way through September. The hatch starts around the State Bridge area; from there, you can follow it for a couple of weeks or so up into the Pumphouse area. Nymph with a bright attractor such as a pink San Juan Worm or pink stonefly and a caddis such as a Dorsey's Mercury Caddis or John Barr's Graphic Caddis.

While the dry-fly fishing can be as good as it gets on the upper reaches of river around Parshall, I have found that down around the Pumphouse to the State Bridge area, trout seem to be more concerned with the nymphs and emergers rather than the dries. I have had good dry-fly fishing down here at times, but generally caddis emergers work best.

By the end of May/early June, you can see the first signs of adult Salmonflies around the Two Bridges boat ramp. The hatch moves quickly upstream, all the way to Hot Sulphur Springs. One thing I like about this area is that you can travel the river system in search of the hatch. Most years the water is at runoff stage and access can be difficult.

On the lower river, as the days become longer, high-country snowmelt begins to fog up the water. Full-blown runoff is still a few weeks away, but you start noticing slight changes in rising water and water clarity. The main flow of the river is controlled by reservoirs upstream, but down here on the lower river, anglers are at the mercy of several tributary creeks (Blacktail, Sheephorn, and Piney) that can alter water flow and especially water clarity. This sounds like a negative, but it can really fish well before the onslaught of full-blown runoff. Water clarity can range from 1 to 3 feet, but this is time to bring out the box of ugly flies—you know, the one you are embarrassed to show other anglers—with the Pink Worms and Chamois Leeches. Not a lot of thought process here: Pick out a section of water that looks fishy, and let it fly. In addition to the Pink Worms and Chamois Leeches, Big Prince Nymphs, Twenty Inchers, and Rubber Legs will all take fish during these conditions. Over the years, I have caught some of my largest trout at this time, partly because I believe the larger trout feel safer poking their noses out in unfavorable water conditions versus when the water has more clarity.

June

Average flow in cfs: upper, 799–987; middle, 2,060–2,390; lower, 8,590–10,200

With the Salmonflies beginning to taper off, usually after the first week of June, the river kind of goes through a transformation era for the next few weeks. Weather conditions are usually pretty mild, but we have seen snow in June. Although some stoneflies will still appear on the river's upper stretches, by the end of June pretty much all stonefly activity comes to a halt as far as transformation of these large insects. During normal precipitation years, water levels begin to rise and runoff is in full swing. Some options for this time of the year are the waters below Shadow Mountain Reservoir, the Williams Fork, Muddy Creek, the Eagle upstream of Wolcott, the Roaring Fork River above the confluence of the Crystal River, and the Frying Pan River near Basalt.

That said, the river can fish better than you think in high water. Not just during runoff but anytime after heavy rains, muddy water can be a factor. The Colorado River system is made up of countless creeks and tributaries, and on any given day rain showers in any one of these areas can turn the water off-color. I have learned over the years to be ready for any situation that arises.

One guide trip that comes to mind was with Mik Aoki, head baseball coach at Notre Dame. I already knew the lower river was muddy, so Mik and I headed up to the Parshall area, right below the confluence of the Colorado and the Williams Fork. After a short time spent rigging our rods, Mik made a couple of presentations and an 18-inch brown came to hand. "We're gonna kill 'em today," I told him. Little did I know that we would not touch a fish for another hour and a half.

Taking a page out of the Peyton Manning handbook, "Hurry, hurry, Omaha," we took off downstream in an effort to save the day. I can vividly remember saying to myself, "What are you thinking, taking him down to water that has eight inches of visibility?" When we showed up at Pumphouse, Mik was looking at me as if I had lost my mind. I said, "Let's go down and at least try it." Tying on a bright pink San Juan Worm and some other junk, I watched his pink presentation disappear within the first foot of the water column, and all of a sudden, the indicator was swimming upstream. That day was marked by numerous browns and rainbows, with not another angler in sight.

Not every muddy water day fishes as well as that one, but it does not mean the trout will not respond either. A box full of flies that will cover your bases should include San Juan Worms in a variety of colors including pink, Chamois Leeches, large Prince Nymphs, large stonefly nymphs, and one of my favorites, the Oh Betty Fly.

SUMMER

July

Average flow in cfs: upper, 295–847; middle, 1,240–2,050; lower, 3,480–8,340

As soon as the water recedes from runoff, around the first week of July, the Colorado River really comes alive. Fish pushed into deeper runs due to the higher water now start to spread throughout the river into more traditional lies such as riffles, deep runs, and water along the banks. Weather tends to be on the warm side with daytime temperatures in the mid-80s, with almost constant afternoon rainstorms.

In addition to caddis, which have been hatching since May, July brings in Pale Morning Duns and Yellow Sallies. PMDs will continue to hatch throughout the river through the end of July, with an occasional sporadic hatch into the first two weeks of August. Yellow Sallies will come off the river consistently through July and into the first week of August.

Mik Aoki takes a stab at a brown while fishing the Crescent Moon Hole located in the river's braided section below Pumphouse. Runs that have nice riffled water followed by big deep holes usually host numerous trout.

BOB DYE

In the middle river, one of the first places I begin looking for the sulphur-colored bugs is at Sunset lease. Other areas of interest during the PMD hatch are the Kemp-Breeze units and the confluence below the Williams Fork, as well as the Williams Fork itself. PMDs also hatch in large numbers in the Glenwood Canyon stretch and the Kremmling to State Bridge section. If the water conditions are right, the PMD hatches can be exceptional. Sometimes there are so many insects on the move, it puts the trout in a feeding frenzy. This is when the river has almost a nervous feel to it; anglers who have experienced this can almost see the water being displaced from active trout. At this time I often fish rigs with both PMDs and Yellow Sallies on them or fish nymphs that do a fair job of representing both insects, such as Mike Mercer's Epoxy Back PMD.

Streamer fishing is also particularly good in July. For whatever reason—warmer water temperatures, oxygenated water, baitfish spread out—the larger fish move into some of the fastest riffles in the river system. After hooking numerous fish during the PMD and Yellow Sally hatches, I have started getting clients to pitch streamers to round out the day. This has become one of my change-ups in the normal rotation of pitches and has brought to net some of the larger trout of the season.

August

Average flow in cfs: upper, 141–289; middle, 1,020–1,260; Lower, 2,440–3,400

August brings some of the hottest days of the year. Rain or snowpack from the previous months can be a determining factor in how the upper river will fish. The Colorado relies on releases from Granby Reservoir and Williams Fork Reservoir to carry the river through the hot months, and some years low precipitation spells hot water temperatures during August and September. In normal water years, if

The author and John Barr watch a pod of feeding fish sipping Trico spinners in August near the Williams Fork confluence. The Colorado River has great Trico hatches that start during the dog days of August and last well into mid-October. JAY NICHOLS

the reservoirs are full, they usually send enough water to keep the temperatures at a level between the low 50s at night and mid-60s during the afternoon. These are great feeding temperatures for trout, especially brown trout.

August usually means the dog days of summer are upon us, and it is true the trout can become lethargic and seem to be napping part of the day. Fortunately, there are a couple things going on that keep their interest, mainly Tricos until about midday, followed by a menu of terrestrials such as grasshoppers, ants, and beetles. You can also encounter sporadic hatches of *Baetis*. In low-water years, I usually find it best to fish early in the morning and late in the afternoon on cloudy days. Trout tend to be more active due to slightly cooler water temperatures during these times rather than in the middle of the day.

As August wears on and depending on water flows, water temperatures can rise into the high 60s. Throughout the entire river system, this pushes feeding fish (browns as well as rainbows) into the faster, more oxygenated water, and anglers should focus their attention here. Anglers should note, however, that in low-water years temperatures can climb above 70 degrees from the mouth of Gore Canyon to Dotsero. This can be fatal to trout that are played to exhaustion, so when this occurs, try to fish in the early morning hours or later in the evening.

If you are floating, sections of rivers with short floats can provide excellent early morning and late evening fishing when water temps turn down a notch. Like most rivers in the West, especially freestone rivers in August, the Colorado can have a magic hour in the evenings. Most anglers have left the river, and trout that have been taking a siesta come to life with the setting sun.

Concentrating your efforts on faster riffles that dump into deep holes will often be your best bet, specifically in the evenings. Trout that were napping during the heat of the day seem to come to life and move up on these shelves and feed vigorously until you cannot see anymore due to darkness. Try fishing patterns that move a lot, such as a Pine Squirrel Leech or a rubber leg pattern, across these faster riffles.

The Colorado high country is in constant change; this holds true the last days of August, when nighttime temperatures can drop to the low 30s. Cooler nights signal that fall is just around the corner. Now that most of the hot days are in the rearview mirror, the river starts to stabilize. While water temperatures remain warm, they cool off just enough to be in that prime feeding zone for the trout—the high 50s to low 60s.

During late summer Tricos are still a mainstay for the trout and will remain that way through September, but Blue-Winged Olives start coming off a little more consistently, and on cloudy days full-blown hatches will occur. Depending on water storage in the reservoirs upstream, flows dip slightly to between 900 and 1,200 cfs from the mouth of Gore Canyon to Dotsero.

FALL

September

Average flow in cfs: upper, 126–144; middle, 855–1,010; lower, 2,170–2,430

September is a transitional time. With cooler nights and shorter days, water temperatures begin to cool down from the hot summer days of August. Anglers begin noticing a certain crispness in the air, and the landscape begins to change. Aspen trees turn a brilliant gold, and the underbrush sports a rainbow of colors around the river's edge. Early fall is an exceptional time to be fishing anywhere, including the Colorado River drainage. After many days guiding on the water through summer, September reenergizes me knowing that some of the best fishing lies ahead.

As the Colorado River transitions from the hot days of August into September, it begins to cool with the colder nights. Daytime temperatures can still be in the 80s, but nighttime temperatures are getting around the freezing mark. This signals change to many plants and animals in the region, and one of the first to respond are the brown trout. While they will not begin their spawning rituals until mid-October, they begin changing color like the trees around them. Some of the more mature fish begin feeding a little heavier in anticipation of the rigorous spawn ahead.

After Labor Day the rafting and kayaking traffic winds down. Even the number of anglers floating in drift boats declines. Water conditions improve for angling, and places that looked unfishable begin unveiling hidden shelves and deep dishes that were hard to read with the higher water earlier in the year. Flows this time of year are typically around 1,000 to 1,300 cfs. These flows are perfect for float fishing the river and are now getting down to where walk-wading becomes an option again. Whether you are floating or wading, concentrate your efforts on riffle runs and shelves that drop off these riffles. Even with the cooler nights of early fall, water temperatures are still optimal for fish to be active in the faster oxygenated water.

Rachel Kohler lands a fat rainbow inside the Kemp-Breeze units during a Blue-Winged Olive hatch in mid-September. The trout ended up taking a no. 22 Stalcup's Baetis Nymph as the second fly in a three-fly rig.

BOB DYE

While this section (Kemp-Breeze Units) can offer great fishing in most months (besides winter), September marks some of the best hatches the river has to offer. Trico hatches are still in full swing throughout the month, but other hatches are on their way. Blue-Winged Olives appear again, along with Red Quills. The Williams Fork, the confluence of the Williams Fork and the Colorado, the stretch above State Bridge, and the Pumphouse to Little Gore Canyon stretch of water can offer good Red Quill action. One of my favorite rigs at this time of the year is a Pine Squirrel Leech and a standard or Soft Hackle Pheasant Tail as an emerging nymph.

As September comes to a close, brown trout begin staging in certain parts of the river for their annual mating ritual, and by mid-October they are in full swing. Mature browns begin making their way to some of the river's tributaries as well as seeking out gravel bars along the river's edge and faster riffles. As these fish congregate, other fish follow to start feeding on the egg trails. Anglers should leave spawning fish alone, but the ones behind them are absolutely fair game.

Barring any late fall rainstorms, the Colorado's water clarity can be about as good as it gets during these months. This is the time when technical tactics work best. It is by no means as technical as Cheesman Canyon or other tailwaters, but fishing with flies the same size, shape, and color as the naturals is definitely important. Fishing this time of year also requires anglers to step down in tippet size. Instead of running 3X to your attractor and dropping with 4X, now is the time for 4X followed by 5X. Not only do the fish have a harder time recognizing your tippet, but smaller tippets allow the fly to drift more naturally. I usually have some sort of worm pattern (annelid) on my rig at this time of the year.

Another insect that can sneak up on you on any given day is the small mayfly known as *Pseudocloeon* (Tiny Blue-Winged Olive), or Pseudo. These little bugs should not be overlooked in the fall; if they come off in numbers, the trout will most definitely key in on them. I hate this hatch, but if you want to catch fish, you

While the low flows of fall can offer the best times to wade the mighty Colorado, it also an extremely slick river. Sometimes wading across the river in groups can be a safer way to navigate the big stream. JIM NEIBERGER

need to roll the way the river does. I usually find fishing normal BWO patterns a little smaller is enough to get the job done. When trout are taking them as emergers, come well armed with size 24 or 26 dark olive Post Foam Emergers. If the trout are rising to these little guys, try a size 26 Parachute Adams. That fly seems to work more often than not during tough situations.

October

Average flow in cfs: upper, 112–123; middle, 695–858; lower, 2,030–2,150

Most of the golden leaves have fallen, and with them most of the anglers. Colorado's big-game hunting seasons are in full swing, and most of the anglers that visited the river in the summer are now pursuing other game. As the Colorado River flows decline in October, so do its hatches. Besides a few remaining BWOs and an occasional Pseudo hatch, the river settles into primarily midges as the trout's major food source. Fishing is far from over, however: Trout will readily feed on eggs and midges through the last few weeks of October and even into November.

While the insect life has gradually become smaller, it does not mean big fly season is over. Besides feeding on eggs and midges, trout will aggressively attack properly placed streamer patterns. They are fired up because of the spawn, so their predatory instincts are in full swing. I generally always carry a rod rigged with streamer presentations to capitalize on overaggressive brown trout. I frequently

Fly fishers generally find solitude when fishing in the later fall months. Most of Colorado's outdoor population is either hunting or skiing, which bodes well for anglers. BOB DYE

nymph-fish a certain section, making sure to cover it thoroughly, then run streamer patterns through that same water.

October is when the self-sustaining population of brown trout in the Colorado typically performs its yearly spawning ritual. When Mother Nature triggers these fish to reproduce, they undergo extensive anatomical and behavioral changes. Males turn darker shades with brilliant markings, and their lower jaws begin to form into a weapon called a kype, kind of like how bull elk grow antlers before the rut. Females put on weight.

About the second week in October, fish begin to pair up and the females start to form a redd, a saucer-shaped depression in the gravel. Trout usually spawn in the faster water in order to keep oxygen and nutrients flowing over the spawning areas. Males guard the spawning areas until the females have finished constructing the redds. A mature female can produce 400 to 2,000 eggs, depending on her size, and once she is ready, she deposits them in the redd. The male then returns to fertilize the eggs, and the two will repeat the process until the female is spent (laid all her eggs). While fishing over spawning beds isn't the mark of a good angler, there are other ways to capitalize on this once-a-year event.

As the spawn reaches full swing about the third week of October, the entire river system comes alive. The brown trout are on the move, and the rainbows start to take note—they know what is coming. When the females deposit eggs in the gravel sections of the river bottom, a certain percentage washes down in the currents. This can create feeding lanes, or egg trails, to the fish that line up below the spawning browns. Eggs deposited in the faster riffles begin tumbling downstream, and the trout that are not spawning line up behind spawning fish like a herd of cattle coming to hay.

Browns in the Colorado drainage often boast large pectoral fins. River flows are constantly changing, and the fish have to adapt to their environment. PAT DORSEY

Trout eggs range in size from 2 to 8 millimeters and differ in color schemes from pale yellow to iridescent orange. After they are deposited in the river bottom, the males spray them down with their sperm (milt), and they then incubate for one to five months depending on flow and water temperature. During these months the fertilized eggs are subject to many pitfalls such as disease, predation, drought, and flooding. The eggs that are well buried in the gravel hatch into alevins, or sac fry, that are about ¾ to 1 inch long. At this stage the sac fry don't move much; rather, they rely on their enclosed yolk sac, which provides nutrients for the young trout until it is absorbed. At this point the young fish become mobile and can begin foraging for food, generally in shallow water to evade predation. During this entire process it is estimated only about 1 percent of these young fish survive until adulthood.

Average growth rates in the Colorado River vary due to the always-changing water conditions. An average or above average snowpack year usually means good aquatic life, which in turn means faster growth rates. The Colorado has its share of drought years as well. This usually equates to lower fry survival and lower growth rates. In turn, the Colorado's upper reaches around Rocky Mountain National Park have much lower growth rates due to higher elevation, colder water temperatures, and less water supply.

Being that this spawning event is so delicate, it is imperative that anglers protect spawning areas. While it's not illegal to fish over spawning fish, it's the sportsman's job to protect the natural resource. Anglers should be wary of wading in these areas in an effort not to disturb the nest. Look for 2- to 4-foot dishes that look cleaner than the natural substrate and simply walk around the beds.

Early snows begin to move in on the Colorado River by late September. By the time October rolls around, the weather can be anybody's guess on any given day. JIM NEIBERGER

While this is a special time to be on the water, anglers need to remember the importance of spawning trout. Without them, trout populations would decline and you would not leave the river a better place than you found it. Presenting flies over spawning beds is not the mark of a good fly fisher, as trout are so engaged in trying to reproduce that they will do anything to protect the nest. Educating anglers on what spawning beds look like and the importance of not walking or fishing over them insures the trout will reproduce effectively. After all, the more successful the spawn, the more fish we all have to catch. While it's the sportsman's responsibility to recognize spawning beds and stay clear of spawning fish, I think the ones below them are fair game.

While some browns will spawn through November, most of them wrap it up the first week of that month. This does not mean fishing season is over, though. Trout that have engaged in rigorous spawning activity begin to feed a little heavier for the upcoming winter.

November

Average flow in cfs: upper, 90–114; middle, 582–680; lower, 1,660–2,020

The lower river doesn't have as many spawning trout as the upper reaches, but it does have an amazing number of mountain whitefish. During the last week of October through the first two weeks of November, they begin spawning. Browns and rainbows stack up in the water column behind these spawning whitefish, and while this is not unusual, it makes for a great day of fishing.

By the time November rolls around, the Colorado River experiences some its lowest boat traffic of the year. This can be a great time to float the river hassle-free. JIM NEIBERGER

Buck and hen browns that have gone through the rigors of their spawn are actively looking to put on a few pounds before the upcoming winter. Most of the bug life has packed it in for the year, with the exception of consistent midge hatches and a few sporadic Pseudos. While midges are readily available, whitefish eggs pack more of a protein punch. Browns will feed heavily on these small ⅛- to ³⁄₁₆-inch eggs, which range in color from a whitish cream to pale peach. I fish a smaller egg, usually tied on a size 22 Tiemco 2487, using Mcflyfoam egg-tying material; the color "Early Girl" matches whitefish eggs perfectly.

Before long, as November wears on, water temperatures begin to slowly shut down the Colorado River. However, the

Mike Lyons prepares to land a fish on a cold mid-November day. Trout in the Colorado River use this month to fatten up before the onslaught of winter takes hold on the water. JIM NEIBERGE

Some anglers are willing to defy the weather to put a few trout in the net on a 12-degree day in late November on the river's upper-middle section near Gore Canyon. BOB DYE

Dr. Eric Atha is one of the state's great anglers. Here the author lends a hand scooping up one of his fish during an outing in mid-November. JIM NEIBERGER

stretch between Hot Sulphur and Kremmling generally will stay open through November, until winter finally takes hold and shuts down most of the water. This is still a productive time, with midges and a few smaller mayflies making up the trout's diet. Trout begin moving back into their slow-water winter homes. Egg-and-midge rigs are money in the deeper, slower-moving water.

As the days roll on through November, winter starts to set in and fishing becomes more difficult. All the hatches with the exception of midges come to an end. Trout still have to feed, but access becomes an angler's biggest obstacle. While the upper river settles in for winter, there is still fishing to be had on the lower sections of the Colorado River.

WINTER

December through February

Average flow in cfs: upper, 78; middle, 515–539; lower, 1,410–1,440

Wintertime usually finds anglers giving up the fly rod for a pair of skis or taking a break until the warmth of spring lures them back into the outdoors. There is no question about it: Winter fishing can be tough, with cold water temps, inactive fish, and less aquatic life. Nevertheless, trout still have to feed, and on the right day, winter fishing can be rewarding.

Mathew Thomas prepares to drop his Boulder Boatworks drift boat at the Dino Hole boat ramp in February. Much of the lower section is floatable year-round. While nearby rivers such as the Frying Pan and Roaring Fork are noted for winter angling, you can have awesome winter fishing on the Colorado as well. PAT DORSEY

While the upper river is locked with ice much of the winter, the lower section from Glenwood Canyon to Silt can be one of the best winter destinations in the state. Furthermore, the Glenwood Springs area is also a launching-off point for the Frying Pan and Roaring Fork Rivers, which fish extremely well during the winter. Glenwood is full of great hotels, restaurants, and bars—and, of course, the hot springs—making it a great place to spend a couple days. Weather can be relatively mild (Glenwood Springs sits at 5,761 feet above sea level) and daytime highs can sometimes be in the 40s and low 50s, making it a great fishing destination at a time when most of Colorado's fishing community has hung up their waders for the season and grabbed their skis.

Not only can winter fishing be excellent, but the low flows in the lower stretches (1,200 to 1,500 cfs) allow you to get to know the river's structure intimately. This knowledge will serve you well when the river is at higher flows during the summer. On milder days you can float the Roaring Fork and the Colorado, though at this time of the year the Colorado offers some of its best walk-wading opportunities.

When planning a winter fishing trip in the Glenwood Springs area, concentrating your efforts around the slower water near Two Rivers Park is a good place to start. Other areas of importance in this section are the Roaring Fork River, especially right in the town of Glenwood Springs; the South Canyon Bridge area; the water down in West Glenwood (Ford Hole); the Canyon Creek area; and the water up from the Dino Hole boat launch. Moving a little farther downstream, the water between New Castle and Silt can offer awesome midge fishing during February and March.

All of these areas have slow, deep holding areas that on the right day can offer great winter fishing.

By the time the end of November spools around, trout are starting to migrate to the deep, slow pools. The flows are at their lowest of the year, and the trout are concentrated. Besides finding the fish, there is not a lot of thought process that goes into catching them. Sure, there is always some kind of insect floating down the river, but midges and annelids are the mainstay over here. "Anything tied small and resembling a midge will work" says Mathew Thomas, longtime guide and resident of these parts. In addition to midges, I like to fish a lot of egg/midge combos this time of year. The reason for this is that the browns and rainbows are used to seeing them coming out of the fall.

On the right day, the Colorado River can boast huge midge hatches. Look for these tiny insects to start popping off the water about 10 a.m. or so and lasting well into the afternoon. There is no reason to get started at the crack of dawn. You want to give the sun time to warm the water. On the Colorado in winter, midges tied with blue and purple highlights seem to work best, particularly when fishing the deeper runs, perhaps because these colors are more visible in deeper water. Midges such as Dye's Purple Flash Midge, Cobalt Midge, OTD Midge, and Annelid and Neiberger's UPS Midge are all good flies to start with. With the number of fly tiers in Colorado, I am sure there are plenty of other patterns that work extremely well. Just remember that size, shape, and color are the three main ingredients of successful midge ties.

In the upper middle river, winter can be tough sledding, but there is still a chance for some good fishing. The Williams Fork tailwater stays open through the winter down to its confluence with the Colorado. During a mild winter the Colorado will

Midge emergers such as Dye's Colorock can fool even the pickiest of trout when the river runs at its clearest during the winter. JIM NEIBERGER

stay open some years down to the Sunset fishing access. Anglers can access the river from the Kemp-Breeze units, located off US 40 or the Williams Fork access off the junction of US 40 and County Road 3.

In the winter, cold water temps (high 30s and low 40s) have an enormous impact on the fishing. I see a great number of anglers simply fishing the wrong water. Trout become so lethargic that they are not going to be in the faster turbulent parts of the river; rather, they are going to be in the slower, deeper parts of the run. There are only so many runs like these in a particular stretch of water, so fish tend to concentrate in these deeper pools. This is good news for fly fishers, but getting them to eat is not always so easy. That being said, fish still have to feed, so it is just a matter of being on the water on the right day.

These winter fish are more apt to eat something that looks real rather than something that has a bunch of bling on it. Tie or buy your patterns small and slender. A little flash is OK—just don't use flies with an overwhelming amount. I generally stay with egg patterns as an attractor, but tying them smaller than usual can draw more strikes than standard egg patterns. Perfect drifts are essential; this water is a lot slower, so trout pick up on subtle movements in your drift. Normally fishing 3X and 4X tippets during the warmer months is acceptable, but during the winter dropping down to 5X and 6X will allow your flies to look more natural.

PART I

The Upper Colorado: Rocky Mountain National Park to Hot Sulphur Springs

When most people think of the Colorado River, they immediately think of big water or the Grand Canyon. But the river's humble beginnings start at La Poudre Pass at 10,184 feet above sea level, and it is up here among the thin air that you can jump across most of the river. The Colorado River is 1,450 miles long, and as it makes its way to the Pacific, it winds through some of the West's most scenic landscapes.

The intimate setting of the Colorado River in Rocky Mountain National Park draws anglers and visitors alike to its natural wonder. The river starts up on La Poudre Pass at 10,184 feet above sea level and travels 1,450 miles to the Gulf of California. JIM NEIBERGER

Overview of the Kawuneeche Valley part of the Colorado River headwaters. JIM NEIBERGER

Much of the upper Colorado runs through the Kawuneeche Valley, where the Never Summer Range rises to the west. As the river makes its way through the valley, its first stop is into Shadow Mountain Reservoir about 18 miles from its headwaters. From there it takes a short jump, about a mile and a half to two miles, into Granby Reservoir, both of which are part of the Colorado–Big Thompson Water Project, designed to divert Western Slope water to the Front Range and the plains.

From Granby, the Colorado River flows through fertile ranchlands and small towns. It's at this point that the Colorado picks up the much-depleted Fraser River and dumps into Windy Gap Reservoir. From this reservoir, there is a 6-mile pipeline back to Granby Reservoir in an effort to further aid the Colorado–Big Thompson project. As the river leaves Windy Gap, it starts taking on the characteristics of a grander western trout stream on its way down to Hot Sulphur Springs.

ROCKY MOUNTAIN NATIONAL PARK

The Colorado is a small stream in Rocky Mountain National Park (RMNP), full of eager trout willing to take just about anything during the summer. It's generally about 10 yards wide and runs about 20 to 50 cfs after runoff toward the end of July. Its shallow riffles host an abundance of aquatic insects, and deep undercut banks create perfect habitat for a dry-fly fisher's dream.

Much of the Colorado River inside RMNP is accessible via US Highway 34. Once you are inside the park, the road is referred to as Trail Ridge Road and parallels much of the Colorado River. Several pull-offs along the road provide unlimited access to the river. The first pull-off is the Never Summer Ranch, located about 8 miles north of the park's Grand Lake entrance. This is a very productive piece of water during the summer and fall and is made up of classic riffle runs that filter into long glass-like flats. Be sure to get flies into some of the many deep cut banks on the river's bends.

Another mile north and you are at the Timber Creek Campground, another stretch of accessible and productive water. Again, the stream is made up of nice riffles followed by undercut banks. Fishing upstream here is the best bet.

I typically find the best time to fish the park is right after runoff, usually about the first week of July. After runoff expect to see large numbers of caddis, PMDs, and Yellow Sallies on any given day, and follow that up with dropper patterns such as a Prince Nymph, Trigger Nymph, or Pheasant Tail. Expect to catch browns, brookies, and a few rainbows in the 8- to 12-inch class.

As early fall arrives, look for good hatches of Blue-Winged Olives starting about the middle of the day. Standard BWO patterns like a Pheasant Tail or Stalcup's Baetis will work for the nymphs, and an Olive Compara-dun or Parachute Adams in sizes 18 through 22 should cover your dry-fly bases.

A little later in the fall if the weather holds, about the first week in October, the browns and brookies begin to spawn and egg patterns and smaller midges will take trout on a consistent basis. However, fall comes early to Rocky Mountain National Park, so cold weather can become an issue starting in September.

Several beaver ponds in the area are worth investigating. They are dotted in and around the river and seem to change from year to year. The brookies that inhabit them will rise to almost any well-presented dry fly, but stealth is key.

Mike Kruise of the Laughing Grizzly Fly Shop fishes the Colorado River in Rocky Mountain National Park just after peak runoff in mid-July. This can be one of the best times to be inside the park. PAT DORSEY

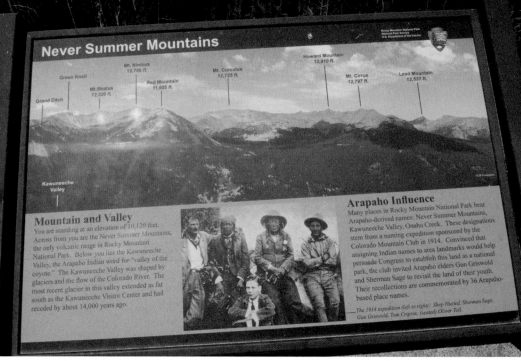

Never Summer Mountains

Rocky Mountain National Park
National Park Service
U.S. Department of the Interior

Howard Mountain
12,810 ft.

Mt. Nimbus
12,706 ft.

Mt. Cumulus
12,725 ft.

Green Knoll

Mt. Cirrus
12,797 ft.

Lead Mountain
12,537 ft.

Red Mountain
11,605 ft.

Mt. Stratus
12,520 ft.

Grand Ditch

Kawuneeche
Valley

Mountain and Valley

You are standing at an elevation of 10,120 feet. Across from you are the Never Summer Mountains, the only volcanic range in Rocky Mountain National Park. Below you lies the Kawuneeche Valley, the Arapaho Indian word for "valley of the coyote." The Kawuneeche Valley was shaped by glaciers and the flow of the Colorado River. The most recent glacier in this valley extended as far south as the Kawuneeche Visitor Center and had receded by about 14,000 years ago.

Arapaho Influence

Many places in Rocky Mountain National Park bear Arapaho-derived names: Never Summer Mountains, Kawuneeche Valley, Onahu Creek. These designations stem from a naming expedition sponsored by the Colorado Mountain Club in 1914. Convinced that assigning Indian names to area landmarks would help persuade Congress to establish this land as a national park, the club invited Arapaho elders Gun Griswold and Sherman Sage to revisit the land of their youth. Their recollections are commemorated by 36 Arapaho-based place names.

The 1914 expedition (left to right): Shep Husted, Sherman Sage, Gun Griswold, Tom Crispin. (seated) Oliver Toll.

The Never Summer Mountain Range is home to seventeen named peaks and all rise above 12,000 feet. BOB DYE

Brook trout like this one can be found in Rocky Mountain National Park and will take most well-presented beaded nymph patterns, especially post-runoff in mid-July. PAT DORSEY

A bull moose looks on cautiously as anglers fish the upper Colorado in Rocky Mountain National Park. Seeing moose and other wildlife is common inside the park. JIM NEIBERGER

There are two ways to access RMNP. The first is to take I-25 north out of Denver to the Estes Park/US 34 exit. Take US 34 west through Estes Park and follow it up and over Trail Ridge. The back side of the pass is the headwaters of the Colorado River. This route is recommended just for the sheer amount of scenery en route to the river. The second route is to take I-70 west out of Denver to the Empire/US 40 exit. Take US 40 north up and over Berthoud Pass and down into Winter Park. From Winter Park, continue through the town of Granby on US 40 until you hit US 34. Take a right, head north, and drive around Grand Lake. Just above the lake you will enter RMNP.

To reach the headwaters of the Colorado, take the Colorado River Trail north; the trail begins where Trail Ridge Road veers away from the river, about 14 miles upstream from Shadow Mountain Reservoir. A well-defined foot trail leads you to the actual headwaters about 3 miles up to Lulu City, an old abandoned mine site. The stream is full of mostly brookies here, and any dry fly with red in it will send these fish attacking your fly as if it were their last meal. If you are willing to make the hike, you will more than likely be the only one there, and if you are really ambitious, you can continue all the way to Little Yellowstone Canyon, which is about 0.75 mile farther.

SHADOW MOUNTAIN, GRANBY, AND WINDY GAP TAILWATERS

All of the Colorado River's upper reservoirs have an impact on the river as a whole. Whether they are adding colder water or just adding much needed water, they define what the river is today. The upper stretches of the Colorado River, more specifically the stretches between Shadow Mountain Reservoir and the town of Kremmling, are a bunch of tailwater and freestone rivers mixed into one. The 2-mile section between Shadow Mountain Reservoir and Granby Reservoir has characteristics of a tailwater fishery. Midges and smaller mayflies make up most of the aquatic life here, but it is one of the reservoirs where *Mysis* shrimp are prevalent.

Moving downstream, the 300-yard section directly below Granby is most certainly a tailwater fishery. Granby is a large, deep reservoir, and with the potential to release water from the bottom, it provides much needed cold water to the river below. As the river leaves Granby, it transitions from a tailwater fishery into a small freestone fishery as it make its way down through the valley to its confluence with the Williams Fork River, another 2-mile-long tailwater that adds much needed water to the Colorado.

These three reservoirs, Shadow Mountain, Granby, and Windy Gap have a great impact on the Colorado River, from controlling the amount of water that flows in the river to altering its water temperatures. While this section doesn't go into detail about fishing the reservoirs, it does cover the tailwaters below them.

Shadow Mountain Reservoir Tailwater

Approximately 18 miles downstream from the headwaters of the Colorado is the tailwater below Shadow Mountain Reservoir. This roughly 1-mile stretch between

Some 18 miles from its headwaters, the Colorado River's first impoundment is Shadow Mountain Reservoir. This unique tailwater allows anglers to catch six different species in one day: browns, rainbows, cutbows, brookies, lake trout, and kokanee salmon. JIM NEIBERGER

Shadow Mountain and Granby can be one of the more diverse fisheries in the Colorado River drainage. There is access down both sides of the river. The trails are fairly evident, but fallen beetle-killed trees sometimes pose a threat when navigating along the river's edge. It is not uncommon to catch multiple species here, including rainbows, browns, cutbows, lake trout, brookies, and kokanee salmon.

This tailwater fishes best during runoff (perfect when the lower river is blown out), when the dam releases generous amounts of water into Granby Reservoir and the different species of trout seem to show up in hoards. Midges dominate as the food source here, but an enormous amount of *Mysis* shrimp get pushed through the dam as well. On any given day, the water right below the dam is often crowded, but you can find solitude by simply walking down the north side of the river and continuing till it dumps into Granby. About 300 yards down on the south side of the river, a small section is closed due to an osprey rehabilitation project; otherwise, the rest of the river here is open. I usually start a fishing trip here by walking down the north side of the river and working my way back up.

This section of river features several nice riffles and midstream shelves along with some deeper pockets. Most of the fish are in the 10- to 14-inch slot, but being that the trout have full range from Granby Reservoir up into the river, expect from time to time very large fish being brought to the net. Fly selection never seems to be too difficult; using beaded patterns like Prince Nymphs and Pheasant Tails will draw strikes at any time, but always have a midge pattern somewhere in your nymphing rig. One of the best fish-producing midges for me is the Rhinestone Midge, a

Mature rainbow trout can be one of the most vividly colored species in the trout world. Trout take on different colors depending on their environment and nutrients in the water, and those from *Mysis* shrimp fisheries are often brilliantly colored. JAY NICHOLS

knockoff of the popular Zebra Midge with a gunmetal bead. Lastly, Laney's Mysis Shrimp is another standard for me here.

Colorado Parks & Wildlife (CPW) puts special regulations on this stretch for spawning kokanee salmon. Fishing is prohibited from October 31 to December 31. To reach the Shadow Mountain tailwater, take US 34 north out of Granby for about 11.5 miles to County Road 66. Take a right and follow CR 66 for about a mile until you hit the Green Ridge Campground. Do not park in the campground; instead, park by the dam access.

Granby Reservoir Tailwater

Granby is the next reservoir down from Shadow Mountain and, in fact, fishing both tailwaters in one day is not unheard of. As the crow flies they are only about a mile apart, but by road they are a 9-mile, 15-minute drive apart. Though there is only about 300 yards of public water below Granby, and the water doesn't have as many fish as the stretch below Shadow Mountain, you can have a shot at some very large trout. This tailwater is home to aquatic life such as *Mysis* shrimp, midges, and occasional BWO and PMD hatches during the summer.

A few patterns that fool these educated fish include size 18 to 24 egg flies, Laney's Mysis Shrimp, Rhinestone Midge, Dye's Colorock Midge, Neiberger's UPS Midge, Dye's Purple Flash Midge, Stalcup's Baetis, Periwinkles, and Post Foam Rs2s. Besides these, do not be afraid to throw something that is fresh off your vise; after all, the trout have not seen it. When there is not a lot of water coming out of the

The tailwater section below Granby Reservoir can harbor some of the largest fish in the system depending on water flows. Here the author admires a hefty rainbow caught on a size 20 Laney's Mysis Shrimp in September. JAY NICHOLS

tunnel below Granby, you will need long leaders, small indicators, and a good deal of stealth to fool these fish.

To get here, take US 34 out of the town of Granby and go north approximately 5 miles. Turn right on County Road 6/Monarch Lake Road and follow it around the lake for about 0.75 mile to the fee station; there is a $6 fee to enter the park. After the fee station, travel another 0.25 mile; the road ends and the gravel parking lot is to the right. From there, access the well-worn trail to the south and follow it down to the river. Access to this area can be difficult. While the trail is only about 500 yards long, it is very steep.

Windy Gap Reservoir

After a short, 300-yard stretch below Granby, the Colorado River travels through quite a bit of private property; it is not until after Windy Gap, 3 miles west of Granby on US 40, that there is a small stretch to fish about 0.5 mile below the reservoir. This stretch is only about a couple hundred yards long, but it holds a good number of trout from time to time and is worth investigating if you have a few hours to fish. Fishing seems to be best after runoff in July and August and then again in the fall. Powerful telescopes set up on the north side of the reservoir offer a great wildlife-viewing area. The distance between this small area to fish and Hot Sulphur Springs is about 9 miles, and there is no other public access until you reach Hot Sulphur Springs and the state wildlife area known as Pioneer Park.

Fraser River

From its headwaters just below the Continental Divide at Berthoud Pass, the Fraser River travels through the towns of Winter Park, Fraser, Tabernash, and Granby to its confluence with the Colorado (8 miles of the river is located inside of Arapaho National Forest). Over the years, though, the Front Range's thirst for water has depleted this once great trout stream, which in turn affects the flows on the Colorado River.

One of the best access points is the Fraser River Trailhead. To reach it, travel 6.5 miles west from Winter Park or about a mile east from Tabernash on US 40. Turn east on County Road 84 towards Devils Thumb Ranch. At the fork in the road, stay left and travel 0.8 mile until you see BLM Road 2751. Turn left and travel another 0.8 mile to another fork in the road, then stay left and continue about 0.6 mile to the Fraser River Trailhead. From the parking area, you can access about 0.75 mile of river.

Ski Granby Ranch, formally known as Sol Vista Resort, also offers access to the Fraser. From Granby, take US 40 south for about 3 miles to Village Road. Hang a left and travel approximately 2 miles until you reach the ranch (888-850-4615). Access can be had here by buying a permit from the resort or by invitation of a guest.

While there are other access points in Winter Park, I believe the best public fishing is below the town of Tabernash in the canyon. To reach this stretch, take Road 84 to the northeast from US 40 neart Tabernash. Turn west after 0.5 mile onto Strawberry Road and follow it for about 1.4 miles to the parking area. The river is mostly lined with lodgepole pines, most of which have been killed by the pine beetle. Native grasses and sagebrush make up the rest of the foliage along the river.

Expect to find browns and rainbows in the 10- to 14-inch range, but do not be surprised to find an occasional 18- to 20-inch fish roaming the river. The Fraser is also home to a fair number of 8- to 10-inch brookies.

I typically like to fish the Fraser around the first week in July after runoff has subsided, and if the flows maintain at a respectable level, through the fall. Starting in July the river boasts some respectable hatches, including caddis, PMDs, Yellow Sallies, Green Drakes, and some Golden Stones. Look for some pretty amazing Green Drake hatches during the month of July, and if that isn't happening, it's a pretty good bet you will hit sporadic hatches of PMDs and Yellow Sallies.

Nymph fishing can pull a few trout out of the deeper runs, but dry-dropper rigs are best when it comes to fishing the river's shallow riffles and mid-seam currents. One fly that has always been a consistent producer for me here, even when prominent hatches are coming off, is the good old Buckskin. Be sure to have a few of these tied up in your box in sizes 18 and 20. The browns eat them like popcorn.

Don't pass up the runs that look too fast to fish. Try running a few fly patterns down these fast currents, and you will be surprised at what comes out. I have had days where I would be chunking on weight to reach the bottom of a 2-foot riffle, thinking nothing could swim in there, and much to my surprise, I'd hook a 12-inch brown, fighting like a 34-inch steelhead.

Taylor Dye, a big right hander on Colorado Mesa University's pitching staff, probes some plunge pools with a dry-dropper rig on the Fraser River near Tabernash. BOB DYE

As fall rolls around, be prepared for smaller insect hatches such as BWOs and midges. Attach these patterns behind a beaded Prince Nymph or an egg fly to fool the fish in the lower water. As the middle of October approaches, expect to find numbers of brown trout spawning. Streamer fishing can be at its best this time of year. One of the most productive streamer patterns on the Fraser is a size 10 white Sculpzilla. I don't know what it is about this pattern, but holy cow, the browns love that thing. ■

Scenic view of early morning fog on the Colorado River downstream of Windy Gap Reservoir. While public fishing is limited in this stretch, it does mark the beginning of Gold Medal water downstream to the confluence of Troublesome Creek. JIM NEIBERGER

Though the Windy Gap project and the diversion of water to the Front Range have dampened the bug life in the upper sections (below the Fraser), they still have prominent insect hatches that fly fishers flock to during the early summer. In fact, CPW has designated the stretch between Windy Gap and the Troublesome confluence as Gold Medal water. There is over 9,000 miles of river to fish across Colorado, but only 168 miles are worthy of Gold Medal status. These waters must meet certain criteria: 12 trout per acre over 14 inches or 60 pounds of trout per surface acre.

PIONEER PARK/HOT SULPHUR SPRINGS

Ten miles west of Granby on US 40, on the northeastern side of Hot Sulphur Springs, lies the first public access downstream from Windy Gap. Pioneer Park lies on the north side of town and can be accessed by turning off of US 40 to the north on Park Street. The park sits between the highway and the Colorado River and has several well-marked parking areas.

Pioneer Park offers a variety of water to fish, from long riffle runs and deep pools to productive bank fishing. The park has some great hatches in the summer, including caddis, PMDs, Yellow Sallies, and the famed Salmonfly hatch. The Salmonflies (*Pteronarcys*) start to come off the lower river in mid-May and reach the Hot Sulphur Springs area the beginning of June. During a normal runoff year, the water is off-color but fishable.

BOB DYE

There are a couple of places to park to access the river. One is the west side of town off US 40. Take US 40 west to Park Street; there you will cross the river and park on the north side. The other is inside Pioneer Park, which lies north of town about 200 yards. Both offer easy access to the water. This section of water sets up nicely, with several riffles followed by nice pools below them. It is one of my favorite places to show up after nightfall and throw streamers to the banks. The park sits just up from Byers Canyon, and while it has a good half mile of river to fish, fishing is not limited to just Pioneer Park. Anglers can work their way all the way down the 5 miles of Byers Canyon and into the Paul Gilbert SWA.

PART II

Middle Colorado: Byers Canyon to Kremmling

The middle Colorado has the most diverse water of the entire river system, from the steep walls and plunge pools of Byers Canyon to the soft, snaking meadow stream around Kremmling, and it is undoubtedly one of the most popular stretches with anglers. It holds a good number of trout that average 10 to 14 inches, with several taken in the 18- to 22-inch range, and has prolific hatches, with everything from midges to giant stoneflies.

The middle section has several tributaries, but the main ones are the Williams Fork, Reeder Creek, Troublesome Creek, Blue River, and below Wolford Mountain Reservoir, Muddy Creek. All of these rivers and creeks contribute to the Colorado and add diversity to the area. "A guy could spend a week over here and never fish every square inch of water that is available," explains Jim Neiberger, longtime fly fisher of the Colorado River. While there is private water in the area, public fishing opportunities abound.

The upper-middle portion of the Colorado flows through prime terrestrial habitat. The cattle ranches that dot the area between Granby and Kremmling offer large hay fields for the insects to thrive. One of the best sections of water for prime terrestrial fishing is the Troublesome Creek area.

Other areas that should receive attention from anglers include the small access points upstream from the Highway 9 bridge; these overlooked fishing areas sit in the widest part of the valley, just above Kremmling. To access these

Jim Neiberger, who fishes the Colorado River on a consistent basis, lands a rainbow on a UPS Midge in the lower Kemp-Breeze units located about 10 miles east of Kremmling on US 40. BOB DYE

areas, take County Road 33 east off of Highway 9; the first piece is 0.75 mile of public fishing east of the highway. The second is a small section about a mile from the old Elk Trout Lodge. This water is slow-moving and does not look like prime trout water, but I have had some amazing days fishing these areas. While I do not frequent them, they can offer some prime terrestrial fishing. Crowds are not an issue down here.

BYERS CANYON

This 5-mile canyon is located 0.5 mile west of Hot Sulphur Springs on US Highway 40, just below Pioneer Park. There is easy access at the top of the canyon and at the bottom just above the US 40 bridge. Parking above the bridge in the dirt parking lot and accessing the lower canyon, anglers can expect a midsize-boulder-laden trail that is fairly difficult to navigate. As you proceed farther into the canyon, the trail dissipates and travel becomes more difficult but not impassable. There are a couple of pull-offs in the middle section of the canyon, but you need to be part mountain goat to reach the river. The upper section of Byers Canyon can be accessed from Pioneer Park by turning north off of US 40 onto Park Street and following the dirt road along the railroad tracks for about 500 yards until the road ends.

If you are lucky to time it right, Byers Canyon can provide great fishing during the Salmonfly hatch. In the high water, trout find refuge by lying along the edges and behind large boulders. Here they can grab food out of the faster current or search for bugs churned up in the pools.

When fishing nymphs in Byers Canyon, I usually find fishing them in the water column is more effective than fishing them on the bottom, as the current is swirling the bugs into the pools rather than keeping them tight to the bottom. Rig a standard nymphing setup, but fish it short and heavy. This allows your flies to sink quickly. Weighted flies such as the Pat's Rubber Legs or Bitch Creek can aid in this technique. When fishing Salmonfly patterns dry, I prefer to slam them off large boulders, imitating a stonefly that has just fallen off a rock. Trout become accustomed to this behavior, so it is important to imitate it. As the bugs hit the water, they begin to twitch and find refuge in the closest boulders, so be sure to give your flies a little movement to entice strikes.

When fishing Byers Canyon, it is important to stay on the move. Fishing one run or pool for a couple of hours isn't a good recipe for success; rather, pick a small section of water, whether it be the rock section of the bank or a pool created by a large boulder. Make presentations in these areas, adjusting your weight and depth accordingly, and then move to the next piece of water. There are probably not 20 fish behind each rock, so staying on the move is your best bet. Usually anglers can make a full day of it fishing the canyon, but for the hard-core angler that likes to stretch it until dark, there's Pioneer Park nearby.

In the low light of summer evenings, or during the fall, one of my favorite things to do is fish streamers in the canyon. I have fished the canyon during the day only to catch fish in the 10- to 14-inch range, but when the light dims in the evening, bigger fish awaken to sounds of streamers breaking the current. This is another strange piece of water. I do not know if these larger fish lie in wait until night to feed in the summer or what, but come fall these larger fish seem to become a little more vulnerable.

View of Byers Canyon from the US 40 bridge at the bottom of the canyon. Byers Canyon offers a variety of water to fish; however, access can be difficult due to large boulders and steep terrain. BOB DYE

PAUL GILBERT AND LONE BUCK

As the Colorado River transitions out of the boulder-laden Byers Canyon, it starts to take on a different attitude. The river in the Paul Gilbert State Wildlife Area is classic trout water due to the long dry-fly runs, fast riffles, and deeper pools. Clients have mentioned during their trips that they feel they are on a different river. In addition to the unique water, the towering pine trees and different undergrowth make you feel like you are fishing somewhere else besides the Colorado River.

John Perizzolo uses all of his 10-foot Sage rod to help land a fish on the lower Paul Gilbert State Wildlife Area. This section of water is known for being one of the better dry-fly sections along the entire Colorado River.

BOB DYE

To arrive at this access point, take US 40 west out of Hot Sulphur Springs for 3 miles. Go past the US 40 bridge and make a left onto the dirt road labeled Paul Gilbert State Wildlife Area. Follow the road down a steep grade until you reach the access area. The other access point is just downstream from Paul Gilbert and is labeled Lone Buck SWA, the two units run together. There is easy access from the parking area, or anglers can walk downstream a mile or so into the Lone Buck lease. While there is access at Lone Buck, I prefer to walk down from Paul Gilbert to allow more access to the water.

The Trico hatch can be huge here. Another great time to be on the water is in the fall, when Paul Gilbert can be an overlooked hot spot. This unit produces all summer, but something happens in the fall. Most of the fish caught and released in the summer seem to average about 10 to 14 inches, with an occasional 16- to 18-inch fish brought to hand. I am not quite sure how far these fish have migrated, but they seem to show up here in force.

This was always a great area for spawning fish, but the high water of 2011 altered the way the river flows. In my opinion, it gave it the cleansing effect it needed to remain a spawning area for years to come. Spawning trout show up here a little earlier than the rest of the river, so timing is everything. I typically find around October 10 to be the magic start time. Fish have been caught in the 22- to 24-inch range, leaving anglers wondering where they were in the spring and summer. The returning browns also bring more rainbows into this stretch, and for a short period of time, Paul Gilbert turns into as good a fishery as anywhere.

In the fall, I usually fish down toward Lone Buck. Do not waste much time in the slower water; you may see some rising fish there, but I have usually found them to be smaller. This is when you want to concentrate your efforts on bigger trout. Besides egg-and-midge combo rigs, browns will acutely respond to streamer patterns. They are aggressive by nature, and nothing gets their primitive instincts boiling like an erratic streamer swimming through the water. When the browns are on streamers, it can be as exciting as it gets—working the banks and long riffles can draw violent strikes. I usually carry a nymphing setup as well as a rod rigged up with streamer patterns. This can be a very effective way to expose all the fish in a run to your flies. Start out by nymphing these areas first, and then bring out the big guns. I have found that larger fish that will not sip a size 22 midge will hammer a streamer pattern.

KEMP-BREEZE UNITS

The Kemp-Breeze units are located 6 miles west of Hot Sulphur Springs (or 10 miles east of Kremmling) on US 40. Remember, after the Lone Buck lease, the next 2.5 miles are private until you come to the Kemp-Breeze units. There are two parking areas about a quarter mile apart, and both offer easy access to the river. The parking area farther west has public restrooms, picnic tables, and handicap access. Colorado

The author and John Barr nymph fish a run just before a Trico hatch near Parshall. Trout will feed on the nymphs early in the morning in anticipation a full-blown hatch midmorning and into the early afternoon. JAY NICHOLS

Rachel Kohler, a guide for ArkAnglers in Salida, works a riffle run near the handicap ramp in the lower Kemp-Breeze units on a beautiful September day. BOB DYE

Parks & Wildlife (CPW) has a "kids only" pond on this lease, designated age 16 or under to fish it. I have found this pond to be a great way to get young kids involved in fly fishing before tackling the rigors of the river. The pond is well stocked and offers youngsters a good chance at hooking trout.

From the confluence of the Williams Fork down through the Sunset lease, there is approximately 3 miles of public water. With access points near the highway, the area can see heavy pressure, especially when everyone figures out a hatch is in full swing. "One thing I've learned over the years is to fish the nonobvious water," explains John Perizzolo, longtime guide on the Colorado. "Fish are spread out everywhere in the summer." I have found this to be true as well; in fact, I have looked up and down the river wondering how I was going to find a spot for my anglers to fish. I usually went the other route, though, walking my clients into the ground while they wondered if they had just signed up for marine boot camp. There are many fish in this stretch and at times a great number of anglers, but there is a lot of access here as well. If you move a quarter mile from the parking areas and fish less-pressured water, you will find yourself working more water, and the end result will be more fish in the bag.

In the fall, brown trout migrate out of the Colorado into the Williams Fork, and a good number of them end up in the confluence. Fishing all the way up the Williams Fork is also very productive; spawning browns bring numbers of rainbows looking for an easy meal. Again, egg/midge combos are the way to go here; pay special attention not to fish over the spawning beds.

SUNSET LEASE

The Sunset state lease is located off US 40, 7 miles west of Hot Sulphur Springs. On the south side of the road is a turnoff with a Sunset Ranch sign; follow the dirt road 0.75 mile south to the parking area. From there it is steep walk down to the river. Access is downstream of the old bridge about a hundred yards all the way upstream into the Kemp-Breeze units, about a mile of water. This section has long riffles, a few deep pools, and some braided sections of river. I have found some decent dry-fly action here. In fact, one of my favorite guide trips during the summer is to start at the Sunset lease and work water all the way to the Kemp-Breeze parking lot. This way anglers can fish every square inch while staying on the move and avoid some of the more heavily fished water.

The Sunset lease fishes well all summer but really turns on in October. It's an important spawning area. Trout that have been vacationing in slower-moving water in the lower stretches begin migrating to this area. Egg-and-midge combos fished at this time of year can be deadly.

POWERS UNIT

After the Sunset lease the river flows through private land for a few miles until the Powers Unit, a 200-yard section of water sandwiched between two private ranches. Access is limited to the north side of the river. This stretch is especially productive right after runoff about mid-July and then again in the fall. Generally around the middle of July, the river is still running between 800 and 1,200 cfs but begins to

Jim Cannon, previous owner of the Blue Quill Angler in Evergreen, holds up a brown trout he caught in the Powers Unit located about 6 miles east of Kremmling. BOB DYE

Jim Neiberger fishes a dry-dropper rig near an undercut bank on Reeder Creek. The creek has generally smaller fish but can be a rewarding dry-fly fishery. BOB DYE

gain quite a bit of water clarity. When some of the major hatches begin to appear, such as PMDs, Yellow Sallies, and caddis, this little stretch can turn on nicely.

One thing to note about this stretch is that when the water is running low, usually around 300 cfs, there isn't a lot of holding water, and the fish tend to vacate the area in search of safer water conditions. When the fall months arrive, browns tend to make an appearance in search of spawn gravel. It is tough to make an entire day of fishing this piece of water; rather, it can be a phenomenal spot for a couple hours during the right time of year!

To get to the Powers Unit, take US 40 east 6 miles from Kremmling (or west 9 miles from Hot Sulphur Springs) and turn onto the dirt road turnout and parking area north of the river. There is a portable restroom at this access.

REEDER CREEK

The next access point, Reeder Creek, is approximately 3 miles downstream from the Powers Unit. Entering the Colorado River from the south about 7 miles downstream from Parshall (or about 5 miles up from Kremmling), Reeder is a meandering meadow stream with hard cut banks, which provide some interesting hiding spots for leery trout and a few heart-stopping moments from flushing blue grouse! It is an excellent place to find some solitude when the upper reaches of the Colorado are busy with anglers.

Years ago, before whirling disease decimated the rainbow trout, they would spawn in Reeder. "I would find fish almost two miles up," says Jim Neiberger. These days, this is not so much the case, but due to the restocking efforts of CPW, this springtime event could once again return to its former glory. However, summertime can still be rewarding with dry-dropper rigs and well-presented flies. Resident trout will pounce on just about anything thrown their way, especially a well-placed Prince Nymph. I have never caught a ton of fish here during the summer, but always managed to squeak out a few. In the summer fish average between 9 and 12 inches, with a few topping 12 inches.

As the summer transitions into fall, this little creek can really light up with migrating brown trout. The browns have historically used the creek to spawn in, but they do not seem to go as high as the rainbows once did.

To reach Reeder Creek from Kremmling, take Highway 9 south 1 mile to County Road 33. Turn left and follow this road east for about 5 miles past the old Elk Trout property, till you reach the parking lot. From the parking lot, the creek will be located just to the east and accesses both sides of the creek for about 0.5 mile. As Reeder Creek reaches the Colorado River, anglers need to observe the private property signs at and around the confluence.

WILLIAMS FORK RIVER

The 2-mile-long Williams Fork adds much-needed water to the Colorado and is a terrific tailwater fishery in its own right. Though the once robust populations of

It doesn't get any better when it comes to fall scenery on the Williams Fork River. Fall can be one of the best times of year to fish in Colorado. PAT DORSEY

rainbow trout have declined, it still has a thriving brown trout population. Expect to catch browns in the 12- to 16-inch range, with a few larger ones. The Williams Fork has long, fast riffles, a few pools, and undercut banks, which create prime habitat. It is not a big river, and anglers can usually stand in the middle casting from bank to bank, searching for rising fish.

There are two ways to get to the Williams Fork, and both require about a mile hike, which serves to thin out the angling crowds. In the spring, anglers should expect snow on the ground, so sometimes this mile seems like a "long mile." If the flows on the Colorado are less than 500 cfs, I usually get to the Williams Fork by parking at the Kemp-Breeze units (there are two parking areas). Park in the one farthest east, then walk about two hundred yards to the east and cross the Colorado River. On the other side, a well-maintained, approximately mile-long trail leads back to the confluence of the Colorado and Williams Fork.

There is a small section of private water below the confluence; anglers should begin their trip above the yellow rope and continue up the Williams Fork. Once above the yellow rope, be aware of the private property (formerly Rocky Mountain Angling Club) on the southeast side of the river.

If Colorado River flows are above 500 cfs, I don't cross the river. Instead, continue on US 40 east and hang a right onto County Road 3. Cross the Colorado River and after approximately 0.75 mile, park at the old barn on the right. To the west, there is a 1-mile-long, well-maintained trail to the Williams Fork.

This tailwater can fish very well early in the year, but since winters can be extremely cold in this part of the state, I usually wait until March and river flows of

Mark Adams landed this fat rainbow on the upper reaches of the Williams Fork. The Willy's Fork can be a tough river to spot trout in, so proceeding with stealth is the key to success on this tailwater. PAT DORSEY

During the fall months, mature browns like this one from the Williams Fork begin migrating towards their spawning grounds in an effort to further the species. PAT DORSEY

at least 40 cfs or higher. Migrating rainbows start showing up in late March and can offer anglers a chance at some sizable fish. Look for sporadic midge hatches to begin mid-March and last well into April. Egg/midge combinations are the ticket this time of year, and some successful patterns include Strawberry Jam, Dye's Purple Flash Midge, Steve Parrott's Chironoflash Midge, Neiberger's UPS Midge, and Dorsey's Top Secret Midge. During this period I like to start at the confluence and work my way up, hitting every pocket and fishing the riffles and long runs. Egg flies are a good point fly, followed by midge or *Baetis* trailers.

As April approaches, be on the lookout for hit-and-miss BWO hatches. It is usually Murphy's Law: If you are not prepared for the hatch, that is when it will come off in force. Fly selection is fairly simple, and I generally stay with the basics. A good old Pheasant Tail or a Stalcup's Baetis will take care of any trout feeding on the nymphs, and a standard Rs2 will take trout that are feeding on the emergers. I have hit it a few times when the fish are rising to BWOs, so carry a few Parachute Adamses for trout breaking the surface.

Reading water and proceeding with caution is the key to fishing the Willy's Fork. Even the tiniest of seams behind rocks will hold trout. Most anglers walk by fishable water in search of "the main run." Instead, try hitting the small stuff such as riffles around rocks and small seams and even presentations along banks where trout are tucked underneath. While solitude can be tough to find on this river, the farther you go upstream, generally the less fishing pressure you will receive.

As a general rule, I like flows between 75 and 300 cfs to maximize fishing opportunities. Be sure to check the river flows on the Williams Fork in the spring;

The Williams Fork has many undercut banks as well as fallen trees to house trout. Dry-dropper rigs will allow you to make presentations to these fish where standard nymphing rigs are a bit cumbersome. JAY NICHOLS

sometimes flows are too low to fish the river effectively. By May and June, when the state's rivers swell due to runoff, the Williams Fork may be unfishable if there is a lot of snowpack. Anything much over 300 cfs makes for tough wading.

If it is fishable during these months, look for deeper runs that the trout congregate in and toss flies such as a Pat's Rubber Legs, Twenty Incher, Red Copper John, and Golden Prince Nymph. Follow those attractor flies with standard bugs such as a Pheasant Tail, Buckskin, Dorsey's Mercury Caddis, and Post Foam Rs2.

In a typical year, the Williams Fork will shape up nicely around July 4 and the summer can bring some of the best insect hatches of the year, including PMDs, Yellow Sallies, and caddis. During these times, especially in the mornings, I nymph with flies such as a Mercer's Trigger Nymph, Pheasant Tail, Mercer's Poxyback PMD, and Buckskin. But by 11 a.m. or so, trout can begin to rise heavily, oftentimes on all three insects. The best combination of dry-fly patterns that I have found consists of the Headlamp Yellow Sally and the PMD Compara-dun; using a standard Elk Hair Caddis in a size 18 will get the job done if any caddis are present. If you see what appear to be rising fish and strikes are hard to come by, try tying on a size 18 Chocolate Post Foam Rs2 below your dry; sometimes emerging takes can be mistaken for dry takes.

As the hot days of August near, the Williams Fork can still fish extremely well, and anglers can look forward to good hatches of Tricos, with the best hatches on the lower third of the river. Tricos will continue to come off strong through the first week of October. The other important mayfly in late August and September

Troublesome Creek

From its beginnings in the mountains northeast of Kremmling, Troublesome Creek flows down through some of the more scenic views in this part of the country. The small creek collides with the Colorado River about 4 miles from Kremmling on US 40 heading east. From the views of Wolford Mountain to the west to the majestic Gore Range to the south, it is an angler's dream and is quickly becoming one of the area's best trophy trout destinations.

Troublesome has two forks before coming together to form the main creek. While typically not a lot of water comes down each fork, the two forks offer some prime brookie fishing. As the two forks come together, the creek begins to offer some unique characteristics, from long riffles flowing into deep bend pools to overhanging canopies that can test the skills of any angler.

Troublesome Creek has browns, rainbows, cutthroats, and the higher you go, brookies. With every bend pool and every riffle, anglers have a chance at 5- or 6-pound rainbows, not to mention some of the undercut banks that harbor brown trout that bring to mind snook fishing in Florida around the mangroves. I can remember catching brookies on the creek's upper stretches when I was a kid; I was not exposed to the lower sections until recently.

Troublesome Creek is a small tributary of the Colorado River and offers anglers great private-water fishing. The creek is home to browns, rainbows, cutthroat, and a few brook trout. LANDON MEYER

While much of Troublesome is private, there is some public access upstream in the national forest via County Road 2. The creek up here holds some small brookies and browns. Several ranches in the area offer access for a rod fee, but Dean Billington of Bull Basin Outfitters (970-724-0417) manages 3 miles of the best water starting about 4 miles up from the confluence of the Colorado River. Billington rotates the beats to offer anglers the opportunity to fish relatively unpressured water in solitude. He also manages the nearby Hidden Valley Pond.

Fishing on Troublesome is usually best just as the peak runoff subsides, usually around the first week of July. Nymphing or fishing with a dry-dropper is the way to

Here the author takes some time to probe Hidden Valley Pond with a Pine Squirrel Leech. This pond is also famous for its damselfly and *Callibaetis* hatches. MARK ADAMS

go on this creek. Carrying dual rods will allow you to cover any situation, from undercut banks to long riffles crashing into a plunge pool. Remember that some of the stream is wide open, while other parts require kneeling and casting under tree branches. While this gem of a stream may be small, the flies used at higher water flows are not. Pat's Rubber Legs, Twenty Inchers, Pine Squirrel Leeches, Copper Johns in all colors, and larger Prince Nymphs are all favorites of Billington's during this time period. As the flows start to subside, around the end of July, the dry-fly fishing really starts to pick up and continues through the early fall months. ■

Dean Billington gets ready to release a nice rainbow back into Hidden Valley Pond, which he manages. He also manages 3 miles of Troublesome Creek. BOB DYE

The confluence of the Williams Fork and Colorado River can be fished year-round but can be spectacular in the fall. Here an angler nymph-fishes the first main run below these two great fisheries. PAT DORSEY

is the Red Quill. This larger mayfly has a way of sneaking up on you, but before you know it, the trout are feeding on them heavily. I have met with little success as far as hooking fish with nymphs, but a size 14 Soft Hackle Pheasant Tail can make the trout look silly. There will be times when you notice the trout steadily rising to these larger mayflies, and this can be when it is most fun. I have tried numerous Red Quill patterns, but the best one seems to be a size 16 A.K. Best's Red Quill.

By September, Tricos and Red Quills still make up most of the trout's diet, but Blue-Winged Olives can add yet another twist. I would call it sporadic at best, but on a cloudy day they can emerge in full force. If this scenario takes place, make sure you're outfitted with a few Pheasant Tails, Skinny Nelsons, Garcia's Darth Baetis, and Stalcup's Baetis for the nymphs and standard Rs2s for the emerging stage of the life cycle. Being that water levels have probably come down a bit during this time of year, you will likely experience some good BWO dry-fly fishing. Having a few well-dressed Parachute Adamses and Olive Compara-duns should cover your bases if the trout are taking dries.

By the time October rolls around, the river generally becomes less crowded due to Colorado's big-game hunting seasons. I am torn this time of year: While hunting can be at its best, so can the fishing. The Williams Fork is home to numerous browns, and while these trout are here for you to try your luck, it is the ones that migrate up from the Colorado River that can put a spring in your step. It is not uncommon to see several spawning fish in the Williams Fork, and while these fish need to be left alone, they bring several other fish into the system. Almost as if they were on a scent trail, browns and rainbows will begin stacking behind the redds of spawning brown trout. Egg flies will take a trout or two during this time, and midges such as a Rhinestone Midge, Dye's Purple Flash Midge, Strawberry Jam, and Dorsey's Top Secret Midge will certainly get the job done in October. Do not forget that tossing a few streamers will surely ignite the leery browns' predatory instinct, and some of the larger browns are taken every year with streamer patterns. A number of streamer patterns are effective, but the ones that consistently work in the Williams Fork are Autumn Splendors, black and white Woolly Buggers, Meat Whistles, and white Sculpzillas.

PART III

Middle Colorado: Kremmling to State Bridge

The Colorado River turns into one of the West's big-water streams in this stretch. With its additions from the Williams Fork and Blue River from the south and Muddy Creek and Troublesome Creek to the north, the Colorado begins to transform from its small-river stature in RMNP to big-water status. I'll guide many different sections of the Colorado in the spring and summer, but I generally run all my trips in this section between Kremmling and State Bridge during the fall. I usually break down this stretch into smaller sections and work a different piece every day.

The Blue River and Muddy Creek join the Colorado River in the town of Kremmling and mark the beginning of one of the state's largest recreation areas. Although the Blue provides some excellent fishing opportunities, it adds something even more important to the Colorado River—cool water.

BLUE RIVER

The Blue starts its path towards the Colorado high on top of Hoosier Pass just south of Breckenridge. From there it flows through high-mountain meadows on its way to Dillon Reservoir. Below Dillon is a local favorite among Colorado fly fishers, as it harbors some large rainbows and a few browns. It is not one of the most scenic areas in Colorado, but can offer anglers a quick fix with its close proximity to Denver. From there the Blue winds its way through the valley, picking up 24 smaller creeks and tributaries before winding up in Green Mountain Reservoir. This is where the Blue is most important to the Colorado River drainage.

Green Mountain was built between 1938 and 1942 by the United States Bureau of Reclamation as part of the Big Thompson Project. The dam itself stands 309 feet high and offers a tremendous tailwater trout fishery below it. Besides its lure as a trout fishery, the Blue also adds much-needed colder water to the Colorado River. This tailwater is one of the most scenic areas along the Colorado River drainage and can give up some pretty sizable fish. Most of the fish range in size from 12 to 16 inches, but several in the 18- to 22-inch range exist.

The best way to access this water is to go north out of Dillon-Silverthorne on Highway 9 about 24 miles. Drive along the reservoir until you reach a sign for Heeney and Green Mountain Dam, then turn left and follow the road across the dam and down into the parking area. The trail follows a steep grade down to the river.

I like to fish this when the flows are between 150 and 300 cfs, but flows up to 1,000 cfs or more are not uncommon in the summer. Wading this stretch can be

Mike Oros of Kremmling, Colorado, fishes a run on the Blue River below Green Mountain Reservoir. The river offers some great walk, wade, and float opportunities. BOB DYE

very difficult due to the sharp boulders that line the river bottom. When flows are higher, take precautions—the water is faster than it looks, and there are plenty of fish lining the edges without killing yourself out in the middle.

Being a tailwater, midges under an attractor fly are always a good bet, but the river has all the great hatches that make up an exceptional trout stream. April and May bring BWOs and caddis, and the summer brings some pretty good PMD hatches to the area, not to mention occasional Yellow Sallies and Golden Stoneflies. Floating this stretch is an option, but there is private water in the area. You can fish out of a boat, but no anchoring or wading is allowed on the private water. Floating with a local guide who knows the area is the best way not to find yourself talking with a law enforcement officer.

Besides the tailwater stretch below the dam, there is a BLM access towards the town of Kremmling. To access this small piece of water, go south on Highway 9 out of Kremmling 1 mile until you reach Trough Road (County Road 1). Turn right, heading west, down to the bridge, then turn right before the bridge and follow the BLM signs down to the river. There is not a ton of water to fish down here, but in the spring and fall, fish numbers increase significantly.

MUDDY CREEK

Almost directly across from where the Blue enters the Colorado River, Muddy Creek also enters the Colorado. Before Wolford Mountain Reservoir was constructed in

May 1996, Muddy Creek definitely lived up to its name—one glance and it looked like nothing could live in it. Now this tailwater runs clear below Wolford for most of the year and is one of the most overlooked fisheries in the area. During the first year of operation, the Division of Wildlife stocked 10- to 14-inch rainbow trout, and with browns filtering into the system from the Colorado River, Muddy Creek below Wolford Dam has turned into an interesting tailwater fishery. Most of the fish in the river average 10 to 14 inches, but several in the 16- to 18-inch class exist, especially in the fall months.

Not only does Muddy Creek add cooler water to the system, but the reservoir holds back silt and other debris that choked out some of the bug life in the lower river. I have seen firsthand the improvements in insect hatches along Gore Canyon all the way down to Radium.

Wolford Mountain Reservoir, owned and operated by the Colorado River Water Conservation District, has benefited both western Colorado and the Front Range. The Western Slope gains 66,000 acre-feet of water storage, and in exchange for financial support, Denver Water can use up to 40 percent of Wolford's water.

To access Muddy Creek, drive north out of Kremmling on US 40 about 5 miles to the Wolford Mountain Dam exit. Turn right and follow the gravel road to the parking area by the dam. Cross the dam and descend to the creek. While Muddy Creek is about 5 miles long, it does have private property along its journey to the confluence with the Colorado River near Kremmling.

The creek is made up of a few classic riffle runs, followed by deeper bend pools. Fishing in the winter can be a little tough, but once spring rolls around and the flows pick up a bit, generally 20 to 100 cfs, the fishing tends to pick up as well. In late March and April, midges and small mayflies will cover your bases under attractor nymphs such as egg patterns, Prince Nymphs, and Red Annelids. Muddy Creek tends to have quite a bit of silt, so midge fishing is a staple year-round.

Once summer rolls around, dry-fly fishing can be at its best. This is my favorite way to fish the creek. Standard dries including size 14 to 20 Stimulators, Royal Wulffs, and Parachute Adamses will get the job done. In August and early September, terrestrial fishing becomes active, especially in the lower stretches that offer public access. Grasshopper, beetle, and black ant patterns all work well along edges and places where the banks are undercut.

A few migratory brown trout start making their way into the river system in the fall. "I helped the Division of Wildlife electroshock this stretch," Teri Parvin of the Bureau of Land Management said. "We saw several trout in the 20- to 22-inch range." I believe these are browns migrating out of the Colorado, but at the right time, anglers can experience catching these fish.

Besides Muddy Creek, Wolford also offers good lake fishing and camping experiences. For anglers visiting the area with campers or RVs, the surrounding reservoir has 48 overnight camping spots with RV hookups. Call 800-472-4943 for campsite reservations.

Below the confluence of the Blue River and Muddy Creek, the Colorado flows through private ranchland for a couple miles before entering the rough and rowdy Gore Canyon. People come from all over the world to experience the whitewater this canyon provides; however, float fishing is not recommended.

GORE CANYON

From the town of Kremmling, the mouth of Gore Canyon makes its presence known right off the bat. It is obvious by the huge V cut in the landscape that this is where the Colorado becomes a powerful river. With the additions of the Blue River and Muddy Creek, the Colorado River transitions from somewhat of a soft meadow stream to a formidable western river.

Gore Canyon is a great escape when it comes to fishing the Colorado River. With other areas seeing so much float and fishing traffic, the canyon can remind you of the way things used to be. Besides the railroad, there are no signs of civilization in sight. Whether you are looking to pursue trout on a fly rod or just get out for some sightseeing or wildlife viewing, Gore Canyon is filled with possibilities.

The headwaters of Gore Canyon sit at an elevation of about 7,300 feet and descend 3 miles to an elevation of 6,900 feet. With its rapid descent, it has some of the biggest whitewater in the state. Rapids such as Pyrite and Tunnel Falls are class IV and V and can be entertaining for whitewater enthusiasts, but I do not recommend this stretch for float fishing. Instead, access the canyon from the Pumphouse Recreation Site. To get to Pumphouse, take Highway 9 south out of Kremmling for about 1 mile. Turn right on County Road 1, or as most locals refer to it, Trough Road. Follow the maintained dirt road 10 miles west until you come to the Pumphouse

The top of Gore Canyon looking from the town of Kremmling, Colorado. BOB DYE

The Pumphouse recreation area marks the first of many boat ramps traveling downstream. BOB DYE

Recreation Site sign. Turn right and follow the road down to the river. From there you will follow the signs that lead you to the Gore Trail. There is a BLM permit fee of $5 a day to use the area. The trail is on the south side of the river, and anglers can access the lower end of Gore Canyon and begin walking upstream. The trail tapers off about a mile and a half upstream in the canyon; steep walls and waterfalls prevent further safe travel.

Anglers should expect fairly easy walking conditions. The trail has a few inclines and the gravel can be slick along its path, but other than that, it is manageable. The canyon receives little angling pressure compared to access points downstream, and for this reason it is one of my favorite areas to fish along the Colorado River.

During the winter, fishing shuts down in the canyon, but it usually starts to pick up a bit around the end of March. Trout that have been wintering in the slower, deeper water begin to notice the longer spring days. Water temperatures that have been hovering between 35 and 37 degrees start creeping into the low 40s. Trout that have been eating just enough to get by begin to feel the water warm and start feeding a little more aggressively. Midge hatches begin to dominate the bug life in the canyon in late March and will continue strong through about mid-April.

Fishing in Gore Canyon can be hit-and-miss. I have had some days when you think you are on the world's greatest trout stream and others when you wonder if anything is alive in there. Anglers need to remember that when you are dealing with a river that is dominated by browns, they can be some of the most finicky fish around. However, on the right day, several fish can be taken in the early spring. Most fish in the canyon range from 12 to 15 inches, with several 16- to 20-inch fish lurking in every hole.

Midges come in varying sizes and color on the Colorado River. Sometimes taking a closer look at the aquatic life can mean the difference between a good day and a great day. JIM NEIBERGER

Nymph fishing is the way to go here, especially in the spring. The fish do not seem to concentrate as much on color as they do size. The Colorado has a lot of silt in its slower sections, and this makes for prolific midge hatches in the spring. Sizes can range from 18 through 26, so it's important that anglers carry a broad range of sizes. One of my favorite midge patterns of all time is the Rhinestone Midge. This knockoff of the old Zebra Midge is one of the most effective midge larva patterns around. One thing I have found over the years is that the trout in the Colorado River below Kremmling are gunmetal junkies. Most fly selections that have a gunmetal bead on them will probably work. Other midge patterns that I have found successful in the canyon include Greg Garcia's Rojo Midge, John Barr's Pure Midge Larva, Dorsey's Mercury Black Beauty, Periwinkles, and Pearl Jams.

I have never really had a good dry-fly day with midges in Gore Canyon, but on the right day, the fish will definitely take midge emergers. I normally run emergers as my last fly in a three-fly rig. Some of the most effective midge emergers are Neiberger's UPS Midge, Craven's Jubilee Midge, UV Midge, Dye's Purple Flash Midge, and Dorsey's Top Secret Midge, all in sizes 18 through 26.

Fishing these flies behind an attractor pattern is the best way to draw strikes from these overlooked trout. One of the best attractors has always been an egg fly, but being that rainbows only make up a small portion of the population in this part of the river, it is not as effective in the spring as it is in the fall. Instead, two patterns that work especially well in this stretch are the incomparable Prince Nymph and a red Copper John. Fish these patterns in sizes 12 through 18 with your midge patterns below, and this will cover most of your bases this time of year.

Grace Smith holds a healthy brown trout while fishing the Beaver Run stretch of water downstream of Gore Canyon. MARK ADAMS

As spring temperatures warm the water, different insects become more prevalent. Blue-Winged Olives hatch in the canyon, but it is not an overwhelming hatch like it is on other parts of the river. As the water warms, fish start moving into faster riffle water and feed on stonefly nymphs, among other insects. While this hatch will not be full-blown until the first week of June, I try to take advantage of early stonefly activity at the beginning of May because most of the time runoff is in full swing by the end of the month. Standard patterns like a Pat's Rubber Legs or Gorilla Stone work effectively, but one pattern that has been forgotten is the Bitch Creek stonefly imitation. This pattern was a must-have in every angler's fly box 20 years ago. Pick up a few representations of this old pattern; it is new to these fish.

During this time when the water temperatures are in the mid to high 40s, the trout start acting like they do in summer, meaning they are not all in the slow-moving pools but rather mid-seam shelves and faster riffled water. Gore Canyon's boulder-filled bottom creates deep seams and plunge pools, along with hard cut banks and a few riffles, so the trout have a bunch of places to hide in. Besides the obvious runs, fish can be found in the tiniest of seams and soft edges along the bank. This is when anglers want to arm themselves with dry-dropper rigs along with conventional nymph setups—and don't forget streamers.

Dry-dropper rigs can be very effective through the summer. This will allow you to cover water that may otherwise be overlooked. "Gore Canyon is an awesome big dry-fly section of water," says Jim Neiberger, longtime advocate of the Colorado River. Trout that are hugging the banks or in the soft riffles are looking for an easy meal. Big dries such as an Amy's Ant, Royal Wulff, Sofa Pillow, or anything big

A well-placed drift boat can be the key to success in certain runs of the Colorado River. Here Jeremy Hyatt plays a fish on the lower stretch of Little Gore Canyon. MARK ADAMS

and bushy will pull trout up from the bottom. Look for the nonobvious—there is usually fish behind every rock.

As late summer approaches, the trout tend to get a little lethargic. I have found streamer fishing to be very effective this time of year; the fish tend to find the faster, more oxygenated water and will move on streamers. Year after year, I have taken larger fish in the canyon in August than any other time of year. Some of the bigger fish that reside in the slower water down past Pumphouse seek out this faster, cooler water in the late summer.

While a multitude of streamer patterns are effective, a few work exceptionally well in the Colorado River. One is the standard Woolly Bugger—this old standby has taken more fish when situations call for big flies than any other bug. Others include the Meat Whistle, preferably in brown and white; Autumn Splendor; Goldie Lox; and various sculpin and leech patterns. One effective way to throw streamers is to fish your larger streamers first, then add a dropper consisting of a smaller leech or Woolly Bugger. This gives the effect of smaller baitfish fleeing the scene, which can put brown trout in a predatory mode.

The water below Gore Canyon is bigger than the smaller atmosphere upstream, and trout take on a different mentality in bigger water. "Trout can be sipping midge emergers in one hole and fifty yards upstream taking larger caddisflies," says John Perizzolo, float guide for Breckenridge Outfitters. This is one reason I enjoy guiding this stretch of water this time of year.

Gore Canyon can fish really well during high, dirty water. The Colorado River inside the canyon is made up of faster runs broken up by large boulders that have fallen from the high rocky peaks above. Browns and rainbows naturally seek out the slower water along the edges and behind boulders in an effort to feed. Remember that even if the water is not pristine, the trout still have to feed. This stretch is conducive to dry-dropper techniques during high or muddy water. The river here moves along at a little faster pace, allowing the angler to place flies in any area where a boulder breaks up the water or one of the larger boulders creates pocketwater along the edges.

PUMPHOUSE TO STATE BRIDGE

As the river shoots out of Gore Canyon, it opens up in the valley floor below. This is kind of the high desert of Colorado; with the Gore Range and the Eagles Nest Wilderness to the south, this section of the Colorado gives the angler a feeling of seclusion, away from towns or major highways. This stretch is lined with willows and a few juniper pines, followed by denser colonies of trees the higher up you go.

As anglers descend to the river from County Road 1 (Trough Road), it is easy to get excited about fishing this stretch, which probably defines the Colorado River to people in this state more than any other section. While I enjoy fishing the Colorado from its start in Rocky Mountain National Park all the way through Silt, I probably spend more time in this stretch. It has everything when it comes to angling

Overview of the Colorado River from Trough Road. This road is the best way to access the river from Gore Canyon all the way to State Bridge. BOB DYE

John Perizzolo, who guides out of the Blue Quill Angler in Evergreen, sets his anglers up to fish Miller Time above Little Gore Canyon. BOB DYE

opportunities, marking the beginning of float fishing and several walk-wade areas, not to mention some of the best fly water in the entire state.

Every major trout fishery has a fabled section of water in it, and this holds true for the Colorado River in this stretch, from its spectacular views of the Colorado high country right down to its holes. Every hole has a story and each hole has a name, and it probably holds more trout per mile than any other section of water except some of the sections below Glenwood Springs. Everything that makes a trout stream in the western states great is found all balled up in the section between Gore Canyon and Little Gore Canyon. As Ned Parker of Breckenridge Outfitters says, "This is the best stretch of trout stream in the West." Ned, a longtime guide and activist for these waters, knows a thing or two about the Colorado River. "It has it all," he explains. "Everything from nymph fishing, to dries, to streamers."

During the fall, this section really comes alive. Larger brown trout that were lurking in the deep waters in Little Gore Canyon begin to migrate into shallow water to spawn. Some of these fish can leave fly fishers wondering where they were in the summer. The brown trout spawn is really something in this stretch, but anglers need to respect this wild trout fishery. Fishing over redds or walking on them does not help the fishery at all. After all, the more fish spawn, the more fish there are in the future.

This section can be busy, receiving over 60,000 visitors annually. The Pumphouse Recreation Site is best reached from Denver by traveling west on I-70 to the Dillon-Silverthorne exit. Take Highway 9 north for 35 miles to County Road 1 (Trough Road), turn left, and follow it 10 miles until you reach the Pumphouse Recreation Site. Turn right and follow the road down to the river. This site has several amenities, including a pay phone, restrooms, three boat ramps, and camping facilities. Day use is $5 a day and that pass is good for Radium, State Bridge, Two Bridges, and Dotsero. To schedule shuttles, contact Rancho Del Rio at 970-653-4431.

Ten individual campsites are available on a first-come, first-served basis and cost $10 a night, and there are two reservable campsites that cost $30 a night. Fees are charged May 1 through October 31. To contact the BLM field office for campsite reservations, call 970-724-3000. Other activities include wildlife viewing, picnicking, and studying the area's rich history.

The first floatable section is the Pumphouse to Radium float (class II/III), which covers about 5 miles and is one of the more popular floats along the Colorado River. The Colorado leaves the valley floor from the Pumphouse Recreation Site and about a mile downstream flows through Little Gore Canyon. Needle Eye Rapid is located in Little Gore Canyon and can be hazardous. This is also one of the few floats that has ample BLM access for walk-wading.

The runs between the boat ramps towards Gore Canyon can provide good fishing. Long flats mixed with a few slower riffles make up this stretch of water. "This part of the river gets overlooked," says John Perizzolo, longtime guide with Blue Quill Anglers. "It doesn't have the notable structure that the lower river does." I agree

The Colorado River has unique scenery throughout its journey to the Gulf of California. Here the author and Pat Dorsey enjoy a day on the water between Gore Canyon and Little Gore Canyon near the Pumphouse Recreation Site. MARK ADAMS

Pat Dorsey, co-owner of the Blue Quill Angler in Evergreen, admires a solid brown in the Pumphouse area of the Colorado River. The stretch between Kremmling and State Bridge has more 12- to 16-inch browns per mile than any other stretch of river. MARK ADAMS

Dr. Eric Atha shows off a nice brown he caught on a Jenny Midge, one of his own creations. JIM NEIBERGER

with John and rarely fish it myself, but on the rare occasion when you see fish rising in there, it makes you think of how many fish are actually in this stretch. Any rock the size of a beach ball will harbor fish behind it. This is also good streamer water; it is wide open and easy to cover a lot of water.

When walk-wading this stretch, I generally park in the lot by the third boat ramp. From this point, there is a trail on the south side of the river. Walking this path is not difficult—it's pretty much flat, with some brushy sections. It's about one river mile to the beginning of Little Gore Canyon, and this is where you want to start. I refer to this piece above the canyon as the Gravel Flats. The river really deltas out here before entering the canyon. This water is made up of soft riffles with 20- to 30-foot dishes peppered throughout.

From here, anglers can go one of two ways. Going downstream, there is really no maintained trail into the canyon and access is tough unless you are floating in a drift boat. So moving upstream, the next fishing hole is Miller Time, so named because it is the last time you are going to enjoy a beer before rowing your buns off in the rough water in the Little Gore Canyon, namely the Needle Eye Rapid. This is classic trout water at its best. The run is 200 yards long and starts with an awesome riffle at the head of it. It is about 6 feet deep in the fall and is a great wintering hole. Trout start gravitating towards these deeper runs as water temperatures begin dipping into the low 40s.

As you leave Miller Time, the next stretch upstream is Public Enemy. It never fails in this hole—every boat in the river will somehow screw up your fishing here. In the fall, however, boating pressure declines dramatically. This is a beautiful piece of trout water, with shelves, bowls, and riffles. I am not sure why, but several rainbows call this water home.

The run directly above this is Goose Egg Run. For years it seemed we could hardly catch anything here except a cold, but the high-water year of 2011 changed this run for the best and numerous trout now reside here. From here you reach the bottom of the islands (braids), and every one of these channels is choked with fish. Beginning on the right side looking upstream, anglers will encounter Beaver Run; this is another long, deep run with an awesome riffle at the head of it. The best way to fish this is on the left side looking upstream. With flows at 400 to 700 cfs in the fall, anglers can cross safely between Goose Egg Run and Public Enemy. While this run always has fish in it, the number seems to double during the spawn. Trout appear to migrate to this area in search of an egg trail. The head of Beaver Run has no shortage of spawning fish, and while anglers should not target these fish, the ones below are fair game.

Staying in the right channel, upstream from Beaver Run, fly fishers will encounter the Crescent Moon Hole. This run makes a hard right turn and creates sort of a back eddy. This hole fishes best from the northwest side of the river, or river right looking downstream. Crescent Moon has no shortage of hard, fast water, so weight (split shot) is your friend here. While at certain flows it looks unfishable, water hydraulics tell a different story.

After fishing the right side of the islands (Beaver Run), I usually walk back down towards Goose Egg Run and head up the left side. This has some great water as well. Starting at the bottom, the river takes on some San Juan River characteristics.

A drift boat sets up a line to float through the Needle Eye Rapid in Little Gore Canyon. The Needle Eye tests the skills of even the most skilled oarsman. This rapid should always be approached carefully, especially at higher flows. MARK ADAMS

With bowls and dishes along with some gravel flats, trout seem to find every nook and cranny here. Farther up the left side is the Toilet Bowl. I think every river in the world has a "toilet bowl" hole, and the Colorado is no exception. This one fishes really well any time of the year but is a difficult hole to fish. It requires the angler to throw 20-foot downstream mends, but with the right drift, it's game on. If this run presents too many problems in achieving a good drift, try tying on a couple of streamers and run those through. There is more than one way to skin a cat.

As you leave the Toilet Bowl, moving upstream, the next piece of fishable water on the left side is Long Riffle Run. The name says it all—this is about a 100-yard riffle. At this point, timing is everything: With cooling water temperatures, trout start to vacate the faster runs in search of deeper, slower water. But certain years when the weather stays nice and the water temps remain in the mid to upper 40s, feeding fish can still be found here.

While Little Gore Canyon is floatable, caution must be used to navigate the river. The Needle Eye Rapid can eat drift boats. If this is your first visit to the area, I recommend hiring a local guide to navigate the water safely. This will give you more time to fish and enjoy the beauty of the area without worrying about crashing into the canyon walls.

Little Gore Canyon has towering walls that funnel the river into deeper pools. This allows for awesome bang-it-off-the-rocks terrestrial fishing. Fish that are hovering in the first 3 to 4 feet of the water column are waiting for something to plop down in their feeding lanes. In other words, these rock walls give the impression of undercut banks.

Streamer fishing can be as good as it gets for the resident brown trout population, but rainbows like this one like to get in on the action as well. JIM NEIBERGER

Some of the areas between Kremmling and State Bridge are pretty deep, including a couple of spots in Little Gore Canyon that are 8 to 12 feet deep. I have spent a little time probing these areas for bruiser browns but so far have only come up with average-size fish. Those bruisers have to be in there, though. As with most things in fly fishing, timing is everything. Therefore, the next time you are fishing the Colorado River in July, try some streamer patterns in the fastest water you can find and do not forget to go into the abyss—who knows what's down there?

Fishing in this section usually starts around Saint Patrick's Day and concludes around the first of December as cold temperatures take hold of the river. Springtime brings warmer water temperatures, and small midge and mayfly patterns usually will get the job done. As spring transitions into summer, Salmonflies hatch. While the hatch begins several miles downstream, this section can be at an all-time best late May through the early part of June. After runoff concludes, usually around mid-July, the river experiences some of the best aquatic hatches of the year. Caddisflies, Yellow Sallies, Pale Morning Duns, and occasional Blue-Winged Olives can offer up some great fly-fishing opportunities during the summer in this section of river. As fall rolls around, brown trout begin their yearly courtship and the fishing season will continue deep into the fall months.

From the end of Little Gore Canyon, the river opens back up and flows by the little town of Radium, where there are also walk-wade opportunities in the area. Radium Recreation Site is located 9 miles upstream from State Bridge on County Road 1 (Trough Road) or 7 miles downstream from Pumphouse and is one of the more user-friendly sites. Easy access and fairly easy wading (when the flows are

Some areas of the Colorado River require a drift boat to fish them thoroughly. Here Mark Adams probes a long, deep run just above the town of Radium. PAT DORSEY

Jim Neiberger and John Gonzales finish the day at the Boat Ramp Hole just downstream of Radium. This piece of water can fish extremely well when midge or *Baetis* hatches are present.
BOB DYE

under 700 cfs) make this stretch a go-to area in the fall. One way to approach this section is to wade across at the lower boat ramp, walk downstream a couple of bends, and fish your way back. There is a lot of good water down here—deep bend pools with long, gradual riffles leading into them. Many anglers just park by the bridge or the boat ramp and never really fish all the water in this area. The second option is to fish the water from the Radium Bridge upstream. This piece is divided by a series of islands that break the river up into more manageable stretches, especially at higher flows.

If you decide to eat lunch at one of the many picnic tables down by the boat ramp, don't be surprised to get a visit from a couple of the local donkeys in search of a free meal. There are some pretty nice fish here as well; I had a client land a 25-inch brown in the fall of 2013, with a mouth that could swallow a baby duck. Most of the trout in this stretch average 12 to 15 inches, with several in the 16- to 19-inch range. This area receives quite a bit of hunting pressure, so wearing white and brown clothing probably is not the smartest thing to do.

The approximately 6.5-mile float from Radium to Rancho Del Rio can be a little less congested than Pumphouse. The float is rated a class II, but the Yarmony Rapid can be a class III at higher flows. From Radium to Rancho Del Rio the river slows down a bit, and while there is walk-wading along parts of the river, this stretch fishes better out of a drift boat. Slow, deep bends require long drifts, which can be tough to accomplish wading this section, especially at higher flows. To arrange shuttles, contact Rancho Del Rio at 970-653-4431. The Radium Recreation Site requires a $5 a day-use fee. Nine campsites are available on a first-come, first-served basis and cost $6 dollars per night. There are restrooms and a pay phone just south of the boat ramps.

This section of river offers a little different outlook than the Pumphouse to Radium section or the one after, Rancho Del Rio to State Bridge. Aside from the Yarmony Rapid, this stretch is slower moving and requires anglers to adjust their approach. Most of the river is made up of long, slow-moving runs, but on closer look there are countless bowls and dishes that provide trout with shelter along with feeding lanes. Knowing where these areas lie is the key to fishing down here. While the insect life and the hatches remain the same, this can be a very productive piece of water—it just takes some time to learn the structure. Fishing from a drift boat is without a doubt the best way to access this water. Often the boat can be used to back-row a stretch, enabling anglers to hit the bowls and long shallow shelves that litter the river. This section in my opinion is one of the best dry-fly portions of the river. Long, smooth runs allow anglers to cover vast amounts of open water, particularly during the summer when hatches are at their peak.

From Rancho Del Rio to State Bridge, the Colorado River takes on a slightly different look, from more-braided stretches of water to faster riffle runs dumping into deeper water. Floating down to State Bridge, one can't help but feel the history of the area. Recent archaeological work has found evidence that people lived in the region over 8,000 years ago. More recently, the Ute Indians inhabited the area a little over a thousand years ago. The names of some of the area's features are a reminder that Indians such as Chief Yarmony once lived along the Colorado River. Aside from the water below Glenwood Springs, this stretch without a doubt harbors some of the largest fish in the system. Browns and rainbows average 12 to 16 inches, with several in the 20- to 22-inch class, and whitefish are also present.

The float from Rancho Del Rio to State Bridge is approximately 4 miles and has a good amount of wading possibilities, and it is recommended when time constraints are a factor. Private put-ins are available at Rancho Del Rio (fee required). To

reach Rancho Del Rio, take Highway 9 from Dillon 35 miles to County Road 1 (Trough Road), hang a left, and travel 23 miles to the Rancho Del Rio sign. Turn right and continue down to the facilities, which include plenty of campsites and a small grocery in addition to the boat launch. The fine folks down here can fill you in on shuttle information and cabin rentals.

This is one section where a drift boat or raft can really make for an enjoyable day. While fishing from a boat can yield

Rancho Del Rio is one of the few places on the river to pick up supplies and has one of the only shuttle services on the upper reaches of the river. BOB DYE

Drift boats can be a very effective way to fish some of the river's hard-to-reach areas. Here the author is in a good position thanks to the rower, Jeremy Hyatt. MARK ADAMS

some fish in the net, it is more useful to employ the boat as a tool to get out and wade fish certain parts of the river. This stretch has numerous braids and islands that typically fish really well during the spring and summer months. Many of the fishing holes require anglers to make subtle changes in their rig rather than "one-timing it" from a boat.

Approximately 3 miles down on this float, closer to State Bridge, the Piney River enters the Colorado from the south. Access can be had to this little gem by simply walking up the south side of the river from the State Bridge launch/parking area or floating down to the river from Rancho Del Rio. One of my favorite things to do on this float is to access the Piney for some dry-fly action. The fish in the Piney are a tad on the small side, but it's a welcome break sometimes from staring over a nymph rig on the Colorado all day. Anglers can fish the Piney River from the confluence upstream for about a mile; after that it is private property.

While this section can appear to be busy with float traffic, it can be less congested than the river's upper sections. Insect life through this stretch is the same as the rest of the river, with one exception. Here the river receives more sunlight during the early spring, which allows slightly higher water temperatures, thus springtime fishing is generally a little better down here versus the river's upper reaches. This is also why Salmonflies start lower on the river and move upstream. Stoneflies need the water to be around 50 to 55 degrees to begin their yearly mating season.

For wading anglers, the stretch above State Bridge is only accessible from the south side of the boat ramp. Crossing the railroad tracks is considered trespassing. There is a lot of water from the boat ramp up to the Yarmony Bridge. Anglers can usually find solitude over here, aside from the occasional drift boat passing through.

Fishing from a drift boat is a popular way to explore and fish the Colorado River; however, sections like this one inside Little Gore Canyon have class III and IV rapids at certain flows. Consulting fly shops or checking flow charts is recommended for a safe floating adventure. BOB DYE

Left: A bird's-eye view from the Radium Bridge inside a drift boat. Here anglers prepare to fish the 12-foot-deep run located just above the bridge. BOB DYE

Pat Dorsey is regarded as one of the state's best tailwater fly fishermen. Here he fights a fish down from the Pumphouse Recreation Site while wading outside the drift boat on a crisp fall day. LANDON MAYER

Landon Mayer is one of the West's most prolific fly fishermen. Here he takes time out from the drift boat to thoroughly work a streamer pattern near Little Gore Canyon in one of the river's many riffled sections. JAY NICHOLS

Mark Adams holds a beautiful 19-inch brown he caught while floating the Pumphouse to Radium section of river. While most of the fish in this section average 12 to 16 inches, it is not uncommon to catch several of these brutes during a day on the water.

PAT DORSEY

Grace Smith cradles a brown she caught while fishing the Gravel Flats at the head of Little Gore Canyon. This braided section of water can have some of the best insect hatches on the upper-middle river. PAT DORSEY

The author and Mike Lyons share a laugh as he plays a nice a brown trout in the Crescent Moon Hole located downstream from Pumphouse. JIM NEIBERGER

Wading is moderate, but for the angler who does not mind a little walking, this can be as good as it gets. Countless riffle runs, pocketwater, and deep holes make up this stretch—not to mention the Piney River dumps in here as well. The Piney can be a little gem of a river; it has awesome dry-fly fishing in the summer, and during the late fall, brown trout stack up in it as well.

Most of the fish caught here are between 10 and 15 inches, but several fish have been caught in the 18- to 20-inch range, with a few topping 24 inches. There is also a better than average chance that anglers are going to catch a few whitefish down here from time to time.

STATE BRIDGE TO DOTSERO

This stretch of the Colorado River (what I consider the lower middle) covers about 42 miles of water and seems wilder than the upper river. You really feel like you have gone back in time when traveling through this stretch. While mountain peaks still tower around you, the valley floor consists of more of a high-mountain desert, with sandstone walls, tall sagebrush, and thick willows lining the river's edge in certain stretches. With all the Colorado River has to offer, this section is probably used the least when it comes to fishing and rafting. Scott Willoughby, outdoor writer for the *Denver Post* says, "It is the most underutilized section along the Colorado River corridor."

With the help of John Stavney, District 12 executive director, and Toby Sprunk, Eagle County Open Space director, along with the support of Eagle County voters, new boat launch areas and walk-wade accesses are being created. Previously this

The Shale Hole II, located about 2 miles downstream of Rancho Del Rio, has countless riffles and long runs to fish. Here the author retrieves a brown that took a size 16 Soft Hackle Pheasant Tail. This fly has a lot of movement and is a favorite among Colorado fly fishers. JAY NICHOLS

One of the best ways to access the river below Kremmling is via drift boat. Here anglers get their gear in order at the State Bridge boat launch site, one of the many access points along the Colorado River corridor. BOB DYE

section of the river was broken up by long floats. For example, State Bridge to Catamount was a 14-mile float, which made for a long day. Now with the new Two Bridges access point, this float has become more manageable. "This kind of proactive approach really opens some doors down here," Willoughby says. "It takes the pressure off the upper river, meaning the Pumphouse and Radium recreation areas." The other thing it does is makes this stretch more accessible to Eagle-Vail residents, not to mention the tourist activity. This was never one of my favorite areas to float, as it was simply too time-consuming to fish the river effectively, but the addition of Two Bridges has opened up a lot of possibilities.

Given the sheer mileage in this section, I think it is easier to break it up into the stretches that are floatable. Remember, down in this section numerous tributaries feed the river, so the water can be muddy during runoff and through the summer.

State Bridge to Two Bridges

Public access at Two Bridges allows anglers even more opportunity to fish the Colorado River. This stretch has a lot of fishable water. From State Bridge there are some long, deep runs followed by a few shelves and drop-offs, but down about a mile and a half you start getting into some braided stretches of water. And like the river's upper reaches, this is when you can start breaking it down into more manageable pieces.

In the early spring, flows here typically run about 400 to 600 cfs depending on snowpack the previous winter. While this is a floatable flow, it makes for great walk-wading. I usually like to walk upstream from the Two Bridges boat ramp and fish the few runs before getting to the first set of islands. Midges and small mayflies are standard fare here, but larger flies such as Prince Nymphs and Rubber Legs will take fish as well.

Lots of silt in the slower sections make for great midge habitat. Around the middle of March, the large midges begin to hatch. They can range in size from

Anglers prepare to launch a drift boat at the Two Bridges launch site. The Colorado River has numerous put-ins and takeouts from Pumphouse all the way downriver to Silt. MARK ADAMS

Colorado River brown trout are unique in size, shape, and color. Here an angler admires a stout male brown she caught down by Bond, a small town a few miles downstream from State Bridge. BOB DYE

16 through 20 and really get the trout feeding actively. It is somewhat hard to believe that the midges get to this size down here, and I have even been fooled into thinking it was a BWO hatch at first. Take advantage of this larger midge hatch, as it seems to be short-lived.

About the second week of April, the Blue-Winged Olives make their return. I have really only caught this hatch a couple of times down here, so I think they are sporadic at best. Still, it is enough to get the trout riled up, so anglers should be prepared. Standard BWO nymph patterns such as Stalcup's Baetis and Flashback Pheasant Tails will work; there is no magic fly, just the way it is presented. Emerger patterns should consist of standard Rs2s and Soft Hackle Pheasant Tails rigged as the last fly in a three-fly setup.

As with the rest of the Colorado upstream, this stretch has a large population of free-living caddis. When water temperatures begin to rise, these insects, like the trout, become active and are a staple food source. When the fishing on the Colorado gets tough, one thing I always do is tie on a caddis (free-living forms). The river has a ton of bug life in it, so something that worked one day may not work the next. Constant change is the norm when fishing large freestone rivers, but caddis patterns seem to bring relatively consistent success beginning in mid-March and can be effective throughout the fishing season.

This float is only about 4 miles long, which makes for a great day of using the boat as a vehicle to get from one wading spot to the next. This is important in the springtime because the Salmonfly hatch is just getting under way. With the right water conditions, this is one of many places you want to be. While the bigger stones can be found throughout the river, they really seem to be in higher concentrations from here (State Bridge to Two Bridges) up through Hot Sulphur Springs. Most anglers are searching for the hatch upstream, and while it will eventually get there, this is where the bulk of it starts.

The best way to plan a fishing trip down here this time of year is to contact a local fly shop or Rancho Del Rio for the latest water conditions. Rancho Del Rio is located on the water, between Radium and State Bridge, so they have a little better

Drift boat anglers prepare for another fishing adventure near the Rancho Del Rio boat ramp. This ramp is a popular put-in and takeout along the Colorado River, with shuttle service to most of the river's access points provided by Rancho Del Rio. BOB DYE

idea of what is going on with the river. They can also run your shuttles, which range from $35 to $45. Their number is 970-653-4431.

Sheephorn Creek near Radium and the Piney River near State Bridge can add lots of flow and really murk up the water down here. If this is the case, moving upstream in search of more favorable conditions is a good bet, though in some years even upstream can be tough. Sometimes the lower stretches of water can fish well on high, dirty water days, but there are times when it is just not going to happen. Rainstorms in the area can sometimes drive you to look for other options; keeping alternate destinations on the back burner can turn a non-fishing day into a fishable one.

In summer flows, the braids and side channels seem to fill with hungry trout. The trout move into these riffles and mid-seam currents waiting for PMDs and Yellow Sallies to become active.

Being that this is a short float, anglers can spend most of the day fishing and not worrying how far the boat ramp is, and because this is a relatively new public access, fishing pressure has been pretty light down here compared to the river's upper floatable areas. This float has jumped up a few notches when it comes to my favorite floats on the Colorado, for as much as I love floating the river, I do not like long, drawn-out floats. To me, unlike the North Platte(Grey Reef section) or the Bighorn, this is not a boat-conducive river when it comes to long drifts out of a drift boat or a raft. Anglers can throw dries and streamers from a boat effectively, but when it comes to getting out and dissecting the river, a boat is just a tool to get you from one place to another.

The author studies the water near Little Gore Canyon before picking the right drift lane. Choosing the right drift lane optimizes the angler's chance of hooking fish in a particular run.
MARK ADAMS

Being that it is a good 35 miles from the closest tailwater, water temperatures affect the river's lower reaches immensely. These temperatures can reach the low 70s on hot days. While this is nothing new to the fish, it is a major reason why the trout populations are predominately brown trout, which can tolerate warmer water better than rainbows. Depending on river flows, which usually average about 1,100 to 1,400 cfs, fishing tends to slow a little in the middle of the day. This is another reason I like these short floats. Putting in early in the morning or late in the afternoon is more of a recipe for success than struggling through the hottest part of the day. In the morning you can have a chance at hitting the Trico hatch. Though not as dense as on the upper stretches of the Colorado, the hatch is still strong enough to get the fish feeding.

There are several rock gardens in this stretch of water, some of which have 2- to 3-foot canals between them with considerable water flow. These areas will hold fish, and they seem to be more apt to take a fly when the other trout seem to have disappeared.

This float has a few primitive camping areas along the way. Two of the campsites, the Double Pine site and Sage Brush Flats, are for float traffic only. Both are on the south side of the river and are located about 1.5 to 2 miles down from State Bridge.

To reach State Bridge from Denver, take I-70 west through Vail to the Wolcott exit, then take Highway 131 north for 14 miles until you hit State Bridge. The boat ramp is on the south side of the river. To reach State Bridge from Kremmling, take Highway 9 south 1 mile to County Road 1 (Trough Road), then take Trough Road approximately 24 miles west until you hit State Bridge. There is a $5 fee to use the area, and this pass is also good at Pumphouse, Radium, Two Bridges, and Dotsero. Restrooms are located at all these sites. For boat shuttle information, call Rancho Del Rio at 970-653-4431.

Two Bridges to Catamount

With the acquisition of the Two Bridges access from a private outfitter, Eagle County Open Space has done something that very few entities have been able to accomplish. This is historic, I think, when it comes to public access. So many times over the years, whether it's hunting or fishing, the public always ends up with the short end of the stick. "This is an exciting time for the Colorado River," says Scott Willoughby of the *Denver Post*. There are not too many places I can think of where the public is gaining ground, and what better place to add boat ramps and fishing opportunities than along one of the state's best rivers? Besides a few outfitters that float these sections, the Colorado River receives very little pressure here compared to the stretches of water upstream. I really think that these new additions are going to change the way the Colorado is fished, floated, and used for other recreational purposes.

This approximately 9-mile float has some interesting features. There are a few braids and side channels, but mostly it is made up of long riffles with a few deeper

runs. Inside this stretch is a little under 4 miles of public access, and all of it is on the north side of the river. Technically, it is illegal to cross the railroad tracks to access some of these public areas, so we will just come at it from a floating perspective.

While navigating any waterway safety should be the number one goal, but this float is one of the easier ones. An interesting feature is the 40-foot-high waterwheel that sits southeast of McCoy. It is the largest waterwheel once used for irrigation in the state of Colorado.

One fly that always seems to work exceptionally well in the lower section of the river is a red Copper John, a great searching pattern that seems to work better on the lower stretches than the upper. I think the reason for this is simple: The water just does not have the clarity down here as long into the spring

Kelli Blue landed this fish on a size 18 Buckskin Nymph, which is one of the most versatile flies on the Colorado River. BOB DYE

as does the river's upper reaches. At any rate, the fish seem to average 10 to 14 inches through here, a tad smaller than other parts of the river. Larger fish do exist, however; I think it's just the way the year classes stack up right now.

One thing that can be special about these lower stretches, if the water clarity hangs on long enough in April, is the caddis. Caddis (Brachycentrus) on the lower river (below Glenwood Springs) can be as good as it gets the first couple of weeks of April, but up here, it is really hit-and-miss. It is definitely a timing thing: If cooler weather hangs around and does not push the river into pre-runoff, fishing the early caddis hatch can be phenomenal. I have hit this several times below Glenwood Springs, but only the last couple of years up here. One reason is the drought that plagued the river in 2012 and 2013, which allowed for much lower water flows. I would probably tell anglers that you have a much better chance of hitting this hatch down in New Castle, but if you are in the area, it is worth giving it a look.

Another effective way to approach this water, especially in the private sectors, is to toss streamers to the bank. While keeping the boat at a manageable casting distance from the bank, anglers should cast and strip to every depression and behind every rock, and work every side riffle. This method covers a whole heap of water in a short amount of time.

There is not a large amount of walk-wade access in the first couple of miles. However, starting upriver from Cottonwood Bend, there is 0.75 mile of BLM land on the northeast side of the river. From there floaters can access several other BLM parcels on their way to the Catamount boat ramp. If the flows are less than 800 cfs in July, walk-wading is an option. Walk-wade access is located where County Road 301 returns back to the river, about a mile from Cottonwood Bend. Note: It is technically illegal to cross the railroad tracks.

The first part of this float has quite a bit of private water, but farther downstream is more BLM access. This stretch has some nice riffled sections with mid-seam shelves dropping into some deep holes. Once you leave the Two Bridges boat ramp, there are a couple areas where you can turn a few laps in the drift boat, but I kind of push hard down to the public stretches, as I would rather

The author displays one of the many quality brown trout that reside in the Colorado's middle sections. Browns make up a large portion of the river's biomass, especially from Pumphouse to Dotsero. JAY NICHOLS

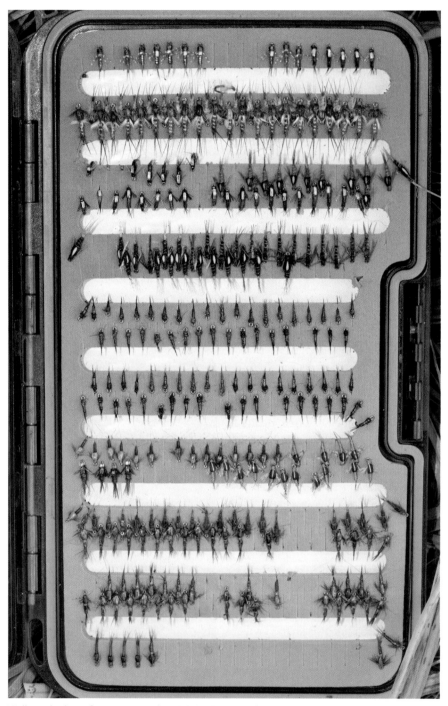

Well-stocked mayfly patterns such as BWOs, PMDs, and Tricos are a must on the Colorado River. Mayflies make up a huge portion of the trout's diet in the Colorado and its tributaries.
JAY NICHOLS

get out and spend some time dissecting the water than make one pass through a hole or riffle run.

It is somewhat interesting that the fish caught in the summer usually average 10 to 14 inches, but then all of a sudden they seem to be on the larger side, which makes you wonder what actually is in here on a daily basis. I have talked to several anglers during the fall months with the same result: "The fish seem to be bigger." When you are dealing with a brown trout fishery, this can often be the case. I do not think there are a bunch of 10-pound fish swimming around, but you regularly pop fish in the 15- to 18-inch range, with an occasional fish over 20. One reason for this, I believe, is that the mature fish begin the early stages of their spawning rituals and while they're not digging redds yet, they are on the move and beginning to stage for the upcoming spawn in October. Many of these fish will feed heavily this time of year before the rigors of the spawn.

This area doesn't get much fishing pressure. Last year we floated it on two different occasions and saw one bank angler and two drift boats. I do not think it holds the sheer numbers of spawning fish, but there are certainly areas where redds are evident. In fact, the run right below Elk Creek had a number of spawning beds, and while we left the spawning trout alone, the fish were stacked like cordwood below them. In these situations you do not need to be a rocket scientist to figure out what to use: egg flies and midges. These fish are already in feed mode with all the eggs coming down the current—all you need is a good presentation and it's game over.

Take advantage of these lower sections and the newly placed boat ramps in the fall. After word starts getting out, you may not have as much solitude.

To get to Two Bridges from Denver, take I-70 west to the Wolcott/Steamboat Springs exit, then take Highway 131 north for 14 miles until you reach State Bridge. Go over the bridge and stay left, then travel about 4 miles to reach the Two Bridges put-in on your left. There is a $5 per vehicle fee to use this area, and the pass is also valid at Pumphouse, Radium, State Bridge, and Dotsero. There is no camping at Two Bridges, but camping is permitted at Catamount. Shuttles can be scheduled through Rancho Del Rio; their number is 970-653-4431.

Catamount to Pinball

Over the many miles of floatable water the Colorado River has to offer, it probably does not get any rougher than this stretch. This is about a 9-mile float, and as much as I enjoy floating the Colorado, the Rodeo Rapid below Burns is not my idea of a good time. I am sure some whitewater enthusiasts would argue this point, but I rather enjoy looking down on the trout, not the other way around. I would recommend putting in at Derby Junction, below Rodeo Rapid; it is a private boat ramp but for a small fee you can save your boat. This eliminates one obstacle, but there are also a couple of class II rapids. Boaters should take time and scout before proceeding.

This is a gorgeous float, however, and just downstream from Derby Junction there is a large amount of public access on the northwest side of the river. This 6-mile stretch is accessible by County Road 301, and while only part of it is on BLM land, it merits a look or two whether you are floating or walk-wading. Generally speaking, most recreational users of this stretch are people that have been on the water for a

Rodeo Rapid is extremely dangerous and not recommended for drift boats. Putting in at Derby Junction, which is below the rapid, is advised. BOB DYE

couple days. The Colorado is famous for its overnight floating opportunities during the warmer months. This area receives a fair share of angling pressure but falls short compared to the sections 20-plus miles upriver.

In my opinion, there is really no need to float this stretch in the spring, when the water is still low enough for effective walk-wading. Several pull-offs are located along the road, and being that the railroad tracks are on the other side, there is no technical reason you can't fish in these spots. I usually find a spot, hit a few of the highlights, and move on to the next pull-off.

Once you leave the Catamount boat launch, so does the accessible road. The road does not make its return until it gets close to Burns. This is "wild Colorado," and even if you do not fish, this is a spectacular float. I would recommend floating with an outfitter that is comfortable with the Rodeo Rapid; it is *not* recommended for drift boats. As mentioned earlier, if you are not an experienced oarsman, putting in at Derby Creek for a small fee is an option.

This is one of the best sections to hopper-dropper fish, especially in the long, narrow stretches. These fish don't typically see flies on a day-to-day basis, so presentations drifted along the edges in front of the boat will usually result in a splashy take or your dry fly disappearing. I have taken several fish on this float using nothing but a size 12 Stimulator followed by a size 16 standard Prince Nymph. I am sure other things will work, but the trout do not seem to be too particular.

Streamers are another preferred choice, as long as you have an oarsman that can keep you within casting distance of the bank. Fish will readily chase well-placed streamer patterns, especially on cloudy or dirty water days. One thing that I have found is that sculpin patterns seem to turn a few more fish in this segment than in other parts of the river. One sculpin pattern that I particularly like is the Sculpzilla in a size 8. It's a buggy pattern that holds its own under the water.

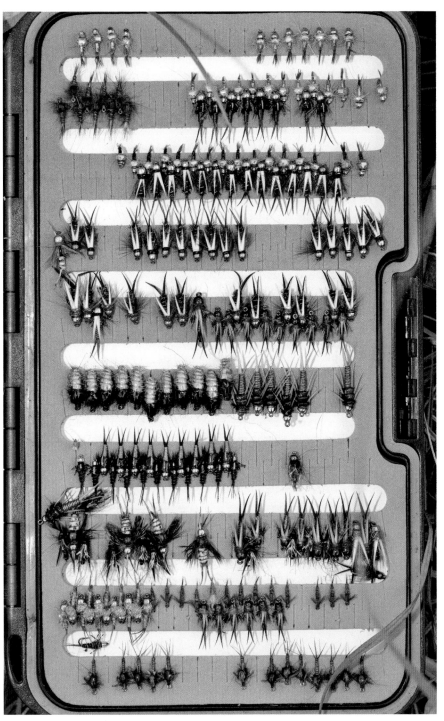

A variety of attractor patterns will help fish notice your presentations as well as hook fish. Prince Nymphs are one of the best attractor and fish-catching patterns ever invented. JAY NICHOLS

The stretch from Dotsero all the way up to Two Bridges is relatively undiscovered in the fall. I think all the great things Eagle County Open Space is doing will change this, just from the standpoint of easier access. To reach Catamount from Wolcott, take Highway 131 north 14 miles to State Bridge, cross the bridge, and stay left until you hit County Road 301. Turn left and follow the road down to the BLM Catamount sign. The boat launch is on the south side of the river. This is a no-fee area with restrooms and camping in addition to the boat ramp.

Pinball to Horse Creek River Access

The new Horse Creek River Access is another great asset that Eagle County has contributed to Colorado River recreation. It breaks up what was traditionally a 14-mile float from Pinball to Cottonwood. Pinball to Horse Creek is now 6 miles, and Horse Creek to Cottonwood is now an 8-mile adventure. The Colorado River in this stretch offers even more stunning views compared to its already impressive setting. The beginning of the float travels through beautiful Red Rock Canyon and is worthy of having a camera ready to shoot some of these stunning rock formations.

While this float is a scenic one, it does have its challenges. The first obstacle boaters will encounter is Pinball Rapid. It is a class II rapid, but mix in the bridge pylon and all of a sudden you can find yourself in a heap of trouble. It is best to slow the boat to a crawl and stay left of the pylon. The next section of difficulty is about a 1.5 miles down from the Pinball Rapid; Posey Creek will be on your left as a marker. This is where County Road 301 and the railroad tracks cross the river (Twin Bridges). While it is not too difficult to navigate, caution should always be used when floating around bridges.

Fishing down here can be excellent, but it can face the same challenges as the preceding sections of water. There are a number of tributaries in this piece of water,

This long but slender brown took a sculpin pattern in the river's lower-middle section. Larger browns would rather eat a big meal than several hundred tiny insects. JAY NICHOLS

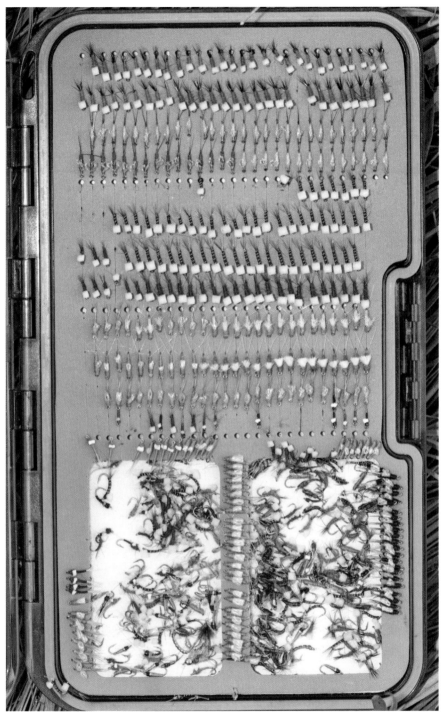

Ample emerging mayfly patterns will ensure a great day fishing the Colorado River. Sometimes emergers can spark the interest of otherwise finicky trout. JAY NICHOLS

This angler does a nice job landing one of the many 16-inch brown trout that reside in the Colorado River's middle stretches near State Bridge. MARK ADAMS

and none of them can ruin water conditions faster than Red Dirt Creek. It certainly lives up to its name and can make for some tough sledding after a rainstorm. Checking water conditions is always a good idea before fishing this section, but when conditions are favorable, it is definitely worthwhile.

Some public access is available to walk-wade; however, most of it is around the Pinball boat ramp downstream. This can fish pretty well the latter part of March and the first couple weeks of April. I would say floating is your best option when it comes to accessing the river, though. Being that it is a relatively short float, using the boat as a tool to walk-wade the public areas and then moving on will allow you to cover the entire portion of the river.

This section can suffer through the spring due to high, muddy water. Similar to the upper reaches, this stretch can be vulnerable to heavy rainfall in the various tributaries such as Red Dirt Creek, Poison Creek, and Willow Creek, besides some of the latest drought years, making it virtually unfishable during the late spring and summer months. Try migrating farther upstream to Pumphouse, Parshall, or some of the Colorado River's tailwater sections. Also, try some of the area's other fisheries, such as the upper Eagle, Roaring Fork, Frying Pan, and Yampa Rivers.

The addition of the new boat ramp at the Horse Creek River Access changes the way you would normally float this in summer. Before, it was such a long float that if you weren't familiar with the river, you wasted half your time trying to find the best water. That was always the frustrating thing about some of the floats along the Colorado. As a matter of fact, I would just concentrate all of my efforts on the best fishable sections and would not worry about the long floats. I know there are anglers that like to fish entirely from a boat the whole day, just making one presentation per run, and sometimes that is the only scenario when you are on private water. However, if you can break your floats down into shorter sections and have the opportunity to wade a couple areas, you are going to catch more fish than the next guy. It's just simple math. This segment is no different from any other—it has private and public access, but now anglers can take time and figure out a run without having to worry about time constraints.

August is a great time to be on this stretch. While other stretches can suffer from warm water, especially in the middle of the day, this section will run a smidgeon cooler with its small tributaries entering the system. While it may not add up to much, I think it is enough. This time of the year, terrestrials surely add to the mix. The couple of times I've done this float basically consisted of casting terrestrial patterns such as hoppers and Chernobyls to the banks and nymph-fishing the faster, more oxygenated runs. One thing I have noticed is that Tricos seem to be a little more numerous down here than in the previous couple of stretches. So fishing these little mayflies in the morning hours is a good bet. This is a very scenic float, and now with the addition of the new boat ramp, anglers should take advantage of this section.

To get to the Pinball launch, take Highway 131 north out of Wolcott for 14 miles. Continue west on Highway 131 after State Bridge to County Road 301, then turn left and travel for approximately 12 miles. You will see the BLM Pinball sign on your left. If you are traveling from the Glenwood Springs area, it is best to take I-70 east for about 15 miles to the Dotsero exit (exit 133). From there take County Road 301 north for about 15 miles. The boat launch will be on your right. The Pinball access has a restroom and a couple of campsites. There is primitive camping at Jack Flats a couple of river miles down from the boat ramp on the south side of the river; some beautiful hiking trails leave from this campsite as well.

As this new boat ramp gains in popularity, hopefully so will its public access points. Right now, there are two stretches of public access around Cottonwood Island; they are on the northwest side of the river and are split up by Sweetwater Creek. I have not floated this stretch, but I have walk-waded the public access points upstream from Cottonwood Island. There the Colorado River bends in several areas, creating some nice shelves and deep bends. At the right flows, this can be a great walk-wade area of the river. I have fished it on numerous occasions in the spring with good success. Coming out of the winter, trout are usually congregated in the slow, deep sections of a river. With the way this section of river runs and the layout of the surrounding hills, this stretch receives quite a bit of sun during the early spring. This can make for great early fishing as water temperatures warm enough to get trout feeding a little more aggressively. On the right day, clusters of midges can be found along the river's snowy banks. I typically find this to be true about the end of March through the second week of April. After that the Colorado River

Many of the trout in the Colorado River system are gunmetal junkies. Try tying some of your favorite patterns with gunmetal beads to fool these fish. JAY NICHOLS

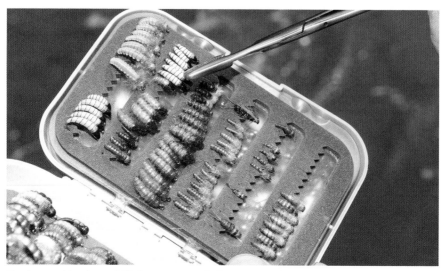

Czech nymphing has quickly become a staple for some anglers. Czech flies can work particularly well on the river's deepest sections and are great weighted flies introduced into a three-fly rig setup. BOB DYE

is subject to dirty water conditions. If the river stays clean through April, keep an eye out for sporadic caddis hatches. This is not common fare, but it has happened.

Mid-April through the end of June can be a tough go over here. I am not saying anglers cannot catch any fish during this time, but there are usually better options this time of year. That is the great thing about the Colorado River and its surrounding tributaries: There is always somewhere to wet a line.

The high water of runoff cleanses the river system and the trout get a break. Returning to the river the first week in July is usually a good bet, and the fish normally cooperate as well. The same shelves and pools that held fish in the spring are now marked with the same fish a little higher on the shelves. Warmer water and additional hatches can put these once lethargic trout into a feeding frenzy. PMDs, Yellow Sallies, and an occasional caddis can really turn the trout on. What's funny about a river that is mostly made up of brown trout is that if there is nothing hatching, fishing can be tough, but if the fish are gorging themselves on a particular insect, you begin to realize how many fish are in a certain stretch of water. This holds true for the entire river system.

I have talked with several guides who work this water, and the same holds true in this stretch as it does in the river's other sections below Catamount. The river is definitely scrutinized for fishing conditions on a daily basis. Rainstorms that pound the river upstream can dirty the water in a hurry, so contacting a local fly shop is the best way to make the most of your fishing trip during the summer.

Horse Creek River Access to Cottonwood Island

By September low flows open a lot of walk-wading access through this stretch, and Cottonwood Island offers a mile of public water on both sides of the boat ramp.

During years when flows are below 1,000 cfs, several points along the river are fairly accessible to the walk-wader, and you can get into position to work a few holes thoroughly. BWO, Trico, and occasional Red Quill hatches can occur during this month. Besides people using the campground and a few recreational floaters, this area can have quite a bit of solitude for angling purposes during the early fall. Being that most of the Colorado River is a brown trout fishery, October has always been a great time to search out these skittish fish. This section is no different.

The main tributary in this section is Sweetwater Creek, and while browns will definitely congregate here, they can be found along other segments in this stretch. I have seen several pairs of mating fish in and around the riffles along the Cottonwood public stretch as well as the 0.5-mile stretch above Sweetwater Creek. Again, anglers should not target the spawning fish, but fishing behind them will surely get your rod bent. Fishing with egg flies and trailing midges will without a doubt take fish here, but do not forget to pitch a few streamers along the way. Most of the fish are between 10 and 15 inches, but I have landed several over 20 inches in this stretch over the years. I have always believed there has to be 10-pound fish in this section. I have never caught one, but you look at some of the runs and there is no way you are getting flies to all these fish.

The new Horse Creek boat ramp is certainly going to open up numerous possibilities when it comes to accessing the river. I do not remember the last time public accesses were on the rise—usually they're on the decline. Over the next couple of years, this boat ramp will surely help with congestion on the river's upper stretches, not to mention opening a few doors on this section of water.

To access the Horse Creek boat launch from the Eagle-Vail area, take I-70 west to the Dotsero exit. From there take County Road 301 northeast for approximately 10 miles. Eagle County Open Space has constructed the new boat ramp at the south end of the Colorado River Ranch under the railroad trestle. There is no fee to use this area. Restrooms are located near the boat launch, and no camping is allowed.

Cottonwood Island to Dotsero

In 2012 heavy rains damaged this section of river, especially the first few miles upstream from Dotsero. The amount of silt and debris dumped into the system was unsurpassed and fish kills were evident. This is nothing new when it comes to the history of the Colorado River; several natural disasters have affected its existence from Rocky Mountain National Park all the way to the Gulf of California. Therefore, this mudslide is a blink of an eye when it comes to the river as a whole. As far as fishing is concerned, it will recover in time. Anglers need to remember that this was a setback, not a total loss; in fact, I fished this section several times since the mudslide and was pleasantly surprised. It was evident that Colorado Parks & Wildlife had restocked several areas with catchable rainbows, and the resilient browns were still hanging around. This is what's so exciting about the Dotsero area: With as many rainbows that were stocked and a little luck, this could turn into the rainbow fishery that many anglers were waiting for.

About 2 miles downstream from Cottonwood Island, the Lyons Gulch access can help break this 6-mile float down to even more manageable sections, especially if

This muscular brown was caught on the river's lower-middle reaches near Dotsero on a size 18 Periwinkle during early April. Browns make up most of the biomass here, but rainbows and whitefish can be found in decent numbers. BOB DYE

time constraints are a factor. The quick float down to Lyons Gulch can be a great early morning or late evening trip and encompasses public access on the northwest side of the river. There is a bit of wading access down here, mostly in the spring or fall months when river levels are at their lowest point of the year.

The other draw to this area, particularly when the Colorado River is running dirty, is Deep Creek. This is a little gem of a creek, especially for the dry-fly enthusiast. Its confluence with the Colorado River is about 4 miles north of Dotsero off of I-70 on County Road 301. Deep Creek shoots off westward, and there is access to the river via Coffee Pot Road. The creek features small brookies and browns, with an occasional rainbow. A few larger brown trout use the system during the fall months for spawning purposes. Any well-placed dry fly during the summer will usually result in a strike from these hungry fish! Along the creek are a few well-marked private property signs, especially just upstream from the confluence, but once you reach the national forest about 2 miles up, you're good to go.

This stretch of the Colorado has some good early spring action, specifically around the Dotsero and Lyons Gulch areas. It seems like for years we would fish the New Castle area all the way up to the Roaring Fork confluence with good success during this time, but on days when things just weren't going our way, we would find ourselves driving back for a quick pit stop in Dotsero. It does not necessarily scream scenic beauty, but at times great fishing can be found. Some of the slower, deeper runs have held fish all winter, and now with midge hatches becoming a little more prominent, these fish will become a bit more active. One thing that will really trigger these trout is the "Big Midge" hatch, which usually comes off the last

Deep Creek is a tributary of the Colorado River located about 4 miles north of Dotsero. The creek features brown, rainbow, and brook trout in the 8- to 12-inch range, with several larger browns migrating into it during the fall months. BOB DYE

week of March through the first week of April. Remember, this stretch was recently stocked with numerous rainbows and the holdovers have not seen much in the way of artificial flies since the previous fall. Using an egg fly as an attractor followed by a larger midge such as a Periwinkle or Black Beauty in a size 18 can be deadly.

About a mile up from Deep Creek there is approximately 2.5 miles of public access on the northwest side of the river. Several pull-offs will enable you to reach the water. Many stretches have good holding water and fairly easy access as long as water flows stay below 800 cfs. I usually do not make a day of it in one piece of water. Moving from point to point by vehicle is the best way to cover this water unless you are floating it.

Like the upper two sections, by mid-April caddisflies can be a factor if the water stays clean enough. Breadcrusts, Barr's Graphic Caddis, and Elk Hair Caddis in sizes 16 through 20 will all get the job done. You can usually count on dirty water in the latter half of April, and while fish can still be caught, there are usually better options.

The fastest way to get to the Cottonwood Island boat launch is to take I-70 to the Dotsero exit (exit 133) and then take County Road 301 north for 7 miles. The boat launch will be on your right. Cottonwood Island is a no-fee BLM access area. Besides the boat launch area, there is a picnic area, and sometimes outfitters provide a Porta-Potty. No camping facilities are available at Cottonwood Island; however, camping is permitted at Lyons Gulch, which is located 2 miles downstream.

To reach the Dotsero boat launch, take exit 133 from I-70. The launch site is just north of the highway on the east side of the river. This site is usually a takeout rather than a put-in because of the Shoshone Power Plant that diverts water out of the Colorado River downstream. Walk-wading can be effective around Dotsero, especially during the spring and fall months when the river is at its lowest flows.

PART IV

Lower Colorado: Dotsero to Silt

Just outside of Dotsero lies the majestic 12.5-mile-long Glenwood Canyon, and with its vertical walls reaching nearly 1,300 feet, it's widely regarded as the most scenic drive along the I-70 corridor. Even if you are not coming over here to fish, traveling through the canyon and stopping at its several tourist points is worth the drive without a doubt.

When driving through the canyon, visitors cannot help but marvel at the engineering that went into creating both the east- and westbound lanes of I-70. Finally completed in 1993, the roadway endured several complications in the building

The Shoshone Hydroelectric Power Plant diverts water in the middle of Glenwood Canyon; however, good fishing can be had during these low-water periods. The plant provides power to towns in the western part of the state. JIM NEIBERGER

Whitewater rafting is extremely popular inside Glenwood Canyon. Here a group of rafters launch from the Shoshone boat ramp, one of many launch sites inside the canyon. JIM NEIBERGER

process along the way. The biggest problem was trying to create a four-lane highway inside a narrow gorge. After several proposals, the final solution was to literally stack the two highways on top of each other. The roadway features over forty bridges and viaducts along with several miles of retaining walls, surprisingly all completed with minimal damage to the ecosystem. Included in the project are four rest areas—Bair Ranch, Hanging Lake, Grizzly Creek, and No Name—complete with parking, interpretive displays, picnic grounds, and access to hiking trails.

This section is also home to some awesome fishing opportunities. Not only is there the Colorado River from Dotsero to Silt, but the Eagle and Roaring Fork Rivers can offer outstanding fishing at certain times of the year. If these larger freestone rivers are not your cup of tea, the area is also home to several small tributaries such as Grizzly Creek, No Name Creek, Canyon Creek, and Elk Creek. All of these contain good populations of trout and offer a variety of fishing possibilities to even beginning anglers.

The Glenwood Springs area might be one of the best places in the country to take a three- or four-day fly-fishing adventure any time of year. With its boundless fishing prospects and all the restaurants, bars, shopping, historic destinations, whitewater rafting, hiking, skiing, and fly shops, it certainly is a top destination for anglers and families alike. Another plus is what an awesome winter fishery this area is. The Glenwood area is lower in elevation, which often makes for daytime winter temperatures in the 40s with some days topping 50 degrees. The Roaring Fork and the Colorado generally stay open year-round, and besides a few days of slushy ice conditions, will usually fish all winter long. I spend most of my winter fishing days over here and quite honestly have not found anything better. There is nothing like topping off a good day of winter fishing with a cold beer at Doc Holliday's and a short stint in the Glenwood Hot Springs.

The section between Dotsero and Silt is home to many walk-wade opportunities as well as several floatable sections. Walk-wading the Colorado is definitely an option in the spring and then again in the fall, but you need to remember that this is big water by the time the Colorado grows to this point. Floating is usually the best option when navigating this section of water. Anglers need to realize that there are not many pull-offs, with the exception of Glenwood Canyon along I-70, to fish. The best way to access the river is from a drift boat or raft; this allows the angler to fish areas not accessible by vehicle.

In this section we will discuss the different floating options that are available and various walk-wade strategies and also take look at the main tributaries, the Eagle and Roaring Fork, along with some of the smaller tributaries that feed the Colorado River.

The lower river can get muddy easier than the upper river; however, if there is at least 1 foot of visibility, you will be able to catch fish. There can be times when traveling over to the Glenwood area in the winter that at first glance you say to your fishing buddy, "Oh, that's ugly!" But other times you think, "I can make that work." More often than not, anglers shy away from muddy water conditions, and rightfully so. But there is a fine line between unfishable and fishable when it comes to the Colorado River. Do not expect trout to be in the river's main currents, however—this can be fast water at these flows. Instead, expect fish to be along the river's edge or behind the numerous large boulders that litter this section, especially in the canyon.

This brown was taken using a Pine Squirrel Leech, which is a very effective pattern throughout the Colorado River. Leech patterns can be used in a standard nymphing rig or fished behind a larger streamer pattern such as a Barr's Meat Whistle or an Autumn Splendor. BOB DYE

Sometimes fly selection can leave anglers in a state of disarray. It's best to start with patterns that imitate several food organisms, such as a Gold-Ribbed Hare's Ear or a Prince Nymph, and then dial it in from there. JAY NICHOLS

I usually use a boat to navigate the river and pull off in stretches where you can work several hundred yards of riverbank. Dry-dropper rigs work best along the river's rocky banks, and having a nymph rod strung up will allow you to get down 4 to 6 feet away from the bank in some of the deeper rock bowls that are close to the river's edge. Being that the water is more than likely going to be off-color, using big, ugly flies can get the attention of a trout or two. Tungsten bead flies like big Prince Nymphs, Psycho Princes, D-Grubs, Hare's Ears, San Juan Worms, and weighted leech patterns will all get down quickly in this turbulent water. From there, matching one of the more dominant hatches like the Pale Morning Duns or Yellow Sallies will pick up the more selective trout. Remember, when nymphing, weight is your friend in these waters.

By August the river has calmed down a bit, but the possibility of muddy water still lingers. It is all at the mercy of what happens on the Colorado's tributaries upstream, including the Eagle River and its tributaries. One substantial rainstorm in any of these areas can blow out the Colorado. I think just knowing the numbers of large fish around the Glenwood area keeps anglers wishing they can spend a day or two on these waters in the summer.

Dirty water can look intimidating at first, but breaking the water up into pieces that are more manageable can yield fish to the net. There will be less clarity in a 6-foot-deep run than there will be in 1 foot of water. Try fishing areas of the river that are broken up around islands, or fishing the edges of the riverbank. Trout that are feeding will move out of some of the darker lies in search of an easy meal. In addition, with the stained water conditions, fish cannot see you as well either.

GLENWOOD CANYON

When you enter Glenwood Canyon, it is hard to take your eyes off the beauty of this natural setting, let alone glance at the water. After all, you are here to fish. This water can appear a little intimidating at first, but breaking it down into smaller pieces is helpful. The water is pretty fast and turbulent, but given a second look, several deep pools and back eddies dot their way down the canyon. The best way to approach this water is to simply use one of the four main access points along I-70: Bair Ranch, Hanging Lake, Grizzly Creek, and No Name Creek. Parking in one of these areas will allow you to access the river on the northwest, or highway, side of the river.

While you can fish any of these points, Grizzly Creek and No Name in my opinion are best. One thing to keep in mind when fishing Glenwood Canyon is that Grizzly Creek and No Name Creek are closed from March 15 through May 15 and then again from October 1 through November 30 to protect spawning trout. In addition, a 50-foot-wide stretch on either side of the creeks on the Colorado River is also closed for spawning trout. Access to these areas is easy, but caution must be used when wading the river's edges. The riverbanks are lined with sharp, jagged boulders and in some instances become extremely deep off the banks. This, however, works to the angler's advantage. Look for trout to find refuge from the fast-paced water

Glenwood Canyon has some of the most scenic views on the Colorado River. Not only does the canyon offer prime fishing, but it also offers hiking, biking, whitewater rafting, and wildlife viewing. JIM NEIBERGER

This brown slammed an Autumn Splendor streamer pattern inside Glenwood Canyon. The canyon offers good streamer fishing year-round but can be epic during the fall months.
JIM NEIBERGER

and seek feeding lanes along the river's edge. Obviously, there are deep holes out in the center of the river, but most of the time working upstream fishing the edge is the key to success here.

Glenwood Canyon's trout are mostly made up of browns and rainbows averaging 12 to 15 inches, but several brutes reside in this water. Over the years I have seen many trout in the 20-inch-plus class brought to the net. It would not be the Colorado River without some whitefish, so expect to catch a few of these hard-fighters as well.

Fishing the canyon year-round is not unheard of, but late March through the middle of April is best for the springtime. After runoff subsides, fishing from the middle of July through August is best for the summer months. Although these are great times to fish Glenwood Canyon, I think September and October are prime time to fish this natural wonder.

If I had to pick two flies to nymph-fish the canyon, it would probably be a Twenty Incher and a Periwinkle. While the trout will surely eat other flies, they seem to find this combination irresistible.

One of my favorite places to fish in Glenwood Canyon is the Grizzly Creek area. To get to the Grizzly Creek access from Denver, take I-70 west for approximately 150 miles. Grizzly Creek is located about halfway through the canyon off exit 121. The access has two parking areas with restrooms, a boat launch, interpretive signs, hiking, and biking. There is no legal place to camp in Glenwood Canyon except for the Glenwood Canyon Resort.

Grizzly Creek's access tends to be a little easier than the other access points in the canyon, not to mention the fact that there's about 400 yards of one hole after another to try your luck in. Nymph fishing is the most widely chosen method in the canyon, but in the summer trout will rise to attractor dries along the riverbanks. I have had several productive days walking downstream from the Grizzly Creek parking lot a few hundred yards. From there casting nymph presentations in the deeper pools will draw strikes, but well-placed dry-fly presentations along the river's banks will bring the trout shooting up from the depths in an effort to engage your fly. Do not be afraid to cast your fly literally inches from the bank's rocks—the river drops off sharply in several areas, so the fish will feed inches from the river's edge. I think many anglers are not aware of this and blow fish out of the pool without even realizing it.

Several dry-fly patterns will suffice, but an Amy's Ant or a Stimulator seems to be the best choice as far as attractor patterns go. Be prepared to encounter sporadic caddis hatches all summer long; when this happens, trout will immediately change gears and begin feeding on the active insects. No secret on fly choice here: An Elk Hair Caddis or a Puterbaugh Caddis will net several fish at this time. If rising fish are few and far between during the hatch, try dropping a Barr's Graphic Caddis off your dry. Often the fish will be taking the emerging caddis before the females return to the surface to lay eggs.

The No Name access is about 2 miles downstream of Grizzly Creek and can offer some great fishing opportunities. The exit (exit 119) is just down the road to the west. No Name has restrooms and access to hiking trails and the Colorado River and is also home to the only legal camping in the canyon at Glenwood Canyon Resort. The resort offers cabins to fit any budget along with RV hookups and tent sites. For more information, call 970-945-6737.

Like other parts of the canyon, this access point receives very little fishing pressure compared to other parts of the Colorado River; it does, however, receive an enormous amount of commercial boat traffic. This seems to have little effect on the fishing, being that most of the trout seem to reside along the river's edges. Fishing tactics remain the same, but of particular note is a run down by the Rock Garden campground that is about 150 yards long. This hole holds a number of fish, but accessing it on low-water days is the key to seeing all the structure and fishing the entire hole.

Summertime is a great time to be in the canyon, but fall is when things really get interesting here. From Glenwood Canyon down to Silt is home to thriving populations of rainbow trout as well as browns. The biomass of rainbows in this stretch outnumber rainbow populations anywhere along the Colorado River. This area becomes very active in the fall. Brown trout that are on the move in the canyon in an effort to spawn will seek out tributary creeks like Grizzly and No Name. Although these creeks are closed during spawning periods, rainbows can line up in a chow line downstream from the creeks eating eggs pushed down by the river's currents. If you are in the area to fish in late October, take a few minutes and just walk along Grizzly Creek (closed to fishing)—you will be shocked at the numbers that have filtered into the tributary. If you were not excited to fish already, this sight will definitely get the juices flowing.

With the number of fish entering the canyon, fly choice is simple. About the only thing hatching this time of year are midges and trout will certainly key in on these, but with the number of fish spawning, egg flies will be the top producer. Color is important, but size is even more important. With so many eggs drifting down the

Grizzly Creek

Grizzly Creek enters the Colorado River about halfway through Glenwood Canyon. Besides its spectacular scenery and great dry-fly fishing in the summer, it is also one of the most beneficial and protected spawning grounds along the Colorado River. Even though the creek is closed from March 15 through May 15 and the again in the fall from October 1 through November 30 for spawning fish, there are some great opportunities to fish this creek during the summer.

I do not think I have ever come across a river or creek that has so much clarity. The water is so clear that you would think you could see every fish in it; this isn't so much the case, but believe me, there are trout here. The trout that live in this pristine water average 8 to 10 inches, with a 12-incher not out of the question. Nevertheless, catching big trout is not the measure of a successful fly-fishing trip. The creek is home to a few browns and rainbows in its lower reaches, with numerous brookies in its upper stretches.

Grizzly Creek is made up of bowling ball–size rocks that seem to stair-step their way up into the canyon. With fallen logs crisscrossing the creek, it is about as gorgeous as a small trout stream can get. There are a few short, deep plunge pools, but most of the fishing is behind boulders and in the small current seams that filter between all of the rocks.

After runoff subsides, usually around the first week of July, the creek displays all the holding water where trout can be found. If there is one square foot of stable water behind a boulder, it probably holds fish. Like most small creeks, picking out a couple hundred yards of water and making presentations into every part of it will be your best bet. These trout are not fussy, however, and well-placed dry-fly presentations will bring fish up to the surface. I like pulling out the old arsenal of dries on these smaller creeks. Flies such as a Griffith's Gnat, Royal Coachman, or Red Humpy and flies that you forgot about will all work. For some of the deeper runs, try throwing a little bigger dry to stay afloat while running dropper patterns such as beaded Prince Nymphs, Copper Johns, and Pheasant Tails.

river's currents, trout become sensitive to presentations that are too big. Trout eggs are only about ³⁄₁₆ to ¼ inch in diameter, so tying your eggs accordingly is important. Any water that looks fishable in Glenwood Canyon will produce with egg/midge combos in the fall, but fishing a little closer to one of these tributaries can really produce numbers of fish. Remember, 50 feet on either side of the creeks is closed to protect spawning fish.

The scenic float from Grizzly Creek to Two Rivers Park is about 6 miles and features mostly class II rapids, but class III rapids are frequent at higher flows. This section can be busy with commercial traffic, but due to the size of the river, it rarely interferes with the fishing. In fact, just about the entire north side of the Colorado River is public access, so using a boat as a tool to fish your way down is certainly a

Grizzly Creek is one of the most scenic tributaries along the Colorado River and one of the most important ones. The creek hosts hundreds of spawning fish during the spring and fall and is closed to fishing during these time periods. JAY NICHOLS

To reach the trailhead for Grizzly Creek, take I-70 west out of Denver for approximately 150 miles to exit 121 in Glenwood Canyon. There are two parking lots on the north side of the Colorado River; the trailhead begins at the northernmost lot. The parking lot closer to the river has restrooms, picnic areas, interpretive signs, and a boat launch. The lower trail is an easy hike; nevertheless, it does become more gradient the farther you travel into the canyon. Expect to see several hikers using the trail but fishing pressure is light, especially the farther back you go. ■

positive in this stretch. This section also has some walk-wading possibilities, especially in the early spring and during the fall. When floating this section, be prepared to spend some time at the Two Rivers takeout after a day on the water. This boat launch and takeout is one of the busiest on the river.

Nearby Two Rivers Park has the Storm King Mountain Memorial, which commemorates the firefighters who lost their lives in the South Canyon Fire. The fire began on July 2, 1994, and by July 6 a dry cold front kicked up winds and caught the firefighters off-guard. Fourteen firefighters died that day trying to save structures in the area.

Floating between Grizzly Creek and Two Rivers Park is certainly a great way to cover this section, but there are a few walk-wade options as well. Wading the Grizzly

Rainbows like this one can't refuse a well-placed *Baetis* pattern during the last week of March on the lower river. Mathew Thomas landed this fish on a size 18 Periwinkle while fishing a strong BWO hatch late in the afternoon. PAT DORSEY

Creek and No Name areas can provide a few hours of fishing if time constraints are a problem, especially in the summer evening hours. I like to show up in the canyon about 5 p.m., after most of the commercial boat traffic has left, and fish till dark. The best way to walk-wade the canyon is simply to park in either of the parking lots (Grizzly Creek, No Name) and access the Glenwood Canyon pedestrian/bike path, from there navigate up- or downstream, giving yourself a few hundred yards of river to work the edges and deeper pockets. Like most rivers, be prepared for prime-time fishing the hour before dusk.

Another piece of water that anglers can take advantage of while walk-wading is the stretch above the Roaring Fork confluence on the north and south sides of the Colorado River. The best way to access this stretch is to park in the Two Rivers parking lot, then walk south until you hit the Colorado River. You will see the Roaring Fork entering the Colorado from this point, and from there you can use the footbridge to get to either side of the Colorado River and the Roaring Fork. This water has a different feel to it than the water farther in the canyon. Although fishing the edges with dry-droppers can be productive, the river is broader down here with a few more shelves and accessible runs, so nymph fishing can be a way to cover the water more proficiently. From the footbridge, anglers can work both sides of the river all the way to the Highway 82 bridge. While this can be great water, it is sometimes hard to ignore the famous Roaring Fork.

This is great water as well, but can be congested at times with anglers and boat traffic at this time of the year.

A person could make a full day of it at the Two Rivers access area. Besides public access in and around Two Rivers Park, anglers can maneuver up the confluence of the Roaring Fork. Upstream from the Two Rivers boat ramp, anglers can take advantage of several riffle runs followed by deep holes, and above the footbridge lies some interesting water, especially around the old bridge platform. This is where one of the many hot springs boils up out of the river.

Look for continuous midge hatches through March and April. Blue-Winged Olives should be in full force towards the end of March into April, and if water conditions warrant, the first caddis hatches can be seen as soon as the middle of April. With all this going on, anglers need to come well-armed this time of year. If that is not enough to get you going, then maybe all the rainbows moving into spawning areas is.

To access Two Rivers Park, take I-70 west out of Denver for approximately 150 miles. As you reach the end of scenic Glenwood Canyon, you will come across exit 116. Turn right at this exit, which is the beginning of Highway 82. Go north one block and hang a left on US 6. From there travel about a mile to Devereux Road, then turn left and travel about two blocks. The park entrance will be on your left. This 22-acre park has a boat launch, restrooms, picnic areas, barbeque pits, horseshoe pits, the Storm King Mountain Memorial, and an amphitheater. Plan your trips

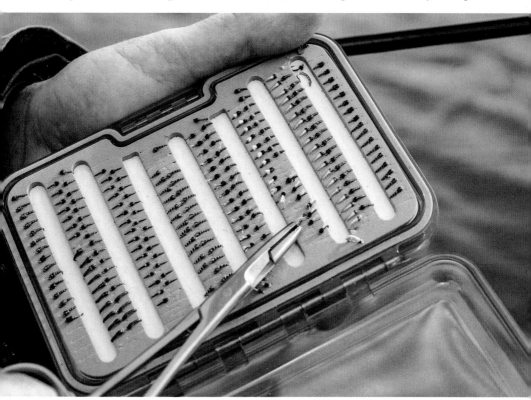

Midge fishing on the Colorado River can be as good as it gets anywhere, especially October through March on the river's lower sections from Dotsero to Silt. MARK ADAMS

accordingly; this can be a very busy area with commercial boat traffic. Putting in early in the morning or later in the afternoon can save a bunch of time.

Being that the Colorado is lower in elevation here, it is home to some of the earliest hatches along the entire river. While winter fishing can be as good as anywhere in the state, spring brings slightly warmer water temperatures and can get the trout really turned on. Midge hatches are common fare, but Blue-Winged Olives will be on the menu as early as the second week of March, and the trout know it. Mathew Thomas, a longtime guide on the Roaring Fork and Colorado Rivers, explains, "The Blue-Winged Olive hatch marks the first of many great hatches in the area." Look for dominant hatches to begin around the third week of March and last well into April.

Because the rainbows are in full spawn, egg flies are still the point fly of choice. Other attractor patterns of importance are Twenty Inchers, Prince Nymphs, and Halfbacks. As the hatch begins, watch for fish slashing in the mid-seam currents and up on gravel shelves. This can be difficult in the Colorado River due to cloudy water conditions. If this is the case, and you are seeing *Baetis*, throwing your presentations off of gravel bars and distinctive shelves is probably going to end up with a fish at the end of your line.

In this stretch, annelids are a staple for trout when other food sources are not accessible. During the last couple of weeks of February and into the first couple of weeks of March, flows on the river are fairly stable. Add cold water to the mix, and there is just not a lot food available besides midges and these small aquatic worms. I am not sure if it's the hot springs peppered throughout the area or the minerals in the water, but they range in color from lime green to chartreuse. Make sure you have plenty of these in your box.

All of the Colorado River experiences midge hatches, but the section between Glenwood Springs and Silt can experience huge blanket hatches, as shown here. This can be one of the best times to be on the water between February and the beginning of April. BOB DYE

Steve Parrott's Electric Caddis is a must-have fly pattern when free-living caddis make themselves vulnerable to trout. MARK ADAMS

If you were not able to get over here in March or early April, chances are 50-50 you missed your window. It seems like in the 1980s and '90s weather patterns kept springtime temperatures cooler, which meant water clarity hung around a little longer into April. Nowadays it is a roll of the dice. However, as long as there is a couple of feet of clarity, anglers can rely on great fishing well into April before early runoff takes hold of the river.

The caddis hatch here can be as good as any river in the state if the water holds up. Most anglers that fish this area wait for the famous Mother's Day caddis hatch on the Roaring Fork, and while this certainly holds true for the Fork, its beginnings start on the lower Colorado. This is an interesting time on the Colorado River. Rainbow trout are still spawning, midge hatches are going strong, Blue-Winged Olives can fire off any given day, and now with water temperatures creeping up, caddis can start to make their appearance. I usually find these active insects around Silt about the end of the first week of April. If the weather stays nice and no serious cold fronts sweep through the area, the caddis hatch will migrate toward the Glenwood Springs area. There have been a couple years where the caddis started to make their appearance around the second week in April up here, but it is usually around the third week.

Summertime terrestrial fishing can also be excellent. From Glenwood Canyon through Silt, most of the river's banks are lined with good-size boulders and most of the banks are steep. This allows deep pockets to form around the river's edges. By the time August rolls around, the trout are already accustomed to looking up. It's hard to imagine big water like this being conducive to dry flies, but some pretty awesome days can be had working dries in close to the banks.

After fishing this water, you might have worked up a thirst. Don't fret—you are right in the heart of Glenwood Springs, home to several bars and restaurants. One of my favorites for grabbing a cold beer is Doc Holliday's, and if dinner is in the cards, it is tough to beat Juicy Lucy's.

TWO RIVERS PARK TO DINO HOLE

This float runs about 9 miles long and is big water. Two Rivers Park is located just north of the Roaring Fork/Colorado River confluence. With the addition of the Roaring Fork River upstream, these lower big-water stretches can be a little confusing when it comes to identifying where to fish. I recommend breaking the river into segments—in other words, break big water down to little water. At first glance it looks huge, but identifying long shelves, bowls, and riverbanks, it starts to become manageable. This is important to recognize because the largest fish in the Colorado River system live in these areas.

It's no secret that the upper reaches of the Colorado are a brown trout fishery, and a great one at that, but a number of large rainbows can be found lurking in these waters. In fact, these stretches harbor more fish per mile than many of the river's other stretches. These fish remind me of the hard-charging rainbows that the world-class trout fishery Grey Reef on the North Platte is known for. The river is made up of browns, rainbows, and whitefish, and in addition to these, expect to catch an occasional squawfish, humpback chub, or pike minnow to round out a day. For the most part these fish average 12 to 16 inches, but believe me, several in the 20- to 24-inch class are here for anglers to test their skills. There are segments of this section that you could send 50 drift boats down and none of them would get a fly to every fish in the river. Parts of the river are extremely deep, so who knows what lurks at these depths? I do know there are 10-pound fish down here.

Floating is the best way to approach this section. There are some walk-wade options, but it is best to utilize a drift boat or a raft to get to these areas. The awesome thing about this float is that it is floatable all year and can provide excellent winter fishing opportunities,

Between Glenwood Canyon and Silt the river is home to strong populations of good-size rainbow trout. Jim Neiberger holds a fat rainbow he caught on a size 22 UPS Midge.

BOB DYE

and anglers have a shot at trophy-size trout. The float is not without its share of hang-ups, though. It is rated as class II/III, but the South Canyon Rapids should not be attempted with a rookie on the sticks. This rapid may not look like much from the highway, but once you are in it, there is no turning back, and the wave train in this rapid can have drift boats looking like the *Andrea Gail* at flows above 7,000 cfs. This float may not be the most scenic along the Colorado River corridor, and can be noisy with I-70 humming in the background, but it is undeniably one of the best places to catch big rainbows at certain times of the year.

Although this stretch is fishable all year long, it is subject, like most of the Colorado, to high muddy water conditions, especially May through August. This does not mean that it is always blown out, but checking with local fly shops can save you a couple hours' drive. That being said, I would say the best times are the late winter and early spring: February, March, and April. Midges make up the bulk of the trout's diet in February and, along with annelids, make up 95 percent of the trout's diet during February and early March. After runoff recedes, the Colorado River below Glenwood Springs is subject to so many rivers that it usually does not shape up until late July. From that point through November, some of the best fishing of the year can be had.

This can be a remarkable float during the late winter and early spring. The stretch has several deep runs, like the water across from the Coca-Cola plant and across from the Ford dealership, and the huge South Canyon Hole that might possibly have more fish in a 200-yard stretch than any other part of the Colorado River. These deeper holes are wintering holes for the trout and are most easily accessed by way of a drift boat.

One thing to keep in mind this time of year is that the South Canyon boat ramp is seasonal and may be closed. Driving by the boat ramp is one way to check the status; the other way is to call Charm Shuttles at 970-379-3966 for information or have them run your shuttle. This float is a little over 5 miles in length, and if the boat ramp is closed, you will have to float down to the Dino boat ramp, which would extend the float to about 9 miles. If this is the case, the float is still doable, but in the late winter and early spring it gets dark around 5 o'clock, so timing this can present a problem. I once made this mistake, and trust me, it's not fun navigating the river in the dark.

Either way, this section can provide some pretty good fishing and some sizable fish at that. Look for strong midge hatches to begin the latter part of February and last well into March. Trout probably aren't going to be up on faster riffles or shelves, so concentrate your efforts in the slow, deep water.

Besides accessing all of the runs out of a drift boat, there are a few sections that warrant parking the boat and spending a little bit of time walk-wading. The first section is just past the South Canyon Rapid. This is where the South Canyon boat launch is located, and from there downriver on the north side is 2 miles of accessible public water. This requires having a bit of mountain goat in you with all the boulders you need to traverse, but there is a cluster of fish here.

The second walk-wade section is the Canyon Creek tributary stretch. The creek is closed March 15 through May 15 for spawning rainbows but is certainly open other times of the year. I like to spend some time walk-wading around the mouth of

Much of the Colorado River remains a dominant brown trout fishery; however, rainbows like this one near Canyon Creek, a tributary of the Colorado River, can grow to lengthy proportions.
BOB DYE

the creek, then walk up the creek where it goes under I-70; there is usually a bunch of fish stacked up here.

The last place is about 0.5 mile down from Canyon Creek, where there is 1.5 miles of public access on the north side of the river all the way to the Dino boat ramp. This is interesting water: It is a huge shelf that takes a 45-degree angle across the river. Be sure to stay river right here. From this shelf down is a vast run that is probably 300 yards long. This hole has it all: a long shelf, riffle water, deep water, edge water. It's also set up to turn a few laps in the drift boat.

If you have never floated this section before, there are a couple of things to be aware of. First is the South Canyon Rapid; this can be a little unnerving, especially if it is your first time. Slowing the boat to a crawl before entering the rapid is recommended, as there are a couple of boulders at the bottom of the rapid that can eat drift boats. The second problem that I have had firsthand experience with is that when the fishing is good, you kind of lose track of time. Timing the float out is imperative due to the amount of daylight this time of year. This is easier said than done when big rainbows are tugging at the end of your line.

If you missed the opportunity to fish this section during the month of March, you have one more chance before the Colorado River is lost due to high water. Flows in April historically run about 1,900 cfs during the first two weeks, but the second half of the month is generally another story. Flows at that time can push well over 3,500 cfs, and that usually spells muddy water. However, the first two weeks can be awesome. The trout are still seeing midges and *Baetis*, but another bug is about to change the way these sections are fished, even if it is just for a short while. The caddisflies begin to make their appearance this time of year, and even with all the time I have logged down here, I only hit it about half the time. It is kind of like hitting the elusive Salmonfly hatch on the river's upper reaches. Water temperature, flows, and water clarity have to come together to be in the right spot at the right time. But when all these factors come into play, it can be as good as it gets when it comes to fishing a caddis hatch.

If you are chasing Salmonflies down here in June, being that these are still big flows, caution must be used when floating through South Canyon. Springtime is dangerous with some of the exposed rocks at lower flows, but at this higher flow the rocks are not the problem—it's the sheer amount of water. I know anglers who think this is fun, and to each his own. But I cannot swim, so I would rather err on the side of caution and live to fish another day. The rapid at these flows makes a huge wave train, with rollers as high as 10 to 12 feet. If you are not comfortable with this, simply rope your boat down the left side of the bank. Other than the South Canyon Rapid, it is a pretty straightforward float, but common sense should always prevail.

By the time August nears, the flows really begin to decrease. The river is still at the mercy of rainstorms affecting the water clarity, but usually there are more chances to fish in August than there are in July. Flows really begin receding at the end of July to an average of 3,500 cfs, and during the month of August, they generally stabilize to around 2,500 to 3,200 cfs. With more stable flows, it's a little easier to determine where the trout will be on a day-to-day basis. I think as a rule trout are going to gravitate to smaller food organisms, especially if water clarity improves. With the flows hovering around 2,800 cfs, the river really begins to express itself. "It's a whole lot easier to pick out the definitive runs at these flows," says Mathew Thomas.

I've had some good days down here in August; with water temperatures in the 60s, the trout are unquestionably in the faster, more oxygenated runs. It is at these flows that I probably spend more time out of the boat than in it, the reason being that you can make several presentations out of the boat in deeper water, but thoroughly working a faster riffle run requires walk-wading it. I usually start by not floating over the riffle I am going fish, but rather row around the section and park the boat at the bottom. From there you have all the time in the world to systematically work the run. Doing this in several runs is obviously going to take hours, but this time of year, it does not get dark till 8:30.

In August, one thing to keep in mind is that if water temperatures are creeping towards 70 degrees, the South Canyon boat launch can break up this float into smaller sections. This is important because anglers can fish these sections early in the morning or late in the afternoon to remedy warm-water conditions. The river mileage between Two Rivers Park and South Canyon is 5.5 miles, and the South Canyon to Dino float is about 4 miles.

In the fall, one of my favorite spots to wade is about a mile down from the Roaring Fork/Colorado River confluence on the south side of the river. The best way to get there is to stay on I-70 to the West Glenwood exit (exit 114). Go south over the river and take Midland Avenue left. Follow the road upstream until you come across the Coca-Cola distributorship; there is a small pull-off parking area on the left side of the road. Most anglers refer to this section as the Coca-Cola Hole. It is a good-looking run, complete with a long diagonal shelf followed by a long, deep

Brown trout are plentiful in most sections of the river. Here the author hoists a 16-inch brown that fell for a Pine Squirrel Leech. MARK ADAMS

run. On the right day, this hole seems to have every fish in the river in it, and if you hit it during a BWO hatch, you will agree. As the hatch starts, trout will be inhaling *Baetis* nymphs in the deeper water, but as it progresses, the fish will begin moving up onto the shelf. Of all the different methods of pursuing trout, there is nothing more amusing than catching fish in a fast riffle. Everything just happens at a faster pace, and the trout do not have as long to study your presentation.

While there are certainly many more sections to walk-wade from a drift boat, one that I like to access by vehicle is the Canyon Creek area. It is easy to reach: Simply take I-70 west out of Glenwood Springs to the New Castle exit (exit 105), then cross over the highway and get back on I-70 east. Being that I-70 is a divided highway, you must take I-70 east out of New Castle to get to the Dino boat ramp and Canyon Creek access. Travel about 5 miles back to the Canyon Creek exit (exit 110). There is a small parking area at this point and a short walk down the big-game fence to the creek. Anglers can fish Canyon Creek from here down to the confluence of the Colorado River.

Besides the creek, there is plenty of walk-wading along the Colorado River. This can be another great place to catch the BWOs or Tricos in September. Pay close attention to the water around the confluence; there are times when numbers of fish use this area. About a hundred yards down from the confluence on the north side, look for trout sipping small mayfly emergers in the surface film of this productive back eddy.

Aside from a few areas more favorable for wading, this section remains float-able as well. Floating it in September can yield some high fish counts, especially if trout key in on a certain hatch. I never see a consistent hatch on the whole river, but rather concentrated hatches on different sections of water. It's at this time of year that the entire river is fishable; using a boat to get from hole to hole is the best way to fish this section.

I feel that spawning fish are hands-off, but the fish behind them are fair game. If you know where the browns concentrate, you can have epic days on the Colorado River. In this section of water, a number of fish will congregate in the Canyon Creek area. Unfortunately the creek is closed from October 1 through November 30 for spawning brown trout, but areas around the confluence of the Roaring Fork, the Coca-Cola Hole, upstream from the South Canyon Rapid, and upstream from the Dino Hole boat launch can offer prime fishing during the month of October. Look for areas with spawn gravel, like the heads of riffles and side channels, throughout the river system. If steelhead can scent 650 river miles up the Columbia River and into the Clearwater River in Idaho to the exact spot they were born, then trust me, rainbows can find their way behind a few spawning browns.

The fishing is not very technical this time of year; in fact, an egg/midge combo will cover your bases for most of your nymph fishing. But the water here can be some of the best streamer water in the Colorado River. As I have mentioned, this water has some deep runs in it, along with nice riffles and miles of rocky bank fishing. These

Selecting the right streamer pattern can be just as important as selecting the right nymph. Some of the river's baitfish include whitefish, suckers, and baby trout. Patterns that have white, brown, and silver tones generally work best when imitating these baitfish. MARK ADAMS

three ingredients spell success for anglers that like to pitch a streamer or two. I have found it best this time of year to have two rods rigged and ready to go. Having one rigged as a nymph rod will allow you to cover deeper seams, riffles, and mid-seam bowls and dishes. Having a tandem streamer rod rigged will allow you to cover all of the above plus banging the banks where the river gets deep quickly. The best way to fish streamers in this prime piece of water is from a drift boat. Using a boat gives the angler a better angle in which to throw towards the banks and strip back to the boat. You can certainly cover water throwing streamers while walk-wading, but from a drift boat you can cover so much water that your arm will be sore before you run out of river.

To reach the South Canyon boat launch and takeout, continue down I-70 west from Glenwood Springs to exit 111. Hang a left and head south towards the Colorado River. The boat ramp is downstream from the South Canyon Bridge. This boat ramp is seasonal, so checking with a local fly shop or shuttle service is recommended. To access the Dino Hole takeout/put-in from Glenwood Springs, take I-70 west for 10 mile to the New Castle exit (exit 105). Go across the New Castle Bridge and take I-70 back to the east for about 5 miles. The boat ramp will be on your right. The boat ramp is in the middle of semi-truck rest area. It is a primitive dirt boat launch/takeout. Charm Shuttles' number is 970-379-3966 and Roaring Fork Anglers' is 970-945-0180.

NEW CASTLE TO SILT

While I surely have stretches of river that I enjoy floating more than others, this section ranks in the top three. The main reason is that it is the best-kept secret that is right under everyone's nose. This segment arguably doesn't have the scenic draw that some of the river's upper reaches have, but it's also probably the least fished. And while the number of trout per mile is a little lower than in other parts, it is the quality of fish that is the big draw here. This portion of river has the same drawbacks as other parts of the river below Glenwood Springs as far as water conditions go, but it has a great deal more structured water than other segments. In fact, it kind of makes you wonder why there are not more trout per mile down here.

Rainbow trout definitely fall off past Silt, but browns can be seen as far down as Rifle. I have caught some hefty browns throughout the Colorado River system, but none as ugly and mean as some of these fish. You need to get into the mindset of catching fewer fish, but having the chance to bag bigger fish. I would say the average fish hovers around that 12- to 16-inch mark, but several in the 19- to 22-inch range roam these waters. Although that might not seem monstrous, it is the girth that some of these fish have that makes them trophy size.

This float is just over 7 miles and is rated a class II. It is a pretty straightforward float with not a great deal of technical water, but anytime you're floating, caution should be used. When the Colorado is fishing well below Glenwood Springs, not only are there sections that can be busy with anglers, but the amount of commercial boat traffic can be frustrating. This stretch does not have that problem. I usually float it in the spring and fall, and there is definitely no pressure at these times. The times I have floated it during the summer, we wondered if there was something wrong with

The river down by Silt offers a wide variety of walk-wade water to fish from December through March, when the water levels are at their lowest of the year. BOB DYE

the river, as nobody was fishing. Well, it turned out that there was nothing wrong with the river at all—everybody is just drawn to the more-famous water upstream.

Sometimes it is hard to leave a stretch of river, especially if you have confidence in it, but trying fresh sections of water can open up new doors. As I once heard an old gentleman say, "Take pride in the whole river, not just one hole."

The water is generally going to be a few degrees warmer here than stretches farther upstream, and in the early season that can make a big difference in fish behavior and hatches. While the water from Glenwood Springs downstream is known for its multitude of midge hatches, this area can see some of the earliest hatches in late February and early March. The river down here can be a little more silty than faster sections upstream, and since midges love silt, you can be right in the middle of a massive midge hatch on any given day during the winter and early spring. I have seen snowbanks covered with the little black insects as well as back eddies that look like midge soup.

I vividly remember one day in particular in 2012. The spent midge shucks were ¼ thick on the surface film in a slow piece of bank water. There had to have been midges below them fighting their way through the soup, because the trout were taking them like humpback whales take krill. I tried tossing my presentation into the mix, but there was no way the fish could find my bugs. It was like trying to find a size 22 midge larva in a haystack. Pondering this situation, I decided to throw on an Elk Hair Caddis and twitch it through the surface film . . . *whack!* They obviously were not taking caddis but rather responding to the simulation of movement of hundreds of emerging midges. While this is certainly not an everyday occurrence, this can be a great section of water to find an early season midge hatch.

The Colorado is made up of countless runs and riffles followed by deep plunge pools. Here the author catches and releases a rainbow near the New Castle Bridge on the river's lower reaches.

MARK ADAMS

As the winter months set in, the trout naturally gravitate towards the slower, deeper runs, and as early spring arrives, this is where you will find the majority of fish. One of these segments is the stretch above the New Castle boat ramp up to the New Castle Bridge. This part of the river has about 0.5 mile of public access on the south side. When walk-wading, the best way is to park a vehicle at the New Castle Bridge and walk down the frontage road to the New Castle boat ramp. From the boat ramp, you can fish your way back to the bridge. There is a good half-day of fishing here, with decent bank fishing, long riffled shelves, and deep holes.

One of the best holes on the river is the one right under the New Castle Bridge; this hole holds a ton of fish and can be best during hatch periods when the trout are 2 to 4 feet deep rather than at the back of this massive run. If you're lucky enough to be here in the spring during a midge or BWO hatch, concentrate your efforts on the shelves and buckets in the long flat sections below the bridge. The center of this hole holds fish, but wade access is difficult due to the depth of the water.

Another area of interest is the section of water down by the Silt River Park Bridge. There is a half mile of public access on the south side of the river, up from the bridge. I have had probably some of my best midge fishing in this area.

There are some pretty darn good midge hatches along the Colorado River, but this stretch seems to take it to a different level. Besides nymph fishing, it can offer great dry-fly fishing when the little insects are prevalent. I have been down there on some days when you wonder if there is anything alive in the river, but during a hatch, especially a midge hatch early in the year, it can seem every fish in the river is in this stretch. There is no reason to be down here at the crack of dawn this time

Mathew Thomas knows the Roaring Fork and the lower Colorado River intimately. Here he sets the boat up in a prime run just downstream from the Dino boat ramp on a spectacular early spring day. PAT DORSEY

of year; rather, showing up around 9 a.m. will allow you to get to know the water before the first bugs are seen. Look for midges to begin around 10 a.m. and be prepared to throw dries in the late afternoon. Do not be surprised to see occasional BWOs in early March, and by the end of the month come well-armed with both midge and Blue-Winged Olive patterns.

This section is floatable pretty much all year and is certainly floatable during the early spring. This float is about 7.5 miles long and is rated a class II. It is a little farther from I-70 and receives very little boat traffic; in fact, the last two springs I have not seen another boat. The water consists of long riffled runs followed by some nice deep pools, but one thing I enjoy about this stretch is the side channels that are found while floating. At the right flows, fish will congregate in these channels and fishing can be at its best!

The Colorado River is generally not busy this time of year, and if you are looking for floating solitude, this is your float. I think one of the best things about the area, especially if you have a few days over spring break, is to float all the sections from Two Rivers Park to Silt. Every section has its pluses and minuses, but it is sure to be a great adventure.

The stretch from New Castle to Silt, if it remains clean, can be the first place to hit the formidable caddis hatch. This hatch begins in this area and moves upstream into Glenwood Springs; from there it makes its way up the Roaring Fork River, where most anglers try to attack it around Mother's Day. This can be as good as it gets when it comes to a caddis hatch. Generally, most years, the group of guys I hang out with have already been fishing the area since late February, with midges and Blue-Winged Olive patterns the mainstay until the first caddis are seen. Once they have been spotted, I immediately look to the long-range forecast. If it looks good

This midsize rainbow fell for a size 16 Elk Hair Caddis skated across the water's surface. The Colorado has good caddis hatches that generally start on the river's lower section around Silt the beginning of April. JAY NICHOLS

Stuart Birdsong, longtime guide and friend, plays a nice rainbow in a hole between New Castle and Silt. The rainbow trout population remains strong in this section of river. BOB DYE

and it does not appear that anything is going to muddy up the water, my next call is to my wife saying that I will not be home for a few days. This does not happen every year, but when the conditions are right, this can really be prime-time fishing.

As a rule, when river flows are between 1,400 and 1,800 cfs, chances are good that enough visibility will allow you to fish the first couple weeks of April. If you start seeing a trend of rising water levels daily, chances are the river will be blown out. That being said, the water is never gin clear down here, so don't fret if you only have a couple feet of water clarity.

When fishing this section in April, it's not always a home run, but in years that the stars line up, it makes you appreciate how many quality fish are in this stretch. If you have spent some time here and caddisflies are tough to come by, try working upstream into the river's other sections. The hatch moves quickly, and you might be behind it.

By the time July rolls around, the river begins to decline and about the second week starts to resemble a trout stream again. Historic flows range from around 8,500 cfs at the beginning of the month to 3,500 cfs at month's end. About the second week of July, flows are around 5,000 cfs, and barring any major rainstorms, this can be a great time to be on the New Castle to Silt segment. While there is some walk-wading at these flows, the best way to approach the river is by drift boat. Even though this float is rated a class II, it does not have the whitewater that some of the river's other floats have, thus way less commercial river traffic will be encountered down here.

In July most anglers are fishing the Roaring Fork, but this stretch of the Colorado has excellent PMDs and Yellow Sallies. Granted, the Roaring Fork can have

With all the thousands of fly patterns and techniques there are to catch trout, sometimes just adding a little extra weight will get the job done. JAY NICHOLS

conditions that are more favorable in July than the Colorado, but that brings the crowds as well. I have only floated this stretch a handful of times in July, but every time had great hatches and good fishing. Mathew Thomas, who floats the area regularly and is no stranger to the Colorado River, says, "It's the best solitude water around." He warns, though, "It's tough to get the conditions right." Thomas's warning refers to the lack of clarity much of the Colorado River suffers from down here. This is true, but I would say that if there is a foot of clarity, plan on fishing. I kind of live by the rule of "fish as far from the bank as there is water clarity."

Although water conditions can be tough, this section certainly has days when there is more than a foot of clarity. When the river allows, this can be a great time to be on the water. PMDs, Yellow Sallies, Golden Stones, and caddis can all be present down here in July. The times I have floated this stretch, we caught fish on all the above in addition to streamers. Be prepared to encounter all of these insects throughout the day and have several rods rigged for any occasion. If the water is dirty, plan on fishing big beaded patterns such as Prince Nymphs, Twenty Inchers, Halfbacks, Colorado River Specials, Copper Johns, and Neiberger's Passion Stones. Do not be afraid of chucking a few streamers close to the banks, especially on dirty water days. If the water has more clarity, widen your fishing opportunities to the main runs and the many shelves and riffles.

Usually when the water clears, anglers need to fish smaller and dial into insects that the trout are feeding on. Imagine yourself being a trout for just a second. In dirty water conditions, your world has just shrunk to a couple feet around you, so anything that resembles a food source, you are probably going to take it. Now turn

Scott Harkins landed this brown on a size 16 Barr's Graphic Caddis. Caddis hatches begin in April and can come off sporadically all summer long. BOB DYE

the tables and imagine seeing 6 feet in front of you. Your world has tripled, and so has the amount of insect life available to you. Being that trout are instinctively intelligent, they are probably going to change their feeding habits to focus on the most abundant food source available. In my opinion, one of the most important things to remember when fishing the Colorado River is that river flows and water clarity are always changing. That being said, and with the number of smaller insects such as PMDs, Yellow Sallies, and caddis and the small aquatic worms that come to the forefront during improved water conditions, you need to be ready.

If you are on the water every day, this can be a little easier to figure out, but if you are coming over to the Colorado River for the first time in the summer, it can be a little tougher. If this is the case, start with attractor patterns such as a Pat's Rubber Legs, Twenty Incher, Prince Nymph, Halfback, or even a Colorado River Special. From there, run patterns that can resemble a multitude of insect life like a Pheasant Tail, Mercer's Trigger Nymph, or Barr's Emerger. This will allow you to net a few fish, take a stomach sample, and dial in closer to what the trout are keying on. If the trout are taking emergers, try tying on a Chocolate Post Foam Rs2 in different sizes. This pattern can cover your bases for all emerging mayflies.

A large amount of the Colorado River does not get fished as hard as some of the more popular places, and this section is one of them. It is not a super-secret, catch-fish-all-the-time section either. But with a little tenacity and the right day, it can rival anything the Colorado has to offer. This is what is so remarkable about the Colorado River as a whole—there is just so much to fish. An angler would have to fish for an entire year to cover all the water in the system.

By August and September in a normal precipitation year, expect flows to average around 2,500 cfs and open up a large amount of fishable water that has not been seen since the spring. There is quite a bit of ranchland mixed into this stretch, and grasshoppers and beetles can be an easy meal for the trout. Staring over an indicator for months can get a little monotonous, so slapping some big hoppers against the rocks can relieve some frustration. An abundance of large boulders line the river in this sector, specifically on the north side, and the trout know it. You could spend your day working the numerous runs and riffles that will all produce fish, but banging the rocks with hopper patterns can be another exciting way to approach this section.

This Colorado River brown smacked an Autumn Splendor streamer pattern with brute force. Streamers can be fished throughout the year, but July through November yield the best results. MARK ADAMS

Woolly Buggers are probably the most versatile fly in the history of flies. Over the years thousands of variations have been tied by some of the West's best fly tiers, and all of them work. Fly anglers should not go anywhere without a few of these must-haves in their box. BOB DYE

The river falls off quickly in this section, which creates some deep pocketwater close to the banks. If trout are not readily taking your dry presentation, try dropping it with a smaller beaded pattern, like a Prince Nymph or Mercer's Micro Mayfly—this should provoke even the most sensitive trout.

Another way to attack this stretch in August is to throw streamer patterns to the rocks. Baitfish abound in this section, and on the right day, streamer fishing can be as good as it gets, particularly if it is a cloudy day. I have had luck with several streamer patterns, but a Sculpzilla followed by a white Woolly Bugger has drawn numerous strikes for me over the years.

Although throwing dries and streamers is always a good bet through this stretch in August, pay close attention to the skyline in front of you, particularly in the late morning hours. Unexpected Trico hatches can send the trout gulping tiny mayflies at the drop of a hat. While the hatch here is not as abundant as the Trico hatches upstream, it is still enough to turn the trout's attention for a couple hours.

In the fall, Elk Creek, about a mile down from the New Castle boat ramp on the north side of the river, can hold large numbers of fish. Unlike the Colorado River's other tributaries, this one remains open throughout the year. Concentrate your efforts around the confluence of the creek and the approximately 200 yards of public water upstream. From the creek downstream, numerous riffles and shelves abound, and with the lower flows, take advantage of the walk-wading opportunities. Remember, this may be the last time to really access the river until next spring.

The next area of interest for public walk-wading is 4 miles down from the New Castle boat ramp on the south side of the river. This stretch covers about 0.75 mile and is worth pulling the boat over for a couple hours of wading. Pay close attention to the river's south bank in this segment. Several fish hang just off the edge of the riffles here in search of an easy meal. Upstream from the Silt River Park boat ramp is another piece of water to maneuver the boat around in an effort to wade the river. The Colorado splits here, and great fishing can be had around the fork. Remember that the boat ramp is located on the I-70 (north) side of the river but the left side of the channel.

To access the New Castle boat launch, take I-70 west out of Glenwood Springs and travel about 10 miles to exit 105. Take a left and go south over I-70 and the Colorado River. At the stop sign go right and travel 0.5 mile to Coal Ridge Park. The boat ramp is located about 100 yards to the north. Restrooms are available, but no camping is allowed. The park is also home to a disc golf course.

To reach the Silt boat launch, take I-70 out of Glenwood Springs and head west to exit 97. Travel over I-70 to the south and take a left on the frontage road. Go about 300 yards to the old motel on your right, then turn right and travel over the bridge. The boat ramp will be on your left. The Silt boat ramp has Porta-Potties; camping is not allowed in the area.

ROARING FORK RIVER

The Roaring Fork is one of the largest tributaries of the Colorado River and is considered one of the best freestone trout streams in the entire state. At its humble beginnings high atop Independence Pass it's nothing more than a small creek, but

Mathew Thomas holds up a nice 18-inch rainbow he caught while fishing the Roaring Fork River near Carbondale in early March. The Roaring Fork has a good populations of sizable rainbows. PAT DORSEY

as the river carves its way 70 miles to the confluence with the Colorado River, it takes on many diverse aspects.

Not only does the Roaring Fork take on many different expressions, so do the people who have inhabited it. The Ute Indians lived in the valley long before Colorado became a state 1876 and named the river "Thunder River" for the thunderous noise it made. In fact, the Roaring Fork descends more in elevation during its 70-mile journey than the Mississippi River does in its entire 2,320-mile length. As the river gains strength from its many tributaries, like the world-famous Frying Pan and the temperamental Crystal River, it takes on the look of a formidable western trout stream. While its upper reaches certainly have numerous opportunities to walk-wade, it is its lower stretches below Carbondale that receive most of the attention when it comes to accessing the river.

I started fishing the Roaring Fork when I was about 10 years old with my dad, and back then probably caught every whitefish in the river. But one thing I've learned over the years is that when you have good whitefish populations, you usually have a great trout stream. The Roaring Fork in its upper reaches is home to good numbers of brookies, browns, and rainbows, and in its lower stretches boasts an abundance of trout and whitefish alike.

Even though the Roaring Fork Valley has added a number of residents over the years, it still has not lost that feeling of serenity. I think in my 30-plus years of visiting the valley, it really has not changed much from an angling perspective. The Roaring Fork's fish counts seem to be about the same, and to mirror that, the insect life is as good as any river in the state. The Fork is known for several prominent hatches that can make any fly fisher take on a "drop what you are doing and go now" attitude. The first major hatch to flood the system is the BWOs; the first bugs can be seen in mid-March and last through April. Look for the nymphs to become active around 10 a.m. and the duns to be on the water in the early afternoon.

The second major hatch, and it can be a big one, is the Mother's Day caddis hatch. Contrary to popular belief, these insects already began to hatch on the lower Colorado River in mid-April; it is just now that they are making their way up the Roaring Fork. Water clarity can sometimes be a problem, as well as trying to find out what section of river the hatch is on. Visiting Roaring Fork Anglers and buying a couple flies is the best way to get up-to-date information; their number is 970-945-0180. If you are lucky enough to catch this hatch right, it can rival any caddis hatch in Colorado. Look for the bouncing bugs to become active around lunchtime and on certain days last well into late afternoon with females coming back to the water to lay eggs.

June will make you understand why the Ute Indians dubbed this river "Thunder River." It can roar down the valley in normal snowpack years with flows exceeding 4,000 cfs. If this is the case, the Frying Pan is a tailwater fishery only 45 minutes away from Glenwood Springs.

One of my favorite times to float the Roaring Fork is right after runoff has peaked, about the first week of July. Those fish have not seen a fly in a while and are

Morgan Dye fooled this nice rainbow on a size 22 Rhinestone Midge behind an egg fly on the lower section of the Roaring Fork River near Glenwood Springs. Fishing an egg/midge combo can be deadly year-round on any river. BOB DYE

generally cooperative. As the flows start to decline in July, the river really begins to light up with several insect hatches. The famed Green Drake hatch begins in mid-July and is one of the more sought-after hatches on any river. The drakes will start hatching on the lower Roaring Fork and keep on trudging until they finally run out of room below Ruedi Reservoir on the Frying Pan in late September. Finding the hatch can be tricky, but when you do, it will most often be in the late afternoon. In fact, I have fished this hatch well past dark a couple of times by the Sunlight Bridge.

In addition to drakes, other bugs will be evident during this time. One is the little yellow stonefly known as the Yellow Sally. Trout seem to eat these bugs like bite-size Snickers. There can be times when both Green Drake and Yellow Sally adults are on the surface at the same time and the trout are taking both. If you encounter this, consider yourself lucky, as most fly fishers go years without seeing this phenomenon.

As if that wasn't enough, throw in a PMD hatch and now you have full-blown fly-fishing nirvana. Mathew Thomas, who runs guide trips on these waters, says, "It's without a doubt one of the best times to experience the Fork." He adds, "Bring lots of dry-fly floatant during this time of year."

If that isn't enough to whet your appetite, there is one more insect that can show up without warning and add to the chaos. Golden Stoneflies make up a large portion of the Roaring Fork's stonefly population and are a big part of the trout's diet, which most certainly accounts for the popularity and consistent success of the Twenty Incher stonefly nymph. I do not think there is a time when I am fishing the Fork that I do not have this pattern on at some point.

As the Roaring Fork transitions into August, it may not have quite the bug life it did in July, but good fishing can still be had. Terrestrial fishing can be at its best during this month, and well-placed grasshopper and ant patterns can draw even the wariest fish up to the surface. August can bring warm water temperatures to the region, and fishing can be slow during the middle of the day. If this is the case, plan to fish in the early morning and then again in the late evening, especially the hour before dark.

September brings a breath of fresh air to the Roaring Fork and a multi-brooded insect back into the fold. Blue-Winged Olives can hatch in full force during the next two months and bring the river back to more-consistent fishing opportunities. River flows have dropped considerably by the time September rolls around, so expect good dry-fly fishing with BWOs during the next couple months. One of the best scenes in the Roaring Fork Valley in late September has to be the scenic views of Mount Sopris. The twin-peaked mountain is 12,965 feet above sea level and is visible throughout the Roaring Fork Valley. With the color change of fall, take a break from fishing and glance towards the southeast for a view of this impressive mountain.

As the fall color change comes and goes, the area begins to lose some of its luster, but the river is just beginning to shift into overdrive. With all of the browns spawning in the Colorado River, the Roaring Fork goes through the same transformation, and, in fact, many of the larger browns end up in the lower Fork. Some large brown trout migrate up the river, and while not common, it can be your chance to latch onto a trophy. Besides the lower Roaring Fork, much of the river fishes extremely well this time of year. Standard egg/midge combos will get the job done, along

Pat Dorsey caught this colorful brown on a size 22 Mercury Midge near Carbondale. The Roaring Fork River is an excellent winter trout fishery when higher-elevation streams are typically frozen over. BOB DYE

with a few smaller mayflies, and don't forget to run a streamer or two for the active browns—after all, streamer fishing can be at its best this time of year.

The Roaring Fork and the Colorado River are among the best winter fisheries in the state. The flows on the Fork during the winter average between 400 and 500 cfs, and at the lower elevation, you can have daytime temperatures in the high 40s to low 50s. The Glenwood Springs area is a great winter destination, and there is no shortage of bars, restaurants, hotels, and fly shops—not to mention Glenwood Hot Springs for a short soak after a long day of fishing.

Roaring Fork Access

Whether you are floating the Roaring Fork or walk-wading it, there are several access points from Carbondale to Basalt, including the Hooks Bridge access, Mount Sopris Tree Farm access, Catherine Bridge access, and Bob Terrell State Wildlife Area. This section of river is technical water, so hiring a local guide is recommended when floating.

One of the best floats is between Carbondale (Bob Terrell boat ramp) and the West Bank Bridge. This is one of the easier floats on the Roaring Fork, and in my opinion the Bob Terrell ramp is one of the best fishing accesses on the river. From

Mount Sopris is one of the better-known landmarks in the Roaring Fork Valley. Here Bob Dye Sr. fishes the Crystal River, a main tributary of the Roaring Fork River. BOB DYE

Glenwood Springs, head south on Highway 82 (towards Aspen) for approximately 10.4 miles. On your right will be the Aspen Glen subdivision. Hang a right on Satank Road and follow it upriver for about a mile. You will see the Carbondale Bridge, and the boat launch is just below it.

The West Bank Bridge is another local favorite and easy to get to from Glenwood Springs. Take Highway 82 south towards Aspen for about 5 miles and hang a right on Old Highway 82. Follow this road about a mile and a half till you hit the West Bank Bridge. Recently Colorado Parks & Wildlife dubbed this area the Sam Caudill State Wildlife Area in honor of Caudill's many contributions to the area. The boat launch is about 75 yards upstream from the bridge.

This float from the West Bank Bridge to Two Rivers Park is about 7 miles and can be rough at times. Take caution when floating this section, especially around the Cemetery Rapids.

These are the main access points from Carbondale to Glenwood Springs when floating this section of river; however, there are many walk-wade accesses. The Roaring Fork is a large tributary of the Colorado River, and at times you are not able to wade across the river, but you certainly can fish this river on foot. One of best accesses is right at the confluence with the Colorado River. The best way to fish this section is to take Highway 82 south from I-70 through Glenwood Springs to 8th Street. Take a right on 8th and follow it through town, cross the Roaring Fork River, and hang a left on Midland Avenue. The entrance to Valgus Park is a couple blocks up on the left. This is a great place to park and fish the Fork all the way down to the confluence with the Colorado River.

Another popular fishing access is the Sunlight Bridge area. This section is a few miles up from the confluence of the Roaring Fork and the Colorado. Take Highway 82 south from I-70 through the town of Glenwood Springs to 27th Street, then turn right and follow 27th to the Sunlight Bridge. There is parking on the east and west sides of the bridge. Pay close attention to the beautiful run above the bridge.

Another way to fish the lower Fork is to simply access the Rio Grande Trail that follows the river. There are several points to access the trail, including in the towns of Glenwood Springs and Carbondale, and from there use the trail to access public points along the river.

The Roaring Fork is truly one of the finest trout streams that Colorado has to offer and one of the best two- or three-day options when it comes to the amount of water to fish in the area and the amenities of Glenwood Springs.

EAGLE RIVER

The Eagle gets its start where the east and south forks come together below Tennessee Pass, and throughout its 60-mile journey before it merges with the Colorado River, it abounds with floating and walk-wading opportunities. The Eagle River never seems to get the press that some of the other Colorado River tributaries receive, and it is kind of a shame. I think over the years the perception has been that the river is mostly private, and while this is certainly true to an extent, it still has many public accesses. As a matter of fact, most of the time when I pull up to one of its many leases, I am the only one there.

The Eagle River is a true freestone stream. Here John Perizzolo probes one of the many riffle runs the river has to offer. MARK ADAMS

The Eagle is a freestone river, which means it goes through the natural progressions like low, clear water to high-water conditions due to snowmelt. For most of the river's journey, it parallels I-70, but in my opinion this does not take away from the river's scenery. I do not think you would even know the highway was there unless someone told you. The Eagle's red sandstone cliffs and varied mountain surroundings make it one of the most scenic and diverse walk-wade or floating rivers in the state.

Its insect hatches are just about as varied as the river itself. Besides its various midge hatches in the spring and fall, it also has good populations of BWOs, caddis, Yellow Sallies, PMDs, and Golden Stoneflies, making this river a must when it comes to fishing in the state of Colorado.

The Eagle is mostly made up of rainbows and browns averaging 12 to 18 inches in length, but a few brookies and an occasional cutthroat can be found at times. If you like a river that has riffles, deep runs, and a ton of pocketwater, then the Eagle is for you. One negative that may haunt the river is that wading it is like trying to walk on an ice rink; there is no doubt that great care needs to be taken when traversing this river.

Beginning in late March, the Eagle has some awesome midge fishing, and as April rolls around, it comes alive with midges and BWOs. April is certainly one of my favorite times for these insects, and the fish just seem more cooperative coming out of the long winter. Look for the "Big Midge" to come off around the first week in April—the trout will engulf them as if it were their last meal. Also look for sporadic BWO hatches that can pop off the river any given day.

The Eagle River is home to good numbers of brown and rainbow trout. Here the author lands a solid rainbow trout taken near the small town of Wolcott. MARK ADAMS

If water conditions warrant, May and June can be the best times to access the river from a raft. You do not see a lot of drift boats on the Eagle due to its rocky nature.

Besides April, I would have to say July is another favorite month to fish the Eagle. Like the Roaring Fork, it can have several hatches coming off at the same time and can send fly fishers into a panic digging through their fly boxes, wondering what the hell they are eating now. The Eagle's PMD hatch is about as good as it gets. I usually start seeing these bugs in force about the second week in July, and they can mix in with the Yellow Sallies about the same time. Green Drakes seem to show up around the end of July, and while the numbers are not as great as those seen on the Roaring Fork and the Frying Pan, the trout cannot resist them.

The Eagle has a strong caddis population, and the insects can be seen in good numbers from mid-June all the way through the second week of September. That being said, look for the strongest hatches to come off in July, especially in the late afternoons. If these insects do not pique your interest, then perhaps the medium-size stoneflies will. Golden Stones seem to be at their most active in July, and fishing these patterns in the dry form can prove to be anything but boring. It seems to me that these bugs were more prevalent in the 1980s and early '90s, but I still see them every year and trout pick them off one by one.

In the fall the water becomes super clear and sight-fishing is the best way to catch the river's larger trout. There is nothing like stalking an 18-inch rainbow in a foot of riffled water. The Eagle can be deceivingly deep, however, and you would be surprised at how many fish are in front of you that you cannot see. Also at this time the browns are in full spawn, and they seem to ignite the river's other fish into a feeding frenzy. Some of the largest rainbows can be taken in the Eagle during this time of year.

The Eagle certainly has its fair share of private property, so there are times when floating it will allow you a little more freedom. If you have never floated the Eagle River, it might be wise to hire a local guide to show you the ropes. There are several outfitters in the area, but two that come to mind are Eagle River Anglers (970-328-2323) and Fly Fishing Outfitters (970-845-8090).

While at times floating the Eagle has its advantages, there is still quite a bit of walk-wading access. Most of the private areas along the river are pretty well-marked, but some of the public accesses includes the Squaw Creek Unit, Bellyache site, Ute Creek, Red Canyon area, Horse Pasture area, Eagle County Fairgrounds, Eagle River lease, and the Gypsum Ponds.

Hatches, Rigs, and Fly Patterns

Whether you get excited by fishing small midge patterns during the winter or giant Salmonflies in early June, the Colorado River has just about every insect hatch fly fishers could ask for. This chapter is not meant as a complete overview of entomology, but instead shares my thoughts on important aspects of each major hatch, as well as techniques and imitations that I have found reliable when encountering a specific insect hatch at a certain time of year.

Remember, the Colorado is a big fishery and there are a lot of different types of food for the fish to eat. Success often depends on your willingness to change. Your best bet is to go with the dominant hatch at the time, but sometimes off-the-wall presentations will yield fish.

Keep in mind the four stages of fooling difficult trout: (1) Adjust your indicator to the depth of feeding fish. (2) Add or subtract weight. (3) Change angles in the

Pat Dorsey long-line nymphs "Miller Time," a run on the Colorado River near Pumphouse. Mastering long-line nymphing takes time and practice, but the rewards can be awesome.
MARK ADAMS

run you are fishing for a different presentation. (4) If all else fails, change flies. It is surprising how these steps can save the day.

HATCH TIMING

When chasing down insect hatches, keep a few things in mind. First is the time of year. Some mayflies, for instance, only hatch at a certain time of year and certain time of day, while others such as Blue-Winged Olives are multi-brooded, which means they can hatch several times a year.

Second is the temperature of the water. During the winter when water temperatures are at the coldest, most aquatic life lies dormant until water temps trigger them to mate. Midges, on the other hand, can hatch year-round but are most useful to the fish during the cold months. Other insects like stoneflies prefer water temperatures to reach 50 to 55 degrees before they begin their annual rituals; however, the juvenile and adult nymphs can be available to the fish year-round. The Colorado is a long river that begins at over 10,000 feet in elevation and drops to around 5,456 feet at Silt. Obviously the water is going warm faster at lower elevations first. As the temperature rises and moves upstream, it triggers many of the insects to hatch, and that's why the hatch moves upstream. Applying this knowledge can help anglers stay with the hatch.

The final factor is the weather. Weather conditions can ignite an aquatic hatch or dampen the hatch. When Blue-Winged Olives first appear on the Colorado in late March and through April, they will be most numerous during a cloudy, darker day. Sunny days don't mean they won't hatch, however—they will just not be as plentiful. Transition into July when the Pale Morning Duns arrive, and it's a different story. These insects are most productive on sunny days and generally won't be seen until late morning. Most anglers miss the Green Drake hatch on the lower Colorado and the Roaring Fork simply because most of them are off the water by 5 p.m., which is usually when this hatch is just getting started.

If this all seems confusing, and it usually is, spending time on the water will help you make more sense of it when it comes to aquatic life. At least once in an angler's life this all comes together and the fish are going crazy during a massive insect hatch and it's as good as it gets!

MAYFLIES

Five major mayfly species (order Ephemeroptera) inhabit the Colorado River: the Blue-Winged Olive, Pale Morning Dun, Red Quill, Green Drake, and Trico. It is important to understand where these species are most abundant and what time of year anglers can take advantage of specific hatches. Understanding their life cycles will also put you in the best situation to catch trout during these hatches.

Green Drakes

Green Drakes (*Drunella* spp.) are among the largest of western mayflies. The Green Drake nymph is a strong crawler that prefers moderate to fast currents with

Green Drakes are an important food source in many parts of the Colorado River and its tributaries but are of most significance on the lower river and the Roaring Fork. JAY NICHOLS

cobblestone substrate. Once the nymph is ready to employ itself into adulthood, it crawls toward slower-moving water in the river. When the conditions are right, it then arches its abdomen forward over the thorax, which eventually causes the wing pad to split. Being that the Green Drake is a large mayfly, it takes time for the now-emerged dun to dry its wings. The good news for anglers is that this makes them very vulnerable to the trout. The most reliable life cycle stage, however, is when the spinners return to the water. Trout will literally gorge themselves during this stage, and it is one of the most exciting times to fly fish.

While Green Drakes can be found in most of the Colorado River, it's the lower sections of the Colorado and the Roaring Fork River that are of most importance to fly fishers. Beginning around late June/early July, Green Drakes hatch on the lower Colorado around New Castle, and by about mid-July the hatch is in full swing, moving up the Roaring Fork. When this event happens, you should use some sick days at work.

Local fly shops such as Roaring Fork Anglers in Glenwood Springs or Taylor Creek Fly Shops (Basalt and Aspen, Colorado) can help you out with fly selection, but there are a few patterns that have consistently worked for me. For the nymphs, a good old size 10 or 12 Olive Hare's Ear or a Beadhead Poxyback Green Drake nymph will get the job done. For emergers, I like a CDC Green Drake emerger; for adults, a size 10 or 12 Colorado Green Drake dry.

When searching out this hatch, concentrate your efforts during the evening hours. This is when the hatch generally turns on, but cloudy days can push it back earlier in the afternoon. There are several places in Glenwood Springs, particularly around the 7th Street Bridge and Sunlight Bridge, where the city lights provide an excellent opportunity to see your dry fly in the late evening hours.

Tricos

Starting in the month of August, Tricos (*Tricorythodes* spp.) begin appearing on the Colorado River and quickly build into epic hatches and spinner falls. Sometimes they come off in such force that it looks like it's snowing in August. They are multi-brooded, which means they can hatch several times a season, so hatches stay strong through September and even well into October some years. Tricos will hatch on most of the Colorado, but some of the largest hatches can be found from the Sunset lease through Byers Canyon and from Kremmling down to State Bridge.

On a typical day, the nymphs become active around 10 a.m. and emergers get the trout turned on shortly after that. The nymphs prefer silty gravel bottoms with medium riffle currents, and before the insects emerge, fishing Trico nymph patterns can be effective. Three-fly nymphing rigs are the way to go here. I usually start with a point fly consisting of a Pine Squirrel Leech or something beaded like a Prince Nymph or Psycho Prince. From there it is just a matter of matching the hatch. Remember, Trico nymphs are small—3 mm to 10 mm—so choosing the right pattern is important. John Barr's Trico Nymph is about as good as it gets. It covers both nymphs and nymphs trying to shake their shucks. Other effective nymph patterns include Pheasant Tails, the Tailwater Tiny, and the Killer Mayfly Nymph.

The third fly in your rig should be something that mimics the little mayflies' efforts to blow their wing out in an effort to breach the surface. There are several emerger patterns that are effective, but only a couple that I come back to time after time. The first is Whitley's Black Rs2, a pattern that should be every fly fisher's box. The second—and the one I use the most for every emerging mayfly on the Colorado River—is the Chocolate Post Foam Rs2. This simple pattern, originated on the San Juan River by John Tavenner, is in my opinion the most effective emerger pattern ever created. When fishing the Trico hatch, fish these patterns in sizes 20 through 26.

Early fall marks the beginning of great fishing to be had throughout the Colorado River. Here John Perizzolo holds a nice specimen that he caught on a size 22 Tailwater Tiny near Parshall. This fly works extremely well for small mayflies such as Pseudos and Tricos when the trout are taking the nymphal stage of these insects. BOB DYE

Landon Mayer fishes a stretch near State Bridge during a Trico hatch in mid-September. Tricos can come off in such force that it resembles a snowstorm during the hottest months of the year. JAY NICHOLS

The trout seem to get turned on when the nymphs start transforming into emergers around 11 a.m. or so, and the fish begin slashing at them off of shelves and mid-seam currents. While several imitations can be used at this stage, it's tough to beat a size 24 Chocolate Foam Wing Emerger. In addition to a three-fly rig with a nymph and emerger on it, sometimes I will simply tie on a Chocolate Post Foam Emerger or Whitley's Black Rs2 in a size 22 below my grasshopper or attractor dry pattern. Use a number 6 split shot about 10 inches above the fly, and you are good to go.

It can be tough to figure out what stage the trout are feeding on, and I have spent countless hours scratching my head wondering what is going on. But when emergers evolve into duns, it seems all hell breaks loose. This can be a technical dry-fly angler's dream. Now is the time, says Jim Cannon, to use "small dries and tiny tippets." Jim owns the Blue Quill Angler and is the guide coordinator. He is constantly trying to get me to switch to fishing nothing but dry flies, but I haven't quite reached that point yet. Some of the best patterns to cover this stage are Stalcup's Compara-dun, A.K. Best's Quill Body Parachute Trico, and John Barr's Vis-A-Dun.

The duns molt into spinners quickly, however—only one or two hours after emergence. This can present a situation where the spinners are falling while the last of the duns are emerging. The best strategy is to use both a dun and spinner dry-fly presentation to try to figure out what stage the trout are feeding on. This will allow you to dissect the problem and take advantage of the hatch.

If the hatch is coming off strong and strikes are rare, try throwing an emerger pattern like a Chocolate Post Foam Emerger or Whitley's Black Rs2 in the event

The Chocolate Post Foam Emerger (#16-24) is one of the best patterns when it comes to fooling fish on emerging mayflies. It is most effective fished as the third fly in a three-fly rig or in the surface film behind a dry fly. MARK ADAMS

the fish are keying in on the emerging cycle of the hatch. I never really seem to catch these fish on Trico dries, but have had some luck on drowning adult Tricos in the surface film. These hatches are short-lived, however, so take advantage of the small window; after all, there is a chance you will land a few more fish than normal.

Eventually the hatch fades, and depending on weather conditions such as unexpected wind or rain, the much-anticipated spinner fall begins to appear. Trico spinners return soon after mating—sometimes a few minutes and sometimes a few hours. This can be obvious by the huge swarms overhead, almost like an isolated snowstorm. After mating, the males fall to the water spent and the females fly to the banks of the river to rest. The females return about a half hour later and fall to the water to deposit the eggs. At this time, the females can lay spent or take off again for another round, and the vast number of naturals on the water can make your fly hard to locate. While trout can be taken at all stages of the hatch, I think the Trico's principal importance is during the spinner stage when they can coat the river's surface and get the fish feeding heavily. Patterns such as A.K. Best's Trico Spinner and Umpqua's Chubby Trico Spinner work effectively during this time.

The Trico hatch can be frustrating at times; you see fish feeding all around and start asking yourself what's wrong with your presentations. I think anglers go into this hatch fishing patterns that are too big or too bulky. "I think the most important thing to remember is size," explains Pat Dorsey, co-owner of the Blue Quill Angler. Tricos can hatch in such force that the trout are used to seeing thousands of bugs at the same time. "If your presentation is a hook size too big, it looks very unnatural," says Dorsey. Trico nymphs range in size on the Colorado River from 20 to 26 and are slender by nature. If you are not a fly tier, select flies that are tied sparsely.

Blue-Winged Olives

By the time March rolls around, water temperatures rise slightly and Blue-Winged Olives (*Baetis* spp.) start hatching as early as the first week of March on the lower river and begin filling the sky on upper reaches of the Colorado as early as April. This is one of the best hatches before spring runoff starts. These little mayflies are a multi-brooded hatch, meaning they can have several hatches between April and even into November.

Out of all five species of mayflies in the Colorado, BWOs are probably the most important just because of their numbers. While these insects hatch on the entire river, there are areas that seem to have a little more activity than others. The first area of interest has to be on the lower river from Glenwood Springs downstream. This area has a milder winter pattern than sections of river upstream; therefore, come the month of March, *Baetis* come off in force and can be the first mayfly hatches of the season on the Colorado River. Other areas of interest include the Kremmling to State Bridge area starting in April and the Kemp-Breeze units starting around the same time.

Here is a little hint: Try turning over rocks in the river to find nymphs; if their thorax is darker than the rest of their body, it is likely a hatch is right around the

Rainbows that are caught on the lower Colorado are generally hard-fighting fish, like this one that fell for a gray Rs2 pattern during a BWO hatch in late April. BOB DYE

corner. Trout will feed on the nymphs year-round, but they become a point of interest during this time. "I've caught fish during a *Baetis* hatch and the nymphs are still wiggling in their mouths," says Billy Berger, longtime guide for Mountain Angler in Breckenridge. Pay close attention to *Baetis* nymphs; if their wing case is dark black with a little bulge, this can be a telltale sign that the BWO hatch is getting ready to start.

Matching the size and shape of the nymphs is important, but adding a little flash to your bugs to help them stand out does not hurt either. Using a bigger point fly such as a Pat's Rubber Legs or a Prince Nymph can draw feeding fish closer to your presentation as well. Flashback Pheasant Tails and Randy Smith's Baetis are good options, but my go-to nymph is a Stalcup's Baetis, which has taken more fish than any *Baetis* pattern I know of.

At maturity, the nymph buoys to the surface, the wing case splits, and the winged dun emerges. You will often see fish slashing at the emergers in the riffles and seams. Typically, when BWOs are hatching, they're coming out of the more oxygenated water, and fish tend to move up on shelves and gravel bars to eat the nymphs. I have seen fish move out of their holding lies and move up to where the hatch is more abundant, almost like they are in competition with other trout in the river. When fishing a *Baetis* hatch, the depth of your presentation is key. Adjusting your indicator to suspended fish or fishing in deeper water is the recipe for success.

I like to fish this hatch with a three-fly rig so that I can imitate both the nymph and emerger. Starting with a point fly, I like to use a Prince Nymph, black Copper John, or anything beaded with a little flash. My second fly of choice is a Stalcup's Baetis or Mercury Pheasant Tail in sizes 18 through 22. Size and shape are

The Chocolate Post Foam Rs2 is one of the best emerger fly patterns to imitate emerging mayflies. As the fly rises through the water column at the end of the drift, its square-cut wing acts as a rudder, giving the fly movement just like the naturals. JAY NICHOLS

Rs2 patterns have evolved over the years, but their importance to fly fishers is second to none. Rim Chung, the inventor of the Rs2, designed the fly to closely match emerging mayflies. Sizes should include 16 through 26, tied in several colors such as gray, black, and all shades of green. BOB DYE

important here; the fish see a ton of insects coming down the water column, so your presentation needs to be spot on. The third fly in my rig is always a *Baetis* emerger pattern. It's tough to beat a size 18 to 22 standard Rs2 or variation such as a Post Foam Rs2, Whitley's Rs2, or Sparkle Wing Rs2. CDC Emergers and Soft Hackle Pheasant Tails are also good choices. Try them all in a variety of colors, including gray, olive, and chocolate. One technique that I like to use is to allow my flies to swing at the end of the drift to imitate the swimming nymphs.

As the duns float on the surface, they are susceptible to rising trout. Trout begin slurping these bugs in an attempt to grab them before they fly away. Pat Dorsey, co-owner of the Blue Quill Angler, explains, "At this stage I like to fish a dry-dropper setup. My dry is usually an Olive Sparkle Dun followed by a Chocolate or Gray Post Foam Emerger in sizes 20 or 22." I generally also go to a two-dry-fly setup, the first being a Parachute Adams in sizes 18 through 24. The trailing fly I usually use is an Olive Compara-dun in sizes 18 through 24. I space the two flies about 24 to 30 inches apart. When fishing dry flies, it is important to set yourself up at the right angle. Casting directly across-stream can line the trout and put them down. I like to work upstream, making presentations up and out rather than down and across.

The lucky duns that escape the reach of hungry fish fly up into the trees and bushes along the riverbank, and this is where they molt and transform into spinners. After mating in the air, the females drop their eggs by diving under the water, or in some cases the eggs fall to the water, and the cycle starts all over again.

I carry a multitude of flies for the BWO hatch, including standard Flashback Pheasant Tails, Stalcup's Baetis, Craven's JuJu Baetis, and Big Bear Baetis for the nymphs, all in sizes 16 through 20. When it's time to fish emergers, a Rim's Rs2, Sparkle Wing Rs2, Post Foam Emerger, and soft-hackle patterns will all get the job done. Fish these emergers in sizes 16 through 20 and have colors to match, such as gray and chocolate. When it comes to dries, it is tough to beat a Parachute Adams, but other flies such as a Sparkle Dun Parachute Extended Body will suffice.

A standard Pheasant Tail will produce strikes, but no pattern resembles the actual nymph like a Stalcup's Baetis in size 22. This fly reaches my line first, before all others. As the hatch progresses, fish begin taking the emergers before they breach the water. Patterns like the Rs2 will always produce fish, but Soft Hackle Pheasant Tails deserve a good drowning as well. Make sure you finish your drifts when fishing emergers; remember, you're trying to mimic the naturals before they breach the surface. As the hatch progresses and trout begin taking the naturals off the surface, your adrenaline can sure start flowing. Look for the trout to begin glancing up about midday or so and feeding on the surface for a couple of hours. If it is a cloudy day, look for these hatches to be more widespread and last longer into the afternoon. Standard Blue-Winged Olive patterns like a Parachute Adams or an Olive Compara-dun in sizes 18 through 22 will bring fish to the surface.

In my opinion, one of the top guides in this area is Mathew Thomas, who has a knack for getting his clients into fish even in the toughest of conditions. According to Thomas, "If fish are refusing your dry presentation, try trailing a greased emerger behind your dry fly." This is good advice, especially since some emerging takes can resemble trout taking dries off the surface. I had a chance to fish with Mathew in

Casey Blue shows off a nice brown that he landed in the Gravel Flats using a size 22 Barr's Emerger. Mayflies can be found in strong numbers throughout the Colorado River, and anglers should carry a multitude of sizes and patterns to work the river effectively. BOB DYE

An angler decides what PMD nymph to use near Gore Canyon before the hatch gets into full swing. PMD hatches are widespread on the Colorado River and at their strongest point during the month of July. BOB DYE

spring 2014, and there was no doubt he knows the area's rivers like the back of his hand. "There is a lot of intimidating water over here, not only from a walk-wading standpoint but floating some of these sections can be dangerous," he says.

One of my favorite nymph patterns is a size 22 Stalcup's Baetis. I know a ton of fly fishers that have their own creations, but this fly is without a doubt a must in any angler's fly box. No flash, no bling, no smoke and mirrors—just a straight-up natural representation of this popular insect. If you cannot catch trout with this fly during a BWO hatch, then you should take up curling. The other nymph that most anglers already have in their box is the standard Pheasant Tail. This fly will work till the end of time; just remember to stay small and slender.

When it comes to the emerging stage of the hatch, it is hard to go wrong with all the Rs2 versions that are out there, but one of the best is a Gray Post Foam Rs2. I think one of the reasons this fly has an advantage over other Rs2 patterns is its design. The fly's emerging wing is made out of foam and is cut square on top of the thorax, giving it a rudder effect as it wiggles (like the natural) to the surface.

Blue-Winged Olives are an essential part of the trout's diet, and trying to fool fish on imitations is not always easy. One of the biggest reasons is that most patterns are tied too bulky. Next time you are on the stream, turn over a few rocks and study the naturals. BWO nymphs are slender and sleek. One thing to keep in mind with any hatch is that trout become selective to a certain size and shape of insect. When there are hundreds of insects in the water column, the trout are going to be a little leery of a presentation that looks out of place. Tie your patterns sparsely, or pick patterns from your local fly shop that match the size and shape of the naturals.

All patterns will work eventually, but the ones you want to get your hands on are the ones that work consistently. It is hard to beat a sparsely tied Pheasant Tail, but one of the best *Baetis* nymphs around is Stalcup's Baetis Nymph. This little fly exactly matches the naturals. In fact, if it were not for the hook protruding from the fly, you would think it was real when wet. Other patterns you should not be without include Dorsey's Mercury Pheasant Tail, Big Bear Baetis Nymph, Barr's BWO Emerger, and WD-40s, all in sizes 20 through 24.

As for emerger patterns, ever since Rim Chung invented the Rs2 in the early 1970s, there have been hundreds of variations of the popular pattern, all of which will catch fish. When fishing the Colorado River, anglers should stock up on the following in sizes 16 through 24: Sparkle Wing Rs2, Dorsey's Mercury Rs2, Flashback Rs2s, Chocolate Post Foam Emerger, and Soft Hackle Pheasant Tail. Patterns should include several color variations such as gray, olive, and chocolate.

Pale Morning Duns

Pale Morning Duns (*Ephemerella* spp.) are the first major hatch when the river levels begin to decline from runoff, usually by the second week of July. While PMDs can be found in the entire Colorado River system, the upper river sees a better population of insects. One of the best places to begin looking for the sulphur-colored bugs is at the Sunset lease near Hot Sulphur Springs. This can be a very prolific hatch, and since caddis and Yellow Sallies can be prevalent at the same time, anglers need to determine what the trout are feeding on.

PMD nymphs are a bit bigger than Blue-Winged Olive nymphs and range in color from chocolate brown to a pale sulphur color. Standard Pheasant Tail patterns are an excellent choice along with Mitchell's Split Case PMD Nymph and Barr's Emerger. Dead-drifting these patterns can produce strikes, but like all mayflies, PMDs need to swim to the surface in order to break through their shuck to evolve into a dun.

I really enjoy fishing this stage when trout become aware of the insects' movements and begin moving towards shelves and drop-offs in the river. I use a multiple-fly rig consisting of a heavy

Mik Aoki, head baseball coach at Notre Dame, caught this brown while fishing a three-fly rig during the PMD hatch in late July. Three-fly rigs can allow the angler to cover all underwater presentations during insect hatches. BOB DYE

point fly such as a Pat's Rubber Legs or Steve Parrott's Electric Caddis. From the point fly, run about 16 to 20 inches of 5X tippet to the second fly (Pheasant Tail, etc.). From there, 90 percent of the time I am using some kind of PMD emerger pattern such as a Chocolate Post Foam Rs2, Crystal Hunchback, or Soft Hackle Pheasant Tail.

Finding the shelf is important, as trout will nose up on it looking for bugs tumbling down the water current or beginning to emerge after hitting a break in water speed. This is why trout seek these areas out during most insect hatches. The other reason I like fishing this faster water is that the fish do not have as long to look at your presentation. They have to make up their minds in a hurry, rather than study your offering in slower water. I usually work a shelf or a drop-off by fishing at a 45-degree angle behind the structure. This allows you to pinpoint fish at the shelf while not spooking or lining fish that are on the shelf. The rule of thumb is to always fish close to you before attempting to cast farther out to other suspects.

As the emergers transform into duns, they spend a few minutes floating down the water column drying their wings before flying off, and trout will begin picking these insects off the surface. When the trout are feeding on PMD dries, I usually stick with a few old standbys such as a Brook's Sprout PMD Dry, PMD Sparkle Dun, or Parachute PMD in sizes 14 to 20, with size 16 being the most common.

Yellow Sallies can hatch at the same time as PMDs. If the trout are taking the duns, it's pretty easy to tell which insect they are keying on, but under the surface, unless you have a snorkel, it can be a little more difficult. Often they are taking both. In these situations, trial and error will solve the problem, but do not be afraid to try patterns that can represent both. Mike Mercer's Trigger Nymph and Poxyback PMD can bring fish to hand in confusing situations. Other times just using these flies to get one fish in the net can make all the difference in the world. After the fish has been netted, using a stomach pump can help you decipher what flies the trout are taking.

Red Quills

Red Quills (*Cinygmula* spp.) are often overlooked, but they are not hard to recognize. Generally larger than Blue-Winged Olives, their rust-colored bodies and elegant flight patterns can get the juices flowing in even the most seasoned anglers. They seem to show up unannounced during the early fall, and if you're caught off-guard, you can miss out on some pretty spectacular fly fishing.

Red Quills can be found throughout the river system and on the right day can provide some exciting fishing during the early fall, but the best place to cross paths with this bug is around the Williams Fork tributary. It's almost like the trout here are programmed for this hatch on a yearly basis.

One way anglers can cut this hatch off at the pass is to periodically pump fish earlier in the day. Being that Red Quills usually come off hardest in the afternoon or evening, this can be a prelude of what's to come, as the presence of Red Quill nymphs in the fish's stomach is a telltale sign of the upcoming hatch. Red Quill nymphs are larger than Blue-Winged Olive nymphs and vary in color from chocolate brown to dark olive, and they become very active before making their way to the surface. Patterns should include standard Pheasant Tails, Mike Mercer's Trigger Nymph, and a dark olive Hare's Ear (the bushier the better), all in sizes 14 through 18.

As the nymphs make their way to the surface, their wing cases darken before emergence, and this makes them vulnerable as well. Tying on an emerger pattern as your third fly can cover your bases. I have found that standard darker Rs2 patterns will suffice in these situations. As with all emerging mayflies, dead-drifting your presentation along with a swing at the end can produce strikes, as you're emulating the naturals. My favorite adult patterns include AK's Red Quill or a standard Parachute Adams in sizes 14 to 18, with size 14 being the most common.

Pseudos

In middle to late September, you may encounter tiny Pseudos (*Pseudocloeon* spp.), which until recently had been classified as *Baetis*. This hatch tends to be an early morning event, but what I have figured out is that they are the staple when nothing else is happening. I have a whole section in my fly box devoted to these little guys, and there are days I lean on them heavily. They can mean the difference between an average day and a great day. Pseudos hatch just about everywhere on the Colorado but seem to be denser on overcast days.

For patterns, a good rule of thumb is to just downsize standard *Baetis* nymphs to sizes 20 through 26 and make sure they are tied sparsely. One of the best nymph patterns out there is Idylwilde's Not Much Fly. Tied with very little material, this fly lives up to its name and ranges in color from bronze to pearl olive. My Bubble Baetis is also a must-have during a Pseudo hatch. I fish this simple pattern in the last of a three-fly nymphing rig or drop it in the film behind a dry fly.

MIDGES

Midges (Diptera) are the most consistent food source for Colorado River trout throughout the year. They flourish in areas of the river where silt deposits at the back of deep pools or along slower parts of the river's edges. Prime time for fishing midges is November through March, primarily because nothing else is hatching and they have the trout's complete attention.

Midge hatches can become so thick that size and shape are keys to success. After a couple hours of seeing the same thing in front of their face, the fish become selective to that particular insect. The Colorado River at Pumphouse is famous for its midge diversity, ranging in size from 16 to 24. If midges are dominant and there are tons of them down here, try to find the most common size and tie on accordingly. Color can vary as well, and while dark olive is the most prominent, color schemes can range from cream to light olive and chocolate brown to black.

At this time of the year, trout will not waste their energy in faster water, so you should concentrate your efforts on the slower, deeper pools. I typically like to use a searching pattern such as egg patterns, Prince Nymphs, free-swimming caddis imitations, and stonefly patterns for the first fly, and then drop off a couple of midge patterns below.

I usually find a standard Zebra Midge with a gunmetal bead works best for the midge larvae in winter. Most commonly the sizes range from 18 through 22. One fly that consistently takes fish during this time is the Periwinkle. I tie this popular

Kelli Blue is all smiles after catching this colorful brown near Radium on a size 22 Dye's Thunderstruck Midge in late October. This multicolored pattern works effectively in the Colorado River's deepest holes. BOB DYE

pattern slightly different at this time of year to match the hatch a little more closely. Instead of olive thread, I use a camel-colored thread, and instead of a gunmetal bead, I use a cobalt blue color. Run this fly under an attractor nymph, and you should be ready to go.

When it comes to the emerging stage, Dorsey's Top Secret Midge in sizes 16 through 20 will cover your bases. Another emerger pattern that works exceptionally well is Dye's OTD Midge.

Until I see fish rising, I usually stay with a three-fly nymphing rig consisting of a 9-foot 4X leader with 3 feet of fluorocarbon attached to my first fly (attractor) and two droppers tied off the attractor. Tying smaller patterns such as midges from the bend of the hook is easier than trying to thread another piece of tippet through the same eye. Placing an indicator 3 to 4 feet below the fly line insures adjustment to the proper depth of feeding trout.

Generally speaking, the best way to approach feeding fish is to start at the back of a run, make presentations in close to start, and then work your way through the run using the grid-system technique. In these long, slow runs, I have found fishing long and light is more productive than short and heavy. Finding the depth of feeding trout, I will make presentations 12 to 15 feet above my target, letting the flies come down naturally to the feeding fish, using split shot no larger than a number 6. Casting out about a foot each time allows the angler to cover the water thoroughly. At the same time, adjusting weight and strike indicators will allow you to cover the water's depth effectively.

Using this system, some of the fly patterns that are deadly include Dorsey's Flashback Mercury Black Beauty, Pearl Jam, Buckskin, Strawberry Jam, Apple Jam, and Periwinkle, all in sizes 18 through 22; and Zebra Midge, Dye's Colorock Midge, Biot Midge, Miracle Nymph, and Sidewinder Midge in sizes 18 through 24. Emerging midge patterns include Dorsey's Top Secret Midge, Neiberger's UPS Midge, UV Midge, Dye's Purple Flash Midge, and Chocolate Post Foam Emerger, all in sizes 18 through 24.

When trout start rising, I use a 9-foot 5X leader, with 5X tippet if the trout will allow. Sometimes finicky trout require anglers to drop in tippet size down to 6X or

Eric Atha holds a solid 16-inch brown he caught while fishing the Crescent Moon Hole near Pumphouse in late November. He deceived this fish using a size 22 Dye's Strawberry Jam.
JIM NEIBERGER

even 7X. I like to use a dual-fly combo when fishing midge dries, usually mixing it up between two different fly patterns to determine which is working best. It's tough to go wrong with a Matt's Midge, Parachute Adams, Griffith's Gnat, or Jim Cannon's Snowshoe Midge, all in sizes 18 through 26. If I am having trouble seeing my flies, I might fish a larger attractor pattern such as a Stimulator or anything easier to see, then tie on the midge pattern the trout are keying in on. One particular thing I like about Cannon's Snowshoe Midge is that you can simply cut the fly down to size and zero in on what the fish are taking.

When fishing a piece of water with one insect dominating the food supply, you need to distinguish your presentation from the hundreds or even thousands of naturals. One thing that I have figured out when this situation arises is to start by tying your flies with oversize segmentation. Midges are truly small by nature, but tying with materials like woven wire midge braid a little bigger than normal can add a three-dimensional look to the old standby patterns. Simply tying a little flash into your patterns can also help immensely. I am not big on flies that look like Mr. T, but a little flash goes a long way. Midge patterns like the Periwinkle and the Rhinestone Midge amplify these points. Sometimes it just doesn't matter, but other times it is the little things that make all the difference between a few-fish day and a 20-fish day.

It does not happen often, but sometimes pods of feeding fish can be found sipping midges in one of the many tailout sections of long runs. If you do not have any dries, that is the time the fish will rise. Dry flies that work well for the Colorado River include the Griffith's Gnat, Parachute Adams, and Cannon's Snowshoe Midge, all

Steve Jordan of Denver caught this beauty using a size 24 Chocolate Post Foam Emerger during a midge hatch in late October. These flies are a must-have on any river, especially the Colorado. BOB DYE

in sizes 18 through 22. Don't forget that when the "Big Midge" comes off, it can sometimes resemble a BWO hatch, but after further review anglers soon realize that it's just an oversize midge. Using larger Zebra Midges will suffice here, but nothing works as well as a Periwinkle in sizes 16 through 18. When the fish are tuned into these bugs, they eat this fly like popcorn.

CADDISFLIES

Caddisfly (Trichoptera) hatches come off in force on the Colorado. While the strongest caddis hatches occur in April and then again from late June through July, sporadic hatches can occur anytime from April through September. The lower river below Glenwood Springs—more specifically, upstream from Silt—can be the first place to engage these insects starting around the second week of April. The beginning of this hatch can rival any caddis hatch on any of Colorado's rivers. Other areas of interest include stretches between Kremmling and State Bridge and the Kemp-Breeze units around Parshall. Also included is the Sunset lease below the Kemp-Breeze units, especially during the month of July.

The fluttering insects begin their life cycle as eggs deposited in the river by the females. Most caddis live underwater for a year before hatching into adults. Some of the most important species for anglers begin life as larvae, building a case around themselves for protection. This cased caddis can be important to anglers, as trout will seek them out when nothing else is hatching. There are several patterns out there for this stage, but Dorsey's Mercury Caddis and Peeking Caddis will get the job done.

When Mother Nature signals them to hatch, the caddis form a gas bubble that shoots them to the surface at a fast rate; there they may drift a while before emerging from their shucks and fluttering away. All this fast-paced action can send trout into a feeding frenzy. It is during this time that anglers should be armed with several pupa patterns as well as dry imitations. When trout are feeding on caddis pupae, it is important to find the right depth and the right speed in which to present your flies. The length of your indicator can accomplish this; remember, length is indicator to weight, not indicator to fly. In addition, the amount of weight can adjust the speed of your presentation. Like all presentations below the surface, the way your flies drift is the key to success. Sometimes when fishing caddisflies this is even more prevalent—some fish want a dead drift, while others are feeding on bugs rising to the surface. This is why trial-and-error nymphing can save your day: If something is not working, change it up.

If I do not see trout feeding on the surface, I start with a standard three-fly nymphing rig. I usually begin with a point fly consisting of what the trout have been seeing for the last month or so, such as stoneflies or worms, or a tried-and-true attractor such as a Pine Squirrel Leech, Breadcrust, or Prince Nymph. I then begin dialing in on the caddis the trout are feeding on. My second fly is usually some sort of larva imitation, such as Parrott's Electric Caddis or Barr's Caddis Larva Fly, followed by a third fly that imitates a caddis pupa. This is almost always a Barr's Graphic Caddis. I typically space my patterns 12 to 14 inches apart, but with the Graphic Caddis I usually drop back of the second fly about 2 feet. This allows the fly to have more movement in the water column. Caddisflies are an energetic insect, so using flies that create movement tends to draw the most strikes.

Other patterns anglers should not be without are Breadcrusts, Lafontaine's Sparkle Caddis Pupa, Bird's Nests, and Soft Hackle Pheasant Tails. Color can be important, but I usually find size to be the most important factor for the fish during a caddis hatch.

Before the hatch starts, the trout will sometimes key in on this emerging stage of the caddis life cycle. I typically see caddis emerging between 11 a.m. and 1 p.m., and by 2 you're usually fishing dries. As I begin to witness the trout's feeding habits, I usually find myself fishing a dry-dropper setup until I see most of the fish rising, and then go to a two-dry-fly setup.

When you have this many insects coming off at one time and your strike ratio is not what you think it should be, try twitching your caddis dries across the surface. Sometimes the naturals do not sit tight and float with the river. Another little trick is to go big: I have tied on larger attractor patterns such as an Amy's Ant or Stimulator and then followed that with a realistic caddis pattern. Occasionally trout see so many bugs jumping up and down on the water's surface that they are ready to pounce on anything that looks buggy. This is why fishing caddis dries is so interesting—there are times when trout want it on a dead drift and times they want it on the bounce. Other times I have found it useful to throw my presentation into the slower water just off the main seam, lift the flies off the water a few feet or so, and then let them travel down the edge of the main current. This draws wary fish from the shallows and initiates their predatory instinct. Sometimes it's just trial and error, but it's fun experimenting.

As the hatch progresses, look for splashy rises along the river's banks and mid-seam currents; trout will be aggressively taking emergers and inhaling the dries. There is no secret formula to catching these trout, and a well-placed size 12 to 18 Elk Hair Caddis, Puterbaugh Caddis, Hemingway's Caddis, or Goddard Caddis should do the trick. If several fish are rising and ignoring your presentation, try giving your fly a little movement; after all, caddisflies do not always remain docile on the surface. Fishing double caddis dries, even when no fish are rising, can also be an effective technique during caddis season.

When fishing dries, I usually start with a 9-foot 5X leader, with an additional 3 feet of tippet to the first fly. Depending on the situation, I will fish two dries or a dry-dropper; either way, stay long, as you will have more opportunities fishing a longer leader. Shorter leaders usually result in "lining" the fish, resulting in missed opportunities. Find a section of water with fish feeding on the surface and make some dead-drift presentations. If the trout do not respond, try skating your flies across the surface. This method of skating really works well in faster riffle water; it is like dropping your favorite fly box in the water and you do not want it to get away. If strikes are inconsistent, try throwing on a dropper below your dry fly; there are times the fish cannot make up their mind, and this way you are covering your bases in the water column.

There are two main types of caddis larvae: case-making and free-living. The case makers are more abundant in the Colorado River system, and anglers are more aware of this type of caddis (Brachycentridae) because of their sheer numbers and on-time hatches. This caddis will start towards the end of April and be off and on through September, but during this time of year, it's the free-living forms that are most important to anglers. Most of these free-living forms are net-building caddis that trap food such as decaying plant material or microorganisms, but there are free-swimming caddis that are predaceous. These caddis are constantly on the move in search of prey, thus making them vulnerable to trout.

While these free-swimming caddis are available to trout year-round, the fish seem to fixate on them early in the spring. My reasoning for this is that they're like the trout. When the water warms slightly, the trout become more active, and it's the same with the free-swimming caddis: When water temperatures climb, the insects become more active. While these insects are found in the entire river system, they seem to have better numbers in the Pumphouse to State Bridge area. Caddis larvae patterns such as Steve Parrott's Electric Caddis, which is one of my best producers, and other imitations such as Dorsey's Hydropsyche, Perizzolo's Zombie Caddis, and Candy Caddis will all draw strikes.

When the wheels come off, Colorado River trout typically turn to caddis. The Colorado is home to huge numbers of free-living caddis, and while many anglers confuse these with scuds, they are an important food source for trout, especially April through November. I have used a number of these patterns, but the best ones seem to be tied by the Czech nymphing community. I think the reason is simply that these flies are tied weighted. Steve Parrott, co-owner of the Blue Quill Angler in Evergreen, has several free-living caddis patterns to his name, one of which he dubbed the Electric Caddis. This pattern is a must among Colorado River fly fling-ers. It is a great fly during April and early May, but is a "save-your-day fly" during the tough times. I fish this fly in a three-fly nymphing rig, usually as my point fly. Not only is it a great pattern, but it is also just a great attractor pattern on many streams where free living caddis are found.

STONEFLIES

Salmonflies

The Salmonfly (*Pteronarcys* spp.) hatch usually starts about the end of May and generally wraps up around the 10th of June, which is also during runoff. Although fantastic fishing can be had this time of year, sometimes muddy water spoils the fun. Over the last 20 years, I have probably only "home-runned" this hatch three or four times, mostly due to the high-water conditions that can affect the Colorado River this time of year. While drought or low-water conditions are not good for the river system, it can usually be the best time to capitalize on this elusive hatch. Look for these big bugs throughout the system, but keep a close eye on the sections upstream from State Bridge to Hot Sulphur Springs.

Like trout, stoneflies require clean, oxygenated water. They generally live in faster water, where the water meets cobblestone or rock garden bottoms. After hatching from eggs deposited by their elders, the little nymphs may shed (molt) a dozen times so that they can grow. They may live in the stream bottom for three or four years before it is their time to repeat the process.

I usually carry two rods with me during this time, one rigged with nymphs and the other rigged with a dry-dropper. This allows me to fish deeper runs along with presentations to the bank. The nymphs tumble through the water column and crawl their way to rock gardens in the river or to the bank, where the winged adult crawls out of the nymphal shuck. Stoneflies generally crawl towards the bank in search of rocks and downed logs or tree branches. Knowing the behavior of these insects can be a difference maker when fishing this water. "I've dead-drifted flies through the water column only to find twitching my flies toward the bank produced strikes," says longtime Colorado River fly fisher Jim Neiberger.

Patterns such as Pat's Rubber Legs, Bitch Creeks, Girdle Bugs, or any beaded stoneflies are the way to go here. Dry-fly patterns include the Rogue Stone, Gorilla Stone, Sofa Pillow, Kauffman's Stone, and anything that looks big and bushy.

Most of the time when I am fishing the Salmonfly hatch, I run an attractor stone, such as a Pat's Rubber Legs or an old-fashioned Twenty Incher. The second fly is a little more natural, like Dorsey's Paper Tiger Stone, or another oldie like the Bitch Creek. Jim Neiberger taught me the trick of fishing a pinkish-cream nymph pat-tern to imitate the molting nymphs. It is amazing how the trout will key in on this off-color stonefly, especially on muddy water days.

The Colorado River has one of the best Salmonfly hatches of any western river. As a matter of fact, biologists from Colorado Parks & Wildlife transported thou-sands of these little critters to the Arkansas River in an attempt to reestablish the population there as well. It is not always a home run, though; runoff and cloudy

Scott Harkins of Simms Fishing Products selects a Bitch Creek stonefly pattern. While the main hatch starts late in May, stoneflies can make up part of the trout's diet any time of year.

MARK ADAMS

Giant stonefly adults. JAY NICHOLS

water this time of year can make this hatch difficult to solve. The last couple of years have been low snowpack years, which meant most of the water was stored in the reservoirs. This translated to low releases from the dams, making it prime time to engage this elusive hatch. In a normal year, however, expect water flows to be at 2,000 to 2,300 cfs and the river more than likely having clarity from 1 to 3 feet. Over the years, I have taken more than a few chances on muddy water days, with several of them successful.

I usually start encountering these insects about the last week in May around the Two Bridges boat launch. I like to concentrate on the braided sections of river from here on up to Gore Canyon, which allows me to break up the hard-flowing river into sections that are more manageable. Whether you are fishing from a drift boat or walk-wading, this will allow more opportunities to engage the hatch more effectively. When searching for the hatch, staying on the move is key. The stoneflies are definitely on the move upstream, but a couple hundred yards either way can mean the difference between success and failure.

I've learned over time that when you're in a stretch of water and the stonefly nymphs are active, meaning they are crawling towards the banks and the fish are on them, return to that area a couple of days later and you should have good dry action. This only works if you know you were in the beginning stages of the hatch. If not, employ trial-and-error fishing tactics. Figure out what the fish want.

I can remember fishing one time with Jim Neiberger when stoneflies were coming off all around us like giant Chinook helicopters. After about an hour of fishing, Jim looked at me and said, "Did you do any good?" "No," I answered. "Did you?" "I got so frustrated," Jim replied, "that I ripped my stonefly patterns through the surface in disgust and a fish hit it." I went, "What?" He said, "The faster I ripped

Stoneflies make up a huge part of the trout's diet in the Colorado River year-round, but fishing this hatch in early May and the first part of June can send even the most seasoned anglers into a frenzy. BOB DYE

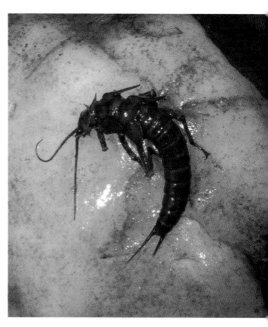

the nymph patterns through the column, the more fish hit it." Note to self: If conventional methods don't work, do something off the wall. This was something that I had never experienced before; ripping nymph patterns to imitate nymphs migrating to the shoreline triggered the brown trout's natural feeding instincts. Most of the time when fishing stonefly nymphs, dead-drifting them is the way to go, but ever since that day, I do at times let them swing towards the banks in an effort to imitate the naturals.

A variety of small stonefly imitations can cover your bases, from attractor patterns to juvenile stonefly nymphs. JAY NICHOLS

While the immature stones take three years to mature, they are still a food source year-round. However, nothing gets the trout more fired up than when the mature nymphs begin crawling to the shoreline. If you are lucky enough to be there on the right day, you will see hundreds of exoskeletons on the river's exposed rocks and female stoneflies hovering above the surface in an effort to deposit eggs for the next generation. The hatch moves quickly upriver, so don't get frustrated if you missed it on a particular day. Remember, at this time of year the fish are accustomed to seeing the large insects.

The second approach is to dry-dropper all the remaining skinny water and riverbanks. Sometimes nymphing rigs can be too cumbersome, and this approach will allow you to cover water for the hidden trout. It never ceases to amaze me where trout will hold in the river; one little 6-inch seam behind a bowling ball–size rock can sometimes yield the largest fish in the run. Tying on dry flies such as a Rogue Foam Para Stone or one of my favorites, the Sofa Pillow, can be a good place to start. Tying on a dropper about 16 to 30 inches below your dry fly will round out this effective rig. Using stonefly nymphs such as a Pat's Rubber Legs or a Bitch Creek is a good idea, but big Prince Nymphs, Twenty Inchers, and Halfbacks are all good fly choices as well.

Yellow Sallies

Yellow Sallies (*Isoperla* spp.) hatch throughout the Colorado River system during the month of July, most heavily on the sections between Hot Sulphur Springs and Kremmling and the stretch between Kremmling and State Bridge. Another area that has tremendous Yellow Sally hatches is the famed Roaring Fork River, one of the main tributaries of the Colorado.

Like other stoneflies, Yellow Sallies prefer the riffles and faster water currents, and they have a knack for appearing right in the middle of a caddis or PMD hatch. "I've seen trout switch gears in the middle of a PMD hatch," says guide Billy Berger. Trout will feed on all three at times, and sometimes it is effective to fish a three-fly rig with caddis, PMD, and Yellow Sally imitations.

When multiple insects are hatching—for example, PMDs and Yellow Sallies— observation is key. I like to start with a three-fly nymphing rig using different patterns, usually a Yellow Sally nymph as a point fly, dropped by a PMD nymph, followed by a Post Foam Rs2. This allows you to cover the water and find out what the trout are eating most. From there you can take it to the next level and dial it in. In addition, try flies that can imitate both insects; for example, Mercer's Trigger Nymph can represent both a PMD emerger and a Yellow Sally stonefly nymph.

Fly patterns that I have found most productive at this stage include Mercer's Poxyback, Iron Sally, and one of my favorites, Oliver Edwards' Stonefly. Yellow Sallies on the Colorado River range in size from ¾ inch to 1¼ inches long, so sizes 14 through 18 will suffice.

Yellow Sallies are an elegant insect, coming off the water as if they already have a purpose in life. Since it is more than likely you are going to encounter Yellow Sallies and PMDs at the same time, successful angling will usually be in the cards.

The author lands a brown trout during the Yellow Sally stonefly hatch that comes off in July. Oftentimes Yellow Sallies can be seen hatching at the same time as Pale Morning Duns throughout the Colorado River. JAY NICHOLS

What is even more amazing is that with all the insects, trout will fixate on one bug at a certain stage of its life cycle.

Nevertheless, anglers need to concentrate on the returning females and prepare to change flies. As the females make their way back to the water's surface, the trout turn their attention upwards. It is almost like throwing a ball for a Labrador retriever. The trout will return repeatedly to pick off the naturals. This is one of my favorite times to take trout on dries (the other being Salmonflies). As long as you have on the right size and shape fly, the trout do not seem to be finicky during this stage in the hatch. Dead drifts are important, but so are a few micro twitches to simulate struggling insects trying to deposit eggs.

There are a gazillion Yellow Sally dry fly patterns out there, but the ones I have found most effective on the Colorado River corridor are the Headlight Yellow Sally, Snowshoe Yellow Sally, Yellow Stimulator, and Parachute Yellow Sally. The Yellow Sallies down in this stretch are a tad bigger than their cousins on the upper river, so carrying sizes 12 through 16 will cover your bases throughout the river system; like all stoneflies, Yellow Sallies prefer faster, more oxygenated water. This will help stack the odds in your favor.

When the females return to drop eggs back into the river system, trout will pick these off as if it were their last meal. When this occurs, try fishing a size 16 Headlight Yellow Sally.

EGGS

As in most trout streams, eggs are an important part of the trout's diet at certain times of the year on the Colorado. Generally speaking, the river's rainbows spawn in the spring and its brown trout spawn in the fall. As the trout lay their eggs, water currents force some of the eggs downriver, and trout will feed on them consistently.

Brown trout eggs are about a ¼ inch in diameter and can range in color from pale yellow to iridescent orange. Hofer rainbow eggs are yellow-colored by nature. Light orange is probably my favorite all-around color, but I use a variety of colors including yellow, orange, red, and all the shades in between.

When spawning fish are active, I like to rig with an egg fly first, dropped by a trailing midge, then a midge emerger such as a Rhinestone Midge or Periwinkle. I have found that the right size and color egg pattern matched with the right midge is a deadly combination. One midge pattern that I always carry with me is the Rhinestone. This knockoff of the Zebra Midge is without a doubt the most effective pattern this time of year for midge larva. I carry it in sizes 18 through 24, with 22s being the most dominant. Concentrate your efforts below riffles and faster currents; browns and rainbows that are feeding on eggs will be in the current that is most likely to bring food into their feeding zone.

Besides the trout being accustomed to eggs drifting along the bottom of the river during the spawning months, egg flies can be a great attractor pattern year-round. It is pretty hard to beat an egg/midge combination during the spring and fall.

AQUATIC WORMS

Another overlooked food source on the Colorado are aquatic worms, or annelids. Aquatic worm, or annelids, live in the river year-round, and fish will seek them out when nothing else is going on. Over the years, stomach samples have revealed these tiny worms along with moss in the fish. That usually sends up a flag that the trout are not seeing many aquatic insects floating down the water column, and therefore have to forage for a meal. Many people mistake these worms for midge larvae and while they are similar looking, the annelids usually have more distinguished segmentation.

These aquatic worms vary in size and color, but the trout love 'em. Whether it's a guided trip or a personal trip, these little worms figure into a successful day 70 percent of the time. When there is not a large amount of insect activity, trout resort to the next best thing, and it is usually annelids. These aquatic worms live in the entire system and are generally fished best when nothing else seems to be happening.

Typically annelids live in the silt and in the moss. Higher water flows will push them down the water current, or the trout will dig them out of the moss beds.

I carry a wide variety of annelid patterns in my box, ranging in size from 14 to 22 and in color from cream to all shades of green to red. I tie these simple patterns in a variety of colors and sizes, but the most consistent one is a size 18 tied in dark olive. Tying in a little flash can help distinguish your flies from the naturals. Fishing these flies under a standard nymph is the way to go. "When I fish these patterns, they're usually my second fly behind an attractor fly," explains John Perizzolo, longtime

Mike Ohara of Evergreen admires a 21-inch fish he caught using a size 18 Dye's Annelid pattern. Annelids are an important food source for trout, which will actively feed on them when other aquatic food sources are not available. BOB DYE

Colorado River guide. They can be a simple tie, usually consisting of a 200R long-shank hook, thread color to match ribbing, and some D-Rib.

There are days throughout the year when it seems insect life has come to a halt and the river resembles something out of the twilight zone. No matter what you try, the fishing just seems dead. Anyone who tells you that every time they go fishing they landed 30 fish is probably full of it. The fish live in the Colorado 365 days a year but we only fish the river a fraction of that time; the advantage therefore goes to the fish. The fish still have to feed, however, and if there's nothing for them to eat, they generally turn to a familiar foe—annelids.

Color schemes include all shades of green, but cream and shades of red should be considered as well. I generally fish chartreuse colors in this section between Glenwood Springs and Silt, but in September red seems to be the dominant color. Every time we have floated any of the sections between Glenwood Springs and Silt, there is always a bunch of red annelids washing around in the bottom of the boat. Sizes range from 14 through 20, but 18s seem to be the most plentiful. The next time you find yourself having a tough day on any river, try one of these—it can change your day.

MYSIS SHRIMP

Mysis shrimp naturally inhabit lakes and reservoirs in British Columbia, but in the early 1970s the Colorado Division of Wildlife began stocking them into the state's lakes and reservoirs in an effort to feed the kokanee salmon populations. While this turned out not to be such a great idea, it did fare better for the tailwater trout in the river below the dams.

Shadow Mountain and Granby Reservoirs are home to these crustaceans, which at times become a formidable food source in the tailwaters. In fact, during periods of heavy runoff or when Denver Water is moving generous amounts of water from Shadow Mountain into Granby, *Mysis* shrimp become a staple for the trout. Besides having a few in your box when fishing below Shadow Mountain, these imitations catch some of the larger fish below Granby Reservoir. Like most fly patterns, there are several versions of *Mysis* shrimp patterns. They will all work, but I like Laney's Mysis Shrimp tied by Joe Shafer.

TERRESTRIALS

The wide-open ranchland through which the lower Colorado flows can offer prime habitat for terrestrials. Grasshoppers make up the majority of the terrestrial food source, but beetles, ants, and crickets also offer trout an easy meal.

Having started my guide career in Wyoming, I learned windy days were not the best of conditions, but then I met Stuart Birdsong, guide for the North Platte Lodge. Stu always seems to have a different approach to any river. I can remember fishing with him on a windy day on the lower Colorado. I was throwing standard nymph rigs, catching a few fish, and every time I glanced up, he was hooked up. "Hoppers!" he yelled. Standing there shaking my head, I figured if you can't beat 'em, join 'em. From that day forward, I realized how important land-born insects were to trout.

Hoppers, ants, and beetles really start to become table fare as the hot months of August and early September roll around. Try these types of patterns, especially on windy days. BOB DYE

In late summer when nothing else is going on, I find myself fishing these patterns a great deal more than in years past.

Being that these insects do not necessarily want to commit suicide by jumping into the jaws of a trout, they usually need a little push from the wind to enter the banks of the river. Making presentations to the bank with a little "pop" is a great way to get the attention of trout searching for a big meal. Bugs that plop into the river seem to spark the primitive instincts in trout, especially brown trout. It is amazing to me how quietly trout will take these large insects.

When fishing terrestrial patterns, spend the majority of your time working in close to the banks and making presentations into the smaller pocketwater closer to the edges. Bugs that survived initial entry will drift out into open currents. Often in the late summer, trout have migrated to the faster, more oxygenated water; this gives anglers the edge, in my opinion. Imitated food sources floating down at a faster rate have a better chance of being eaten than presentations made in slow water.

Billy Berger says, "I've caught larger fish on terrestrials than I have during a Blue-Winged Olive hatch." I have to agree—larger fish, especially browns, seem to transform their feeding habits as they get older. A few of these bruisers are taken in the winter and spring, but more regularly during the dog days of summer and then again in the fall. While larger browns usually seek out smaller fish, they have learned that feeding on terrestrials can supplement their diet when these land-born bugs are present. Fishing *Baetis* hatches in the spring, I have not really spied these larger fish in the faster riffles searching for a meal, but as soon as grasshoppers are present, they seem to show up unannounced.

Anglers should keep a close eye on the most unlikely places for trout to hold. Where the fastest part of a riffle enters the main pool, train your eye to pick out the nonobvious. This is the nice thing about fishing big bugs: Anglers can work every stretch of water, but it's most exciting watching large trout move 3 feet out of a riffle and gently take your fly. Older trout are well-oiled machines—they do not expend energy unless it is worth their while.

I have found that you do not need a ton of terrestrial patterns to be successful, but rather more of a wide variety of sizes to get the job done. When the water is higher, stick to larger patterns; when the water is low and clear, smaller patterns are your best bet. During terrestrial season I generally only carry one box with hoppers, ants, and beetles.

Afternoon winds that usually come up on the lower Colorado can make the trout extremely active when it comes to terrestrial insects being blown into the water. I do not carry a ton of terrestrials with me, but I do carry enough to get the job done. Grasshoppers seem to be the most productive, but do not forget about ants and beetles. One walk through the willows on the bank, and you will have ants crawling all over you. It does not take much wind to see why fish will takes these insects as a simulated hatch.

A couple hopper patterns that stand out for me are a yellow Streambank Hopper and a tan Stalcup's Hopper. Carrying hopper patterns in sizes 8 through 14 will suffice. As far as ant patterns go, a Hi-Vis Foam Ant in black is probably my favorite, followed by Pilatzke's Ant. The ants on the Colorado vary widely in size, so carrying patterns from 14 through 20 should cover your bases. I do not fish many

Out of all the ways to hook a trout, there is probably nothing more rewarding than watching one slowly engulf a large dry fly. Sometimes one fish on a dry is worth ten fish on a nymph rod. Terrestrial fishing can be at its best during August and September, especially on the ranchland sections of the Colorado River. JAY NICHOLS

beetle patterns, but fly tier Rich Pilatzke is starting to change my mind with his version. I have used his beetle pattern on a couple of occasions with great success.

Often on guided trips, I will carry an extra rod rigged as a dry-dropper or double-dry. This allows you to cover more water effectively, casting to rising fish in the riffles or nymphing the deeper pools. On any given day, as the hatches begin to recede, try casting larger terrestrials against banks and in the choppy water. I've found there are always eager fish waiting for a big meal.

I have had days in the late summer when nothing seems to be happening, but with a little closer observation I've found trout feeding in not-so-prime lies. Water temperatures can rise into the high 60s and low 70s, meaning trout are going to seek out more oxygenated water. During these times I like to tie on big, ugly, bushy flies such as a Pine Squirrel Leech, Water Walker, or Amy's Ant. Casting these searching flies can draw strikes from otherwise lethargic trout. Find water that has not been worked to death and cast your fly in fast riffles, along shelves in the river, and against riverbanks. Sometimes fishing the nonobvious can make your day during slow times.

STREAMERS

Most of the baitfish in the Colorado and tributaries are juvenile brown trout, sculpins, rainbow trout, mountain whitefish, and suckers, and I have found streamer patterns that have white and brown tones seem to work best, such as Barr's Slumpbuster, Barr's

Mike O'Leary landed this 20-inch brown on a white Meat Whistle during the month of October. Fishing these patterns, especially on cloudy days, will draw violent strikes from the river's resident brown trout. BOB DYE

Scott Harkins fooled this midsize brownie on a brown Barr's Meat Whistle inside of Little Gore Canyon. Streamer fishing can be about as good as it gets in the canyon due its geography, with the sun providing low-light conditions for most of the day. BOB DYE

Meat Whistle, Autumn Splendor, Galloup's Circus Peanut, Galloup's Barely Legal, Scott Sanchez's Double Bunny Streamer, and black, white, and olive Woolly Buggers.

When the opportunity presents itself, I usually run tandem streamer rigs consisting of a larger pattern as a lead fly, followed by a chaser (streamer). After tying one of these on, I usually follow it with a smaller pattern about 24 to 30 inches from the lead fly. There are a bunch of different ways to go here, but Pine Squirrel Leeches and Woolly Buggers are the best bet. Having a smaller pattern trailing a larger one helps cure short strikes as well.

Fishing streamers from a drift boat is very effective, especially when the river is experiencing higher water flows. When numbers of baitfish get spread out through the river system because of higher flows, this can really trigger larger brown trout's predatory instincts. While pitching streamers to the bank from a drift boat is always effective, try fishing these flies in the faster water currents as well—you will be surprised at the results. Fishing streamers while wading is also effective, particularly during low-water conditions such as in the fall or during low-light conditions in the evenings when floating in a drift boat probably isn't the safest thing to do. Some of the best times to fish streamers are on cloudy days, in the low light of morning or evening, and during the fall.

When fishing streamers from a drift boat, concentrate your efforts in the faster riffles and toss a few against the river's rocky banks or wherever rocks along the edges create a seam. Fish don't normally lie in shallow banks; rather, they prefer some sort of structure to help camouflage them, like riverbanks with large boulders or riffled water near the edge.

Brown trout are a predatory fish by nature, and their willingness to smack streamers is legendary. This brown was taken on the Sunset unit about 6 miles east of Kremmling. BOB DYE

Fly Patterns

Periwinkle

Originated by Adrian Keeler
Tied by Bob Dye

- **Hook:** #18-20 Tiemco 2457
- **Bead:** Gunmetal Spirit River (x-small)
- **Thread:** Olive 70-denier UTC
- **Rib:** Black UTC Wire (brassie)
- **Underbody:** Olive 70-denier UTC
- **Abdomen:** Black UTC Wire (brassie) over olive thread
- **Thorax:** Olive Hareline Ice Dub

The Periwinkle is one of the most versatile patterns out there. Originally tied as a *Baetis* shuck on the Grey Reef in late April, it can cover the "Big Midge" in late March. It is most effective as the second fly in a three-fly rig. Trout in the Colorado River system are gunmetal junkies; this pattern made a name for itself on the North Platte and continues to produce on the Colorado.

Buckskin

Originated by Ed Marsh
Tied by Bob Dye

- **Hook:** #16-22 Tiemco 3761
- **Thread:** Black 6/0 UNI-Thread
- **Tail:** Brown saddle hackle fibers
- **Underbody:** Black 6/0 UNI-Thread
- **Abdomen:** Cut chamois strips

Make sure you cut your chamois strips thin; a razor knife and a metal straightedge works best. The Buckskin is one of the oldest fly patterns around, and yet remains one of the top fish producers on any river, especially in the Colorado River drainage. I run this fly 70 percent of the time when fishing the Parshall area on the Colorado.

Beaded Prince Nymph

Originated by Doug Prince
Tied by Bob Dye

- ■ **Hook:** #8-18 Tiemco 5262
- ■ **Bead:** Gold bead
- ■ **Thread:** Black 6/0 UNI-Thread
- ■ **Weight:** Tungsten bead-substituted
- ■ **Tail:** Brown turkey or goose biots
- ■ **Rib:** Gold or silver UTC Wire
- ■ **Underbody:** Black 6/0 UNI-Thread
- ■ **Abdomen:** Peacock herl with gold or silver rib
- ■ **Thorax:** Peacock herl
- ■ **Hackle:** Brown saddle hackle
- ■ **Wing case:** White turkey or goose biots

Like most flies that produce a number of strikes, this one doesn't necessarily resemble one particular insect. The Prince Nymph can be fished year-around and never seems to get old. I generally run this pattern as my point fly in a three-fly rig. The Prince Nymph is also one of the best "dropper" patterns around.

Pabst Blue Ribbon Midge (PBR)

Originated by Bob Dye
Tied by Bob Dye

- ■ **Hook:** #18-24 Tiemco 2487
- ■ **Bead:** Mercury bead
- ■ **Thread:** Red 70-denier UTC
- ■ **Rib:** UTC Flat Pearl Tinsel (medium)
- ■ **Underbody:** Red 70-denier UTC
- ■ **Abdomen:** UTC Flat Pearl Tinsel (medium)
- ■ **Thorax:** Pearl Hareline Ice Dub
- ■ **Wing case:** Pearl Hareline Ice Dub

When wrapping the Pearl Tinsel for the body, space evenly for a ribbing effect. This pattern started out as a joke, as if to look like a beer can, and quickly became a top fish producer. It is best fished in the winter in the Glenwood Springs area on the Colorado River and the Roaring Fork, and is also a great tailwater pattern.

Chocolate Foam Wing Emerger

Originated by John Tavenner
Tied by Bob Dye

- **Hook:** #18-26 Tiemco 200R, or 2488 for smaller sizes
- **Thread:** Chocolate 8/0 Dark BrownUNI-Thread
- **Tail:** Brown saddle hackle hen fibers
- **Rib:** Gold wire (small; optional)
- **Underbody:** Dark Brown thread
- **Abdomen:** Brown Super Fine Dubbing (optional)
- **Thorax:** Brown Super Fine Dubbing (optional)
- **Wing case:** White Wapsi Razor Foam

Cut the razor foam into ⅛-inch strips for the wing. I remember coming across this pattern on the San Juan River years ago, and why I lost track of this tremendously effective fly is a mystery. I probably use it more as the third fly in a three-fly rig than any other pattern. The versatility of this pattern is uncompromised: In smaller sizes it can cover emerging insects such as midges and small mayflies, and in larger sizes it can cover most mayflies like Pale Morning Duns and Red Quills.

Dye's Midge Emerger

Originated by Bob Dye
Tied by Bob Dye

- **Hook:** #18-24 Tiemco 2488
- **Bead:** Black-Killer Caddis glass bead
- **Thread:** Olive 8/0 UNI-Thread
- **Rib:** Black 8/0 UNI-Thread
- **Underbody:** Olive 8/0 UNI-Thread
- **Abdomen:** Olive thread dyed black for ribbing
- **Thorax:** Black Hareline Ice Dub
- **Wing case:** Wapsi Razor Foam with black Hareline Ice Dub behind bead

Dye olive thread with a black magic marker and then use for the ribbing. This simply tied pattern seems to work best during a midge hatch, fishing it in the film behind a dry-fly pattern, especially when the trout are leery of dry-fly presentations.

Mercer's Trigger Nymph

Originated by Mike Mercer
Tied by Umpqua Feather Merchants

- **Hook:** #14-18 Tiemco 3769
- **Bead:** Gold bead (match to size)
- **Thread:** Camel 8/0 UNI-Thread
- **Tail:** Ringneck pheasant tail fibers
- **Underbody:** Mercer's Buggy Nymph Dubbing
- **Abdomen:** Rusty turkey biot
- **Thorax:** Mercer's Buggy Nymph Dubbing
- **Legs:** Partridge hackle
- **Wing case:** Pale yellow Hareline Dubbing

Mike Mercer is, in my opinion, one of the best tiers around. Not only are his flies versatile, but they all have that "buggy" look to them. This fly is no different. Generally fished during the PMD and Yellow Sally hatches on the Colorado in July, it is also a great attractor pattern any time of the year.

Mitchell's Split Case PMD

Originated by Joe Mitchell
Tied by Solitude Fly Company

- **Hook:** #16-20 Daiichi 1710
- **Bead:** Black tungsten bead (optional)
- **Thread:** Brown 8/0 Danville flat waxed nylon
- **Weight:** Black tungsten bead (optional)
- **Tail:** Natural mallard flank fibers
- **Rib:** Gray UTC Ultra Wire (small)
- **Underbody:** Brown 8/0 Danville flat waxed nylon
- **Abdomen:** Mahogany brown Super Fine Dubbing
- **Thorax:** Mahogany brown Super Fine Dubbing
- **Legs:** Natural mallard flank fibers
- **Wing case:** Black goose biots/yellow marked (0.5 mm)

Sometimes when PMD nymphs are just starting to emerge, their wing case opens up slightly; this may not be visible to the angler, but it is certainly visible to the trout. This fly represents this stage, and fly fishers should be well stocked with this pattern. I usually fish it as the second fly in a three-fly rig. It is a very effective pattern for selective trout.

Soft Hackle Pheasant Tail

Originated by Frank Sawyer
Tied by Bob Dye

- ▪ **Hook:** #12-20 Daiichi 1150
- ▪ **Bead:** Optional
- ▪ **Thread:** Brown 8/0 UNI-Thread
- ▪ **Weight:** Optional
- ▪ **Tail:** 3-6 pheasant tail fibers
- ▪ **Rib:** Copper wire (fine)
- ▪ **Underbody:** Brown 8/0 UNI-Thread
- ▪ **Abdomen:** 5-6 pheasant tail fibers or peacock herl with copper wire rib
- ▪ **Thorax:** Peacock herl
- ▪ **Hackle:** Partridge hackle

This old standby has fooled fish for years and should be in every fly fisher's box. Generally fished as a mayfly or caddis emerger, the movement of its soft hackle catches the eye of even the wariest trout. I usually fish it as the last fly in a three-fly rig and extend the tippet 20 to 24 inches to give the fly a little more freedom of movement.

Stalcup's Baetis Nymph

Originated by Shane Stalcup
Tied by Solitude Fly Company

- ▪ **Hook:** #18-22 Tiemco 200r
- ▪ **Thread:** Olive 70-denier UTC
- ▪ **Tail:** Olive partridge fibers
- ▪ **Underbody:** Olive 70-denier UTC
- ▪ **Abdomen:** Olive brown D-Rib
- ▪ **Thorax:** Olive Super Fine Dubbing
- ▪ **Legs:** Olive partridge fibers
- ▪ **Wing case:** Brown Medallion Sheeting

This is one of the most natural-looking patterns ever tied. There are tons of *Baetis* patterns on the market, but none represent the BWO nymph quite like this one. During prime BWO season in late March and April and then again in September, I use this fly as my second fly in a three-fly rig, followed by a Chocolate Post Foam Emerger.

Parrott's Electric Caddis

Originated by Steve Parrott
Tied by Steve Parrott

- **Hook:** #12-18 C300BL or Hanak H300 BL
- **Thread:** Black 70-denier UTC
- **Weight:** Flat lead wire (medium)
- **Under rib:** Pearl Crystal Mirror Flash
- **Over rib:** Clear UTC Monofil (.006)
- **Body:** Caddis green Life Cycle Nymph Dubbing
- **Thorax:** Dark brown SLF Spikey Squirrel Dub
- **Back foil:** Lime green Jan Siman Magic Shrimp Foil Pearl Strip
- **Legs:** Pick dubbing away from underside of thorax region

Once the fly is finished, color the thorax region with a brown Sharpie. Steve Parrott turned me on to his creation a couple of years ago, and this bug has become a staple in my arsenal. Being that it is a weighted fly, it typically works best as a point fly in a rig. Caddis are an important part of a trout's diet on most rivers, including the Colorado. This insect becomes active towards the end of March on the lower Colorado (New Castle to Silt area) and can be a difference-maker early in the season. I use this fly as an attractor nymph throughout the year when caddis are present. It can be an excellent dropper pattern under a large dry fly, especially in fast riffled water.

Dye's Annelid

Originated by Bob Dye
Tied by Bob Dye

- **Hook:** #16-22 Tiemco 2487
- **Bead:** Mercury bead (optional)
- **Thread:** Olive 70-denier UTC
- **Underbody:** Olive 70-denier UTC 70
- **Abdomen:** Clear Micro Tubing over olive 70-denier UTC 70

Once the fly is complete, color the top of it with a black Sharpie. Annelids make up a big portion of the trout's diet, especially during the winter. When nothing seems to be happening on the river, these little worms can save a tough day. Tie a multitude of colors, including all shades of green, cream, and red. Typically I run this pattern as the second fly in a three-fly rig.

Big Bear Baetis

Originated by Bear Goode
Tied by Bob Dye

- **Hook:** #18-24 2X long
- **Thread:** Cream or light cahill 8/0 UNI-Thread
- **Tail:** Pheasant tail fibers
- **Rib:** Cream or light cahill 8/0 UNI-Thread
- **Underbody:** Cream or light cahill 8/0 UNI-Thread
- **Abdomen:** Pheasant tail fibers pulled over body, ribbed with thread
- **Thorax:** Dark brown thread or brown Super Fine Dubbing
- **Legs:** Black Antron
- **Wing case:** Black Antron

This slender little pattern works exceptionally well for Pseudos. During the fall months, these tiny mayflies can sneak up on you without warning, and the fish can turn their attention to them. This pattern will cover your bases for these smaller-than-average mayflies.

Dye's Purple Flash Midge

Originated by Bob Dye
Tied by Bob Dye

- **Hook:** #18-24 Tiemco 2487
- **Bead:** Black glass bead (x-small)
- **Thread:** Black 8/0 UNI-Thread
- **Weight:** Black tungsten bead (optional)
- **Rib:** Black UTC Ultra Wire (small)
- **Underbody:** Black 8/0 UNI-Thread
- **Abdomen:** Black 8/0 UNI-Thread ribbed with black wire
- **Thorax:** Purple Hareline Ice Dub

This fly is very effective, especially below Glenwood Springs during blanket hatches in late March. Trout see in ultraviolet light, making this a productive pattern in the deeper runs below Glenwood. Run this as a second fly behind an egg pattern during the winter and early spring.

Dye's Blueberry Jam

Originated by Bob Dye
Tied by Bob Dye

- **Hook:** #18-22 Tiemco 2487
- **Bead:** Gunmetal Killer Caddis glass bead
- **Thread:** Purple 8/0 UNI-Thread
- **Underbody:** Purple 8/0 UNI-Thread
- **Abdomen:** Purple UTC Midge Braid
- **Thorax:** Olive brown Hareline Ice Dub

The midge braid material offers excellent flash for deeper runs, off-color water, or low-light conditions. This fly can be placed anywhere in the rig, and is an excellent wintertime midge pattern. On heavily pressured rivers, it can be a fly that not too many fish have seen.

Strawberry Jam

Originated by Bob Dye
Tied by Bob Dye

- **Hook:** #18-22 Tiemco 2487
- **Bead:** Red glass bead or Killer Caddis mercury bead
- **Thread:** Red 8/0 UNI-Thread

- **Underbody:** Red 8/0 UNI-Thread
- **Abdomen:** Red UTC Midge Braid or red rainbow Montana Midge Body Thread

There are a thousand ways to tie a red midge pattern, but this one adds a little flash, which is especially useful for the stained water conditions that are often encountered on the Colorado River. It's the kind of fly that can turn slow days into rewarding ones, specifically during the winter.

Apple Jam

Originated by Bob Dye
Tied by Bob Dye

- **Hook:** #18-22 Tiemco 2487
- **Bead:** Gunmetal or mercury Killer Caddis bead
- **Thread:** Olive 8/0 UNI-Thread
- **Underbody:** Olive 8/0 UNI-Thread
- **Abdomen:** Dark olive UTC Midge Braid
- **Thorax:** Olive brown Hareline Ice Dub

This pattern was derived from the different colors of midge braid. It can pass as an annelid or even a free-living caddis. It's fished best as the second fly behind the point fly and generally works best in late March and early April in the Pumphouse to State Bridge area.

Elk Hair Caddis

Originated by Al Troth
Tied by Bob Dye

- ▪ **Hook:** TMC 100SP-BL or 100
- ▪ **Thread:** Brown 6/0 UNI-Thread
- ▪ **Rib:** Grizzly saddle hackle
- ▪ **Underbody:** Olive dubbing
- ▪ **Thorax:** Olive dubbing
- ▪ **Hackle:** Grizzly saddle hackle
- ▪ **Legs:** Grizzly saddle hackle
- ▪ **Wing case:** Elk or deer hair

I've used a bunch of different caddis dries along the Colorado River and all had some success, but the old Elk Hair Caddis continues to be a top producer for me when adult caddisflies are present. I generally fish it beginning in early April on the lower river and off and on again throughout the summer. If strikes are tough to come by, try skating the fly across the surface. It's also tough to beat the fly's floatability.

Snowshoe Midge Emerger

Originated by Jim Cannon
Tied by Jim Cannon

- ▪ **Hook:** #18-24 Tiemco 2488
- ▪ **Thread:** Black 8/0 UNI-Thread
- ▪ **Underbody:** Black 8/0 UNI-Thread
- ▪ **Abdomen:** Black goose biots or Micro Tubing
- ▪ **Thorax:** Spirit River Fine & Dry Dubbing
- ▪ **Wing case:** Black and natural snowshoe hind foot mixed with white Hareline Ice Dub

This little pattern is a cool bug; not only can it represent a midge cluster, but it can also be cut down in the field to represent the smallest of adult midges. Midges are a food source year-round, and on the right day trout will rise to them in the middle of January, but the fish really key in on the dries in late March throughout the river system.

BWO Snowshoe Dun

Originated by Jim Cannon
Tied by Jim Cannon

- **Hook:** #18-26 Tiemco 101
- **Thread:** Olive dun 8/0 UNI-Thread
- **Tail:** Dark dun micro fibbets
- **Underbody:** Olive dun 8/0 UNI-Thread
- **Abdomen:** Olive dun 8/0 UNI-Thread
- **Thorax:** BWO Spirit River Fine & Dry Dubbing
- **Wing case:** Snowshoe hind foot with olive brown Hareline Ice Dub

This is an elegant tie by Jim Cannon, and most importantly it works. The fly seems to defy gravity and with its soft presentation can fool even the pickiest of trout. Mix dubbings thoroughly.

PMD Snowshoe Dun

Originated by Jim Cannon
Tied by Jim Cannon

- **Hook:** #16-20 Tiemco 101
- **Thread:** Dark brown 8/0 UNI-Thread
- **Tail:** Ginger micro fibbets
- **Underbody:** Dark brown 8/0 UNI-Thread
- **Abdomen:** Dark brown 8/0 UNI-Thread
- **Thorax:** PMD Spirit River Fine & Dry Dubbing
- **Wing case:** Light dun snowshoe hind foot mixed with PMD Hareline Ice Dub

Like Jim Cannon's other patterns, this dry fly will fool a great number of trout when the PMDs are in full swing. I like his patterns when you're trying to fool one particular trout at a time. Long leaders and a soft presentation will usually find you reaching for your net.

Autumn Splendor

Originated by Tim Heng
Tied by Bob Dye

- ▪ **Hook:** #2-10 Tiemco 5263
- ▪ **Bead:** Copper conehead (large)
- ▪ **Thread:** Dark brown 140-denier UTC
- ▪ **Tail:** Brown Woolly Bugger marabou
- ▪ **Rib:** Copper wire (small)
- ▪ **Abdomen:** Medium brown chenille with copper wire rib
- ▪ **Hackle:** Grizzly saddle hackle
- ▪ **Legs:** Yellow round rubber legs (medium)

Many different streamer patterns work well on the Colorado River, but anglers need to remember that most of the baitfish are smaller browns, whitefish, and suckers that have brownish-yellow tones to them. This is why the Autumn Splendor is a great streamer pattern. It can be fished all year, but fall and high-water conditions are best.

Meat Whistle

Originated by John Barr
Tied by Umpqua Feather Merchants

- ▪ **Hook:** #3/0-1/0 Daiichi 90 Degree Jig Hook
- ▪ **Bead:** Copper conehead (large)
- ▪ **Thread:** 140-denier UTC
- ▪ **Tail:** Zonker rabbit strip
- ▪ **Underbody:** 140-denier UTC
- ▪ **Abdomen:** Holographic Diamond Braid
- ▪ **Thorax:** Woolly Bugger marabou
- ▪ **Legs:** Hareline Barred & Speckled Crazy Legs
- ▪ **Wing case:** Rabbit strip

I came across this streamer pattern a few years ago and was amazed at the way it draws fish, or more importantly, large fish. Often streamer patterns lack movement, but not this one. Tie this pattern in white, olive, black, and rust. I really like it in white during July when the water is higher and the baitfish are more spread out.

Two Bit Hooker (Brown)

Originated by Charlie Craven
Tied by Umpqua Feather Merchants

- **Hook:** #14-18 Tiemco 3769
- **Bead:** 2 copper beads (¹⁄₁₆ inch)
- **Thread:** Rusty brown 6/0 Danville flat waxed nylon
- **Tail:** Mottled brown hen saddle fibers
- **Rib:** Black 14/0 Gordon Griffiths Sheer Ultrafine
- **Underbody:** Rusty brown 6/0 Danville
- **Abdomen:** Rusty brown 6/0 Danville
- **Thorax:** Rusty brown Super Fine Dubbing
- **Legs:** Mottled brown hen saddle fibers
- **Wing case:** Opal Mirage Tinsel (medium)

Charlie Craven's innovative patterns are effective because he understands entomology; his flies are slender and match insect specifications to a T. The Two Bit Hooker has many purposes, but the thing I like most about it is that it is a great dry-dropper fly in the fast riffles of the Colorado River during the summer.

UPS Midge

Originated by Jim Neiberger
Tied by Jim Neiberger

- **Hook:** #18-22 Tiemco 2488
- **Bead:** Gunmetal Spirit River (x-small)
- **Thread:** White 17/0 Trico UNI-Thread
- **Abdomen:** Brown and fluorescent orange UTC Ultra Wire (small)
- **Wing:** Oral-B Dental Floss

Start with the bead on the hook first, then begin wire wraps at the bend of the hook with superglue, wrapping forward. One of the positives of this midge is that the wire adds extra weight for some of the deeper runs on the Colorado. Being that it is an emerging fly, I usually fish it as the last fly in a nymphing rig. It can be a very effective pattern late in March on the lower Colorado.

Passion Stone

Originated by Jim Neiberger
Tied by Jim Neiberger

- **Hook:** #6-10 Dai-Riki 065
- **Bead:** Optional
- **Thread:** 17/0 Trico UNI-Thread White
- **Weight:** Lead wire (.020)
- **Tail:** White goose biots, colored with a pink Sharpie
- **Underbody:** White 17/0 Trico UNI-Thread, lead wire, and tapered packing foam
- **Abdomen:** Hareline Natural Nymph Stretch Skin
- **Thorax:** Fluorescent pink and beige (50/50) Ligas Dubbing
- **Legs:** Cream Wapsi leg material
- **Wing case:** Pheasant back feathers, burned with a wing burner
- **Antennae:** Shaft of wing case feather laid forward and colored with a pink Sharpie

Color the tail, abdomen, and antennae with a pink marker. When stoneflies molt, they become a pinkish-cream color. Trout seek these out like beer at happy hour. During the month of May and first week of June, the Colorado is usually off-color; this stonefly pattern is easily visible in dirty water.

Catch All Midge

Originated by Jim Neiberger
Tied by Jim Neiberger

- **Hook:** #18-22 Tiemco 2487
- **Bead:** Gold Killer Caddis glass bead
- **Thread:** Olive 70-denier UTC
- **Rib:** Black and olive UTC Ultra Wire (small)
- **Underbody:** Olive 70-denier UTC
- **Abdomen:** Oliver 70-denier UTC
- **Thorax:** Olive brown Hareline Ice Dub
- **Wing:** Oral-B Dental Floss

This little bug can pass for a midge and smaller emerging mayflies. I have always used flies that can represent a number of insects, and this one is no different. Jim Neiberger has a unique tying style, and his flies usually result in a bent rod. This pattern is fished best in March and April as the third fly in a three-fly rig, and it is also a great tailwater pattern.

Paper Tiger

Originated by Pat Dorsey
Tied by Pat Dorsey

- **Hook:** #4-10 Tiemco 300
- **Thread:** Brown 6/0 UNI-Thread
- **Weight:** Lead wire (.020)
- **Tail:** Black goose biots
- **Underbody:** Brown yarn
- **Abdomen:** Tyvek strip
- **Legs:** Natural pheasant tail fibers
- **Wing case:** Tyvek strip
- **Antennae:** Black goose biots

Color the Tyvek strips with a brown Sharpie. The Colorado certainly doesn't have a shortage of stoneflies, and this pattern will get the job done, especially if the water has a bit of clarity. I usually fish this stonefly as my point fly, followed by caddis or mayfly imitations.

Mercury Pheasant Tail

Originated by Pat Dorsey
Tied by Umpqua Feather Merchants

- **Hook:** #16-22 Tiemco 101
- **Bead:** Mercury Killer Caddis bead
- **Thread:** Black 8/0 UNI-Thread
- **Tail:** Pheasant tail fibers
- **Rib:** Gold UTC Ultra Wire (x-small)
- **Underbody:** Black 8/0 UNI-Thread
- **Abdomen:** Pheasant tail fibers with gold wire rib
- **Thorax:** Peacock herl
- **Legs:** Pheasant tail fibers
- **Wing case:** Pearl Mylar tinsel

The Pheasant Tail needs no introduction, but the mercury bead incorporated into it adds a little life to the fly. Mayflies that are swimming to the surface sometimes trap a gas bubble; this looks more natural to selective trout. I have a ton of these flies in my box, and while they will work throughout the river system, they produce particularly well in the Parshall area year-round. Try this pattern with dyed red pheasant tail fibers.

Hydropsyche

Originator unknown
Tied by Pat Dorsey

- **Hook:** #14-18 Tiemco 2457
- **Bead:** Black tungsten (optional)
- **Thread:** Black 6/0 UNI-Thread
- **Weight:** Lead wrap (optional)
- **Rib:** Brown D-Rib
- **Underbody:** Black 6/0 UNI-Thread
- **Abdomen:** Front and rear, peacock Wapsi Life Cycle Dubbing; middle, olive brown Wapsi Life Cycle Dubbing, ribbed with brown D-Rib

This fly is like sitting next to a bag of Lay's potato chips: Eventually you are going to eat it. The Colorado is full of free-living caddis, and on certain days the fish key in on these food organisms. I use this bug year-round, but it seems to fish best starting in April and through the summer. Tie this fly weighted and use it as a point fly.

Sparkle Wing Rs2

Originated by Rim Chung
Tied by Bob Dye

- **Hook:** #16-22 Tiemco 101
- **Bead:** Mercury bead (optional)
- **Thread:** Gray 8/0 UNI-Thread
- **Tail:** White Fluoro-Fiber
- **Underbody:** Gray 8/0 UNI-Thread
- **Abdomen:** Gray Super Fine Dubbing
- **Wing:** Pearl Flat Sparkle Midge braid

Where would the fly-fishing world be without the invention of this fly? Anytime insects are hatching, anglers should have some form of this fly on. I use it as the third fly in a three-fly rig, but it also can be used under a dry fly or fished in the surface film. This fly can be fished virtually year-round but works best when the trout are taking emerging mayflies. Try tying this pattern in several colors, from gray to all shades of green and black.

Pat's Rubber Legs

Originated by Pat Bennett
Tied by Bob Dye

- **Hook:** #4-10 Tiemco 300
- **Thread:** Black or brown monocord or any "big fly" thread
- **Weight:** Lead wire (0.20)
- **Tail:** Brown Spanflex
- **Underbody:** Tying thread with lead wire
- **Abdomen:** Black, coffee, orange/black variegated chenille
- **Legs:** Brown Spanflex
- **Antennae:** Brown Spanflex

Ever wonder why when you go to your local fly shop, certain fly bins are empty? It's usually because those are the hot flies. This fly has everything a fly fisher wants when it comes to durability and effectiveness. Besides being a great stonefly pattern during the months of May and June, it is an awesome attractor pattern year-round. Try tying this pattern in pink for dirty water days.

Bitch Creek

Originator unknown
Tied by Bob Dye

- **Hook:** #4-10 Tiemco 5262
- **Bead:** Black tungsten (optional)
- **Thread:** Black 70-denier UTC
- **Weight:** Lead wire (0.20)
- **Tail:** White round rubber (medium)
- **Abdomen:** Black and orange woven chenille
- **Hackle:** Brown Whiting rooster cape
- **Antennae:** White round rubber (medium)

This is one of the first patterns that I ever learned to tie. It was a new pattern in the '80s, but has kind of made a reintroduction to trout in western rivers. I generally fish it during the stonefly hatch the first week of June, but it can be a good dirty water fly as well.

Rogue Stone

Originated by Jack Schlotter
Tied by Umpqua Feather Merchants

- **Hook:** #4 Tiemco 200R
- **Bead/head:** Natural brown elk hair
- **Thread:** Orange 6/0 Danville Flat Waxed Nylon
- **Underbody:** Orange 6/0 Danville
- **Abdomen:** Orange closed-cell foam (3 mm)
- **Legs:** Black round rubber
- **Wing case:** Wing Brown Mottled Web Wing over hot yellow Krystal Flash over Wing natural brown moose hair

Color the body with a brown marker. This is quickly becoming my dry fly of choice when the big stoneflies are present. Sometimes presentations require banging the fly off of rocks and other river structure, and this fly holds up to the punishment. Another positive about this pattern is its ability to hold up dropper rigs in heavy currents during the summer.

Mercer's Poxyback PMD

Originated by Mike Mercer
Tied by Bob Dye

- **Hook:** #16-20 Tiemco 200R
- **Bead/head:** PMD Mercer's Buggy Nymph Dubbing
- **Thread:** Camel 6/0 UNI-Thread
- **Tail:** 3 ringneck pheasant tail fibers
- **Rib:** Pearl Flashabou
- **Underbody:** Camel 6/0 UNI-Thread
- **Abdomen:** PMD Mercer's Buggy Nymph Dubbing
- **Thorax:** PMD Mercer's Buggy Nymph Dubbing
- **Hackle/gills:** Ginger marabou
- **Legs:** Golden brown partridge fibers
- **Wing case:** Dark mottled oak turkey tail, epoxied

This very buggy nymph works well as a PMD but also passes as a Yellow Sally. It's best fished as the second fly in a three-fly rig, generally during the month of July. The ginger marabou breathes underwater, giving this fly movement.

Barr's Graphic Caddis

Originated by John Barr
Tied by Umpqua Feather Merchants

- **Hook:** #14-18 Tiemco 2499 SP-BL
- **Bead/head:** Natural gray or black ostrich
- **Thread:** Olive or black 6/0 Danville Flat Waxed Nylon
- **Underbody:** Olive or black 6/0 Danville with silver Holographic Flashabou
- **Abdomen:** Olive Wapsi Stretch Tubing
- **Legs:** Hungarian partridge

Caddis hatches have a way of sneaking up on an angler along the Colorado River, but before the fish turn their attention to the adults, they will voraciously feed on the emergers. This pattern has saved many a day on the water when caddisflies are present. Generally fished as the last fly in a nymph rig, it can also be used in the film behind a caddis dry fly. When using the fly in a nymph rig, extend the tippet 2 feet for added movement to the emerger. Caddis begin to emerge along the lower Colorado River as early as the first week of April and will hatch off and on throughout the summer.

Barr's Emerger BWO

Originated by John Barr
Tied by Bob Dye

- **Hook:** #18-24 Tiemco 2487
- **Bead:** Optional
- **Thread:** Gray 8/0 UNI-Thread
- **Tail:** Brown spade hackle fibers
- **Underbody:** Gray 8/0 UNI-Thread
- **Abdomen:** BWO Super Fine Dubbing
- **Thorax:** Gray muskrat
- **Legs:** Lemon wood duck
- **Wing case:** Lemon wood duck

John Barr's patterns simply work, and his emerger series is one that fly fishers should not be without. I can't even begin to imagine not having these in my box. They can be fished year-round, but Barr's BWO Emerger really comes into play the middle of March on the lower Colorado and in mid-April on the Roaring Fork's upper stretches. A deadly combination in the spring is an egg fly as an attractor, followed by a Barr's BWO Emerger as the second fly, and finally a Post Foam Rs2 as a trailer.

Pine Squirrel Leech

Originated by Seth Kapust
Tied by Bob Dye

- ▪ **Bead:** Optional
- ▪ **Hook:** #8-14 Tiemco 200R
- ▪ **Thread:** Black 140-denier UTC 140
- ▪ **Weight:** Lead wire (optional)
- ▪ **Tail:** Natural Pine squirrel strips (micro)
- ▪ **Underbody:** Black 140-denier UTC 140
- ▪ **Abdomen:** Palmered pine squirrel strips

Parts of the Colorado River drainage are full of leeches. This simple-to-tie pattern is a great point fly, and on certain days the browns have a hard time refusing it. It also makes a great windy-day fly because you don't necessarily have to get the best drift with it. I also use it as a trailer behind larger streamer patterns.

Mercer's Tungsten Pheasant Tail Prince

Originated by Mike Mercer
Tied by Umpqua Feather Merchants

- ▪ **Bead/head:** Black tungsten bead and pheasant tail Hareline Ice Dub
- ▪ **Hook:** #12-18 Tiemco 3761
- ▪ **Thread:** Red 70-denier UTC
- ▪ **Tail:** Prince Nymph brown goose biots
- ▪ **Rib:** Silver wire (small)
- ▪ **Underbody:** Red 70-denier UTC
- ▪ **Abdomen:** Red 70-denier UTC
- ▪ **Thorax:** Peacock herl
- ▪ **Legs:** Partridge Fibers
- ▪ **Wing case:** Amber goose biots

This fly is basically just a color change from the original Prince Nymph, but it never hurts to have a little twist in your box. I've found it to be extremely effective during the Yellow Sally hatch in July, and it is quickly becoming one of my top five dropper patterns along the river.

| Flossy Worm (Pink) | Rainbow Warrior |

Originated by Zac Collins
Tied by Bob Dye

- **Hook:** #10-14 Tiemco U202
- **Thread:** Pink 140-denier UTC
- **Rib:** Dark red or brown 70-denier UTC
- **Underbody:** Pink 140-denier UTC
- **Body:** Pink Wapsi Spanflex

Tie this pattern long with a lot of movement, and try it in colors such as red and dark brown. Typical San Juan Worm patterns that are tied out of chenille are extremely effective during high water along the Colorado River, but this change-of-pace fly adds a little more movement than its predecessor and is quickly becoming a favorite among Colorado fly fishers. The best time to fish this pattern is late April through the first couple weeks of July, when the river is washing down these food organisms.

Originated by Lance Egan
Tied by Bob Dye

- **Hook:** #14-20 Tiemco 2487
- **Bead:** Glass or silver tungsten bead
- **Thread:** Red 70-denier UTC
- **Tail:** Pheasant tail fibers
- **Underbody:** Red 70-denier UTC
- **Abdomen:** UTC Flat Pearl Tinsel (medium)
- **Thorax:** Rainbow Wapsi Sow-Scud

Try this pattern in pearl and red. The best part about this fly, besides the fact it catches fish, is it's so simple to tie. This is the kind of pattern that you tie on when there's nothing else going on in the river; the Rainbow Warrior has been known to come through and save the day. There is no special time to fish it—just throw it on from time to time and see what happens.

Amy's Ant

Originated by Jack Dennis
Tied by Umpqua Feather Merchants

- ▪ **Hook:** #6-10 Dai-Riki 710
- ▪ **Head:** Butt end of the foam back
- ▪ **Thread:** Olive 6/0 UNI-Thread
- ▪ **Rib:** Brown hackle, trimmed
- ▪ **Underbody:** Tan foam extending to form a tag and a head
- ▪ **Body/back:** Olive brown Crystal Chenille; brown foam clipped to form forked tail
- ▪ **Thorax:** Olive Super Fine Dubbing
- ▪ **Legs:** Brown rubber legs (medium)
- ▪ **Wing:** Rainbow Krystal Flash and light elk hair

Every now and then a fly comes along that quickly becomes a "must-have" in every fly fisher's box, and this is one of them. I've seen finicky fish in Cheesman Canyon take this dry when nothing else would bring them to the surface, and it certainly works on the Colorado River. Many stretches of the Colorado are broken up by side channels and rock gardens, and Amy's Ant has a way of pulling the trout out of the tiniest of seams. It also makes a great indicator fly for dry-dropper rigs.

WD-40

Originator unknown
Tied by Bob Dye

- ▪ **Hook:** #18-24 Tiemco 2487
- ▪ **Thread:** Brown or ginger 8/0 UNI-Thread
- ▪ **Tail:** Partridge or wood duck fibers
- ▪ **Abdomen:** Brown or ginger 8/0 UNI-Thread
- ▪ **Thorax:** Gray Super Fine Dubbing
- ▪ **Wing case:** Partridge or wood duck fibers

Sometimes I think this effective little pattern gets forgotten. It's one of those flies that can represent mayflies and midges and is without a doubt one of the simplest to tie. It's more of a silhouette fly and takes fish year-round. One of my favorite times to use it is during a full-blown BWO hatch. Fishing it in the surface film behind a BWO Compara-dun dry fly can be deadly.

Twenty Incher Stonefly

Originated by Brad Tutor
Tied by Bob Dye

- ■ **Hook:** #6-16 Tiemco 200R
- ■ **Bead:** Gold bead (optional)
- ■ **Thread:** Black 70-denier UTC
- ■ **Tail:** Brown goose biots
- ■ **Rib:** Silver or gold wire
- ■ **Underbody:** Black 70-denier UTC
- ■ **Abdomen:** Peacock herl
- ■ **Thorax:** Tan Super Fine Dubbing
- ■ **Legs:** Partridge fibers
- ■ **Wing case:** Turkey tail fibers

This pattern originated in the Roaring Fork Valley and remains one of the best freestone patterns around. Whether it's the peacock herl or the movement of the partridge legs, this fly is a must-have in the Roaring Fork and the Colorado River drainages. Generally used as a point fly in a three-fly rig, it continues to be one of the top fish-producing flies on these two rivers. It produces best during the multitude of different stonefly hatches in the summer, but is also a great winter pattern along the Roaring Fork.

Breadcrust Nymph

Originated by Rudy Sentiwany
Tied by Pat Dorsey

- ■ **Hook:** #10-18 Tiemco 5262
- ■ **Bead:** Gold bead (optional)
- ■ **Thread:** Black 6/0 UNI-Thread
- ■ **Underbody:** Black yarn, tapered
- ■ **Abdomen:** Ruffed grouse
- ■ **Hackle:** Grizzly hen neck feather

This fly was developed in the 1940s and remains a top producer in the Colorado River drainage. Like the Buckskin, it is timeless; it never ceases to amaze me that with all the new fly-tying materials available today, some of the "old-school" patterns are still among the best. I fish this pattern the most when caddisflies are present and usually as a point fly. A deadly combination in the Parshall area during July is a Breadcrust Nymph followed by a Soft Hackle Pheasant Tail or a Barr's Graphic Caddis.

Headlight Yellow Sally

Originator unknown
Tied by Umpqua Feather Merchants

- **Hook:** #14-18 Tiemco 100
- **Thread:** Yellow 6/0 UNI-Thread
- **Tail:** Ginger hackle barbs
- **Underbody:** Light yellow floss
- **Abdomen:** Yellow Vernille tipped with a red Sharpie
- **Thorax:** Yellow 6/0 UNI-Thread
- **Hackle:** Light ginger wrapped parachute style
- **Wing case:** Wing Upright white calf tail and yellow deer hair

Yellow Sallies have a strong presence on the Colorado River. I have used several imitations, but this one seems to draw more strikes than any other. Oftentimes Yellow Sallies coincide with the PMDs during July and the first week of August.

Tailwater Tiny

Originator unknown
Tied by Idylwylde Fly Company

- **Hook:** #18-24 Tiemco 2487
- **Bead:** Copper, brass, or tungsten bead
- **Thread:** Black 8/0 UNI-Thread
- **Tail:** Natural wood duck fibers
- **Rib:** Silver UTC Ultra Wire (small)
- **Underbody:** Black 8/0 UNI-Thread
- **Abdomen:** Black 8/0 UNI-Thread
- **Thorax:** Olive brown Hareline Ice Dub
- **Legs:** Olive Krystal Flash
- **Wing case:** Black Hareline Scud Back (⅛ inch)

This is a very effective pattern for small mayflies such as Tricos and Pseudos. Tie it in rust and chartreuse as well. I started using this little bug on our crowded tailwaters and soon found out it was also effective on the larger freestone rivers. It works best in the months of August, September, and October, when the river begins to decline and water clarity is magnified. The food sources become much more visible to the trout, and they tend to get a little more finicky. Certain stretches of the Colorado, like the Parshall area and Pumphouse to State Bridge, have Trico hatches in good numbers, and this little pattern will cover your bases when the trout are feeding on the nymphs.

Idylwylde's Not Much Fly

Originator unknown
Tied by Bob Dye

- ▪ **Hook:** #18-24 Tiemco 2488H
- ▪ **Thread:** Brown 8/0 UNI-Thread
- ▪ **Tail:** Brown hen saddle hackle fibers
- ▪ **Underbody:** Brown 8/0 UNI-Thread
- ▪ **Abdomen:** Bronze tinsel
- ▪ **Thorax:** Black Hareline Ice Dub

The Not Much Fly lives up to its name; it's very simple to tie, and it can produce as a midge or a mayfly. I carry a few dozen of these in bronze and in olive. It can be a great wintertime pattern on the lower Colorado and the Roaring Fork. It is usually fished as the second fly in a three-fly rig, but is also a great surface film fly.

Heavy Metal Beetle

Originated by Richard Pilatzke
Tied by Richard Pilatzke

- ▪ **Hook:** #12-14 Dai-Riki 305
- ▪ **Thread:** Black 6/0 UNI-Thread
- ▪ **Underbody:** Lime/black Hareline Speckled Chenille
- ▪ **Abdomen:** Self-adhesive foam (2 mm) with rainbow metallic foil
- ▪ **Legs:** Black Hareline Krystal Flash
- ▪ **Indicator:** Yellow Evazote foam (⅛ inch)

I never really fished many beetle patterns over the years, but Richard Pilatzke changed my mind. During the month of August, this fly can be effective plopping it off of the banks on a windy day, but on Troublesome Creek and Hidden Valley Pond, it is dynamite. It also floats like a cork, making it a great indicator for dry-dropper presentations.

Madonna's Bloomer

Originated by Richard Pilatzke
Tied by Richard Pilatzke

- **Hook:** #10-12 Dai-Riki 710
- **Thread:** Fire orange 6/0 UNI-Thread
- **Tail:** Tuft of tan marabou
- **Underbody:** Strip of white craft foam (2 mm) tied down along shank
- **Abdomen:** Strip of red craft foam (2 mm) tied down fore and aft
- **Legs:** Orange Rainey's Round Rubber Legs
- **Indicator:** Yellow craft foam (2 mm)

This is an effective terrestrial pattern on Troublesome Creek and Hidden Valley Pond.

Streambank Hopper

Originator unknown
Tied by Solitude Fly Company

- **Hook:** #8-10 Tiemco 5212
- **Head:** Black/tan/yellow laminated foam rubber
- **Thread:** Tan flat waxed nylon
- **Tail:** Red hackle fibers
- **Rib:** Green monofilament
- **Underbody:** Tan flat waxed nylon
- **Abdomen:** Black/tan/yellow laminated foam rubber
- **Wing:** Canary polypropylene/Wing Post
- **Legs:** Mottled yellow tubular foam (1 mm)
- **Overwing:** Natural elk hair/Krystal Flash

A number of grasshopper patterns are available, but this one seems to work the best on the Colorado River. Typically as the hot days of August roll around, the terrestrial fishing shifts into high gear. Ranchland sections in the Parshall to Kremmling stretch are a good place to start, as are sections from Pumphouse to the Dotsero area and from Glenwood Springs to Silt. Throwing hoppers off the bank on windy days will produce strikes, but also try giving the fly a little movement by twitching it on the surface.

Darth Baetis

Originated by Greg Garcia
Tied by Greg Garcia

- **Hook:** #16-22 Tiemco 200r
- **Thread:** Dark tan 16/0 Veevus
- **Tail:** Dark brown tailing fibers
- **Rib:** Dark-Lagartun Copper (fine)
- **Abdomen:** Dark tan 16/0 Veevus
- **Thorax:** Mahogany brown Super Fine Dubbing
- **Legs:** Dark gray MFC Midge Body Thread
- **Wing case:** Black Hareline Flashback

Greg Garcia is one of Colorado's premier tiers; his flies are to exact proportions, and besides that, they catch fish. I was fortunate Greg gave me some of these *Baetis* patterns to try out, and they are quickly finding space in my fly box.

Fold Over Baetis

Originated by Greg Garcia
Tied by Greg Garcia

- **Hook:** #18-24 Tiemco 101
- **Thread:** Brown 16/0 Veevus
- **Tail:** Dark pardo
- **Rib:** Lagartun Copper (fine)
- **Underbody:** Brown 16/0 Veevus
- **Abdomen:** Brown thread with copper wire rib
- **Thorax:** Gray Super Fine Dubbing
- **Wing case:** Black Spanflex

One of Greg Garcia's latest patterns, it is tied sparse and spot on for a *Baetis* nymph. I used this fly last September with a great deal of success; it worked particularly well as a trailing nymph behind a BWO Compara-dun dry fly.

Icebreaker

Originated by Greg Garcia
Tied by Greg Garcia

- **Hook:** #16-20 Tiemco 200R
- **Head:** Red 8/0 UNI-Thread
- **Thread:** Olive 16/0 Veevus
- **Tail:** Natural wood duck
- **Rib:** Lagartun Copper (fine)
- **Underbody:** Olive 16/0 Veevus
- **Abdomen:** Olive brown D-Rib (small)
- **Thorax:** Black nickel tungsten bead (2 mm) and olive brown Hareline Ice Dub
- **Hackle:** Dark dun hen hackle

Greg knocked it out of the park with this emerger pattern, which is rapidly becoming one of my favorites. It's best fished as the third fly in a three-fly rig, keeping in mind that adding a little extra tippet gives the fly more movement. Next time you find yourself in the middle of a mayfly hatch, give this neatly tied fly a chance.

Sculpzilla

Originator unknown
Tied by Solitude Fly Company

- **Hook:** #4 Gamakatsu Octopus for the trailer/any 2X long cut off at the shank/ tying purposes only
- **Bead:** Black Spirit River Cross Eyed Cone (⅜ inch)
- **Thread:** Black Danville's 3/0 Monocord
- **Eyes:** Red 3D eyes glued to cone
- **Body:** Olive Hareline Ice Dub
- **Gills:** Red guinea body feather
- **Skirt:** Marabou wrapped as collar
- **Wing:** White rabbit strip

The Roaring Fork and parts of the Colorado River are full of sculpins. Sometimes larger trout don't make a meal of smaller insects, like they did when they were younger fish, and instead seek out larger prey. I've done well fishing this pattern early in the morning and at last light in the evening. Sculpins are bottom-dwellers, so fishing this pattern near the bottom of the river is key.

Dye's Colorock Midge

Originated by Bob Dye
Tied by Bob Dye

- **Hook:** #18-24 Tiemco 2487
- **Thread:** Tan 14/0 Veevus
- **Rib:** Color body thread black
- **Underbody:** Tan 14/0 Veevus
- **Abdomen:** Taper tan thread, black marker for the ribbing
- **Thorax:** Olive brown Hareline Ice Dub

All rivers have a substrate that makes up their bed, which can change colors at different points in the river. The Colorado has several areas where large amounts of silt deposits make for prime midge habitat. This fly is simply designed to match the color of the river bottom and is best fished from late fall through the winter. Normally I fish this pattern as my second fly behind an attractor such as an egg fly. The third fly is usually an emerging pattern tied the same way, except for adding four strands of Purple Krystal Flash for the wing.

Mint Julep

Originated by Jim Neiberger
Tied by Jim Neiberger

- **Hook:** #14-18 Tiemco 2487
- **Thread:** White 17/0 Trico UNI-Thread
- **Tail:** 2 wraps of peacock herl
- **Underbody:** White 17/0 Trico UNI-Thread
- **Abdomen:** Caddis green #3 Ligas Dubbing over foam to create a fat tapered shape, ribbed with Hareline Nymph Stretch Skin/Natural
- **Head:** Peacock herl

About the time April rolls around, water temps begin to climb a few degrees and caddisflies start to emerge from their shucks. Trout definitely take notice, and this Jim Neiberger tie will put a few fish in the bag. While full-blown caddis hatches are still a few weeks away on the lower Colorado, this can be a prelude of what's to come. I fish this fly as my second fly behind an attractor pattern but still have a midge as my third fly. As water temperatures begin to climb on the river's upper reaches, this fly will become more productive.

Sage Flashback Midge

Originated by Jim Neiberger
Tied by Jim Neiberger

- **Hook:** #18-22 Tiemco 2487
- **Thread:** Black 17/0 Trico UNI-Thread
- **Abdomen:** Black and golden olive UTC Ultra Wire (small)
- **Thorax:** Peacock herl
- **Wing case:** Thin sheet foam and Flashabou

This was always a great tailwater pattern, but is quickly gaining popularity on the Colorado River. I've had good luck with it in the Hot Sulphur Springs area and on the Williams Fork. Like many of Jim's patterns, it can represent several aquatic insects. Did you ever notice that flies that are tied exactly don't work as well as ones that represent several insects? A bushy Hare's Ear is a perfect example of this.

Thunderstruck Midge

Originated by Bob Dye
Tied by Bob Dye

- **Hook:** #18-24 Tiemco 2487
- **Bead:** Cobalt blue Hex Bead (x-small)
- **Thread:** Black 8/0 UNI-Thread
- **Body:** Veevus Midge Thread Iris

This colorful midge pattern captures light from all angles. Whether you are fishing it in a foot of water or an 8-foot-deep run, the trout will definitely know that it is there. With its different shades of blue and purple, it is a perfect wintertime pattern. Without a doubt it is a proven fly on the Roaring Fork and lower Colorado River.

Appendix: Maps

MAP LEGEND

Recreation Symbols

🅰 🄰	Stream Access with Parking, Access with Pulloff
⛴	Boat Launch with Access
⛺	Campground
🚶	Trailhead
🆁	Rest Area

Transportation

═══	Highway
───	Local Road
------	Trail
▪▪▪▪▪	Railway
89	Interstate
50	US Highway
26	State Route
61	County Road

Boundaries

	National Park / State Park
	National Forest
	Public Land (BLM)
	Wilderness Area

Hydrology

◉	Rapids

Lulu City to Grand Lake

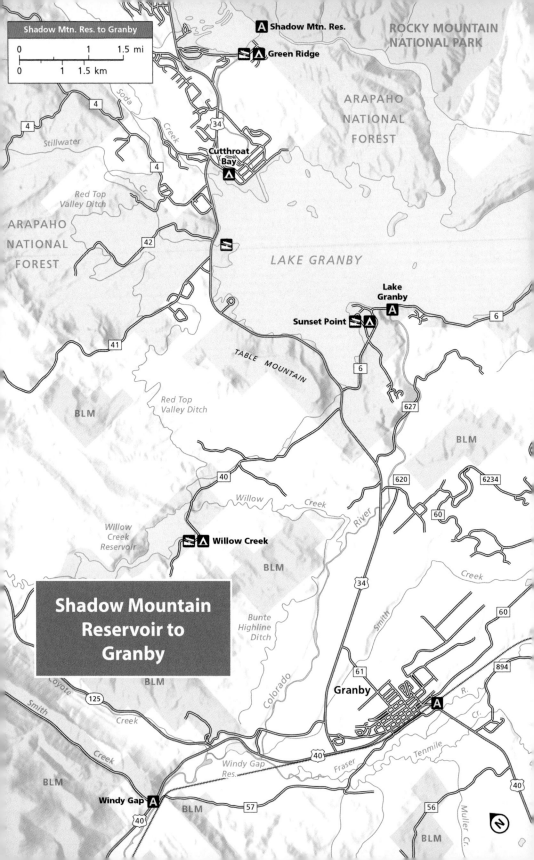

Shadow Mountain Reservoir to Granby

Shadow Mtn. Res. to Granby

0   1   1.5 mi
0 1 1.5 km

A Shadow Mtn. Res.

Green Ridge

ROCKY MOUNTAIN
NATIONAL PARK

ARAPAHO
NATIONAL
FOREST

Stillwater

Soda Creek

Cutthroat Bay

Red Top
Valley Ditch

ARAPAHO
NATIONAL
FOREST

LAKE GRANBY

Lake
Granby A

Sunset Point

TABLE MOUNTAIN

Red Top
Valley Ditch

BLM

BLM

Willow Creek

Willow
Creek
Reservoir

Willow Creek

BLM

Bunte
Highline
Ditch

River

Colorado

Smith

Creek

BLM

Coyote

Smith

Creek

Granby A

Creek

Fraser

Tenmile

Windy Gap A

Windy Gap
Res.

BLM

BLM

Muller Cr.

N

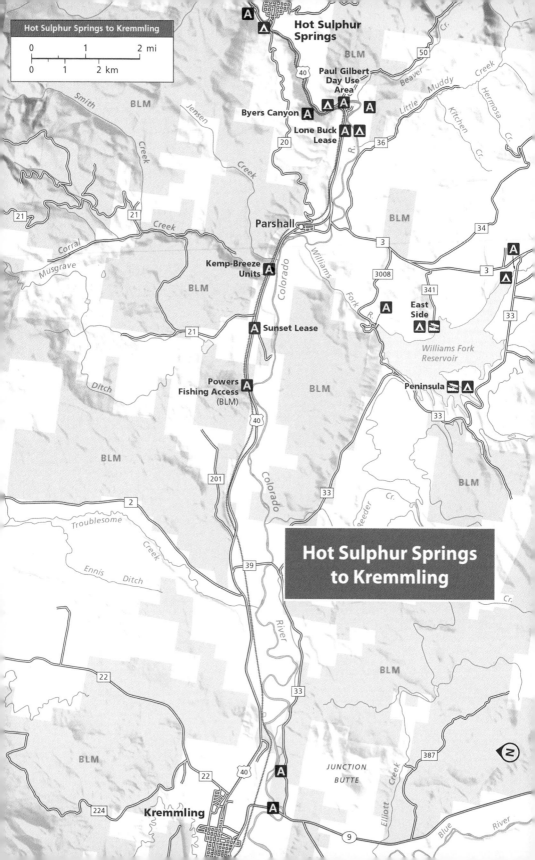

Hot Sulphur Springs to Kremmling

Hot Sulphur Springs

BLM

50

40

Paul Gilbert Day Use Area

Byers Canyon

Lone Buck Lease

20

36

Smith

BLM

Jensen

Creek

Creek

Little

Muddy

Beaver

Cr.

Kitchen

Hermosa

Cr.

Creek

21

21

Creek

Corral

Musgrave

Parshall

BLM

3

34

Kemp-Breeze Units

Colorado

Williams

3008

341

33

3

East Side

Sunset Lease

21

Fork

R.

Williams Fork Reservoir

BLM

Powers Fishing Access (BLM)

Ditch

40

BLM

Peninsula

33

201

Colorado

BLM

2

Troublesome

BLM

33

Reeder

Cr.

39

Ennis

Ditch

Creek

Hot Sulphur Springs to Kremmling

River

22

33

BLM

22

40

JUNCTION BUTTE

387

Cr.

N

224

Kremmling

Elliott

Creek

Blue

River

9

Kremmling
to Radium

BLM

Wolford Mountain
Reservoir

BLM 224

22

40

40 227 **Kremmling**

BLM 33

JUNCTION
BUTTE

387

BLM

A

A

14

12

A BLM Fishing Access

9

BLM 1

12

City Res.

River

Colorado

Sheep

Muddy

Creek

14

14 14

BLM 1

Dry Cr.

Blue

River

Elliott
Creek

TROUGH

GORE CANYON

BLM

Beaver

BLM

French

Canyon

Creek

ROUTT

NATIONAL

FOREST

Creek

Colorado

1

A Pumphouse

106

11

BLM

Blacktail

Cr.

Cr.

Thomas

Beaver

Blacktail Cr.

Creek

11

A

River

Radium
SWA

A

11

Sheephorn

401

Creek

BLM

Little

Creek

Radium

111 A Benches

1

BLM

Kremmling to Radium

0   1   1.5 mi

0   1   1.5 km

N

Radium to State Bridge

Map Labels

Little Blacktail Creek

Blacktail Creek

NEW TROUGH RD

BLM

11

Radium SWA

Sheephorn

Radium

Sheep Creek

Creek

111

Island

Colorado

1

Cottonwood Creek

BLM

Creek

111

Trail

BLM

Colorado River

Radium to State Bridge

2

Yarmony Rapid/Red Gorge

1

GARDEN GULCH ROAD

Rancho Del Rio

Yarmony Bridge

BLM

WHITE RIVER NATIONAL FOREST

YARMONY MOUNTAIN

Colorado

BLM

1

BLM

Elk Creek

Horse Creek

Cr.

Cable Rapid

Crazy Creek

Castle Creek

BLM

River

State Bridge

State Bridge

Piney River

131

N

Dotsero to Glenwood Springs

Cottonwood
Lyons Gulch
BLM
Colorado R.
Dotsero
301
Eagle River
BLM
6
70
RED HILL RD.
COTTONWOOD PASS RD.
BLM
Cottonwood Creek
Creek
Deep Creek
POT RD.
BLM
Spruce Creek
Spruce Cr.
Ike
Bair Ranch (Rest Area) R
BLM
COFFEE
WHITE
French
Creek
East Fork
Dead
Horse
Cr.
W. Fork
Dead
Horse
Creek
RIVER
Dead Horse Creek
Dead Horse Cr.
Hanging Lake (Rest Area) R
Colorado River
Cinnamon
Devil's Hole Cr.
BLM
Consolidated Reservoir
BLM
Creek
6
GLENWOOD
NATIONAL
Grizzly
70
Shoshone Rapids
River
Hopkins Reservoir
FOREST
CYN
Creek
Grizzly Creek
Landis Cr.
115
119
No Name
Creek
120
BLM
115
Rock Garden & No Name (Rest Area) R A A
A
Oasis
East Glenwood Canyon
Glenwood Canyon
Tombstone Rapid
Glenwood Springs
Mitchell
Creek
BLM
A
Two Rivers Park
82
Roaring Fork R.
A
A
6
70
DEVEREUX ROAD
MIDLAND AVE.

Dotsero to Glenwood Springs

0   1   2 mi

0   1   2 km

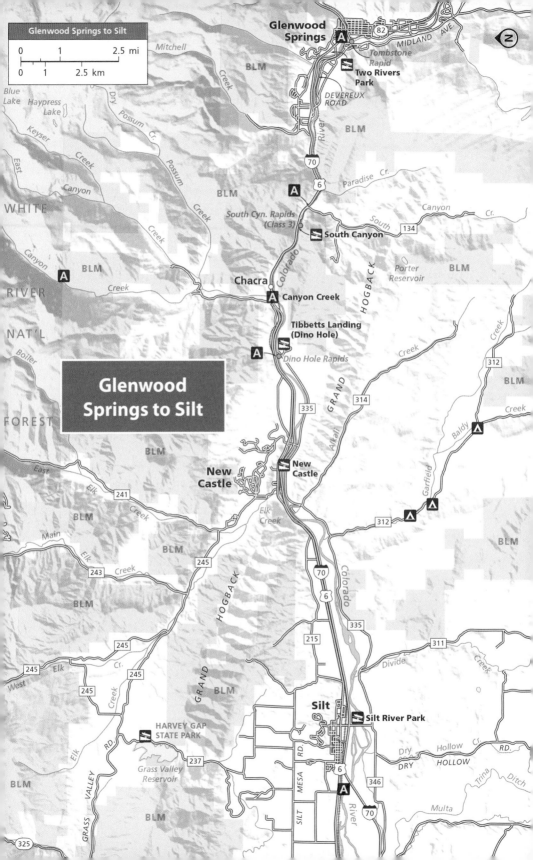

Regulations and Resources

REGULATIONS

The Colorado River is a tremendous trout fishery from its headwaters in Rocky Mountain National Park through the town of Silt. As the river makes its twists and turns toward lower elevations, so do the regulations that are stamped on the river to keep it fishing for generations to come.

The following is an overview of the regulations for the Colorado River; keep in mind that the Colorado inside Rocky Mountain National Park has different regulations, as do many of the river's numerous feeder creeks and tributaries. When fly fishing, a maximum of three fly rigs may be used, and fishing barbless is always recommended. Picking up a copy of the current Colorado Parks & Wildlife (CPW) regulations before fishing is advised. Special regulations include:

From Lake Granby Dam downstream to the US 40 bridge approximately 3 miles west of Hot Sulphur Springs, bag and possession for trout is 2.

From the US 40 bridge approximately 3 miles west of Hot Sulphur Springs downstream to the confluence with Troublesome Creek (approximately 5 miles east of Kremmling), artificial flies and lures only and all trout must be returned to the water immediately. No more than 3 flies can be used.

From the confluence with Troublesome Creek downstream to the I-70 exit 90 bridge at Rifle (excluding 50 yards upstream and downstream of the confluences with Grizzly, No Name, and Canyon Creeks), bag and possession for trout is 2.

Releasing trout into oxygenated water helps revive them faster, ensuring their survival for another angler to enjoy. BOB DYE

From 50 yards upstream and downstream of the confluences with Canyon, No Name, and Grizzly Creeks, bag and possession limit is for trout is 2 and fishing is prohibited from March 15 through May 15 and October 1 through November 30.

The Colorado has a section of Gold Medal water from the confluence of the Fraser River downstream to the confluence of Troublesome Creek. Gold Medal waters are designated by CPW as providing great opportunities to catch large trout. These stretches are defined as being able to produce 60 pounds of trout per acre, with at least twelve 14-inch or larger trout per acre. Only 322 miles of Colorado's 9,000 miles of trout streams carry this Gold Medal status.

Remember to obtain permission from landowners to fish on private lands.

SHARING THE RIVER

Colorado law states that no wading or anchoring is allowed on private property at any time without written permission from the landowner. If the landowner owns both sides of bank, he or she also own the river bottom. This can put a lot of pressure on public access, and every angler seems to get packed into a half mile of river when it comes to walk-wading, rather than being spread out over several miles. I find myself starting guide trips at the crack of dawn and usually walking clients into the ground just to stay ahead of the masses.

One thing I have found is that most anglers tend to fish the easy-to-get-to access points or a river that has just received some press in the local paper. I can vividly remember talking with an old gentleman in the Kemp-Breeze units soon after CPW opened them to public access. He simply said, "Take pride in the whole river, not just one hole." Over the years I have stuck with that motto when it comes to guiding the river on a daily basis. You never know when someone will beat you to your favorite section of water, so always have a plan B.

There are times, especially on weekends, when waterways have a ton of pressure on them and you feel there is just nowhere to move. First of all, we are all part of the problem, and second, there is always something that we could have done to avoid fishing crowded waters. One of the best things to do is plan your trips in the evenings. Most guides and anglers generally are off the water by 5 o'clock. This leaves the fish feeling less pressured, and usually some

Fishing the hour before dark can sometimes pay dividends along the Colorado River and its tributaries. Here Rachel Kohler nymph-fishes a run in the last light in hopes of one more fish. BOB DYE

Jeremy Hyatt shows off his skills landing a fish in the river's middle region. Landing fish quickly helps the trout's survival rate, especially in warm-water conditions. BOB DYE

of the best fishing can be found in the evening hours of low light.

Another thing I have found myself doing, or I should say have been forced into doing, is fishing the nonobvious water. There are times when you show up on the water and people are standing in all the obvious spots. Well, that's fine—I would have been there too if I were able. Instead of moving to another location, which is definitely an option, try fishing a section that might be all riffles or change tactics and throw big dries against the river's edge. I have found that pressured fish (big fish) tend to navigate away from highly pressured areas anyways, especially in low water. During the summer, fish can be found throughout the entire stream, in fast riffles, behind every rock, hiding underneath structure, etc.

When fishing the nonobvious water, you are sooner or later going to have to move past another angler. Remember this was his or her water first. I have found that the best way to handle this situation is to simply engage in conversation: "How is your day going?" "How far can I go up and be out of your way?" Usually some short, friendly words are greeted by mutual respect and the problem is solved. If you run into another angler and this is not the case, he or she might have a whole lot of other issues to deal with and it's probably better to just stay away. I have found that common sense usually prevails, and you can find yourself not dealing with the problems of crowded river systems in the first place.

The Colorado River certainly receives its fair share of pressure from anglers, commercial rafting trips, kayakers, drift boats, and just general users of the area. While spring and fall are generally quiet, summer is a different story. First, I should point out that everyone has the right to enjoy the river, whether fishing or just floating for fun. Boat ramps can be congested, especially around the Pumphouse, Radium, and State Bridge areas, and then again around Grizzly Creek and Two Rivers Park. While commercial boat traffic is on a time schedule, anglers are not. Try putting in between the hours of 6 and 8 a.m. or wait until after 10 a.m., when most of the commercial boats have left. One piece of good news is that with the help of the BLM and Eagle County Open Space, new boat ramps have been constructed below State Bridge at Two Bridges and at Horse Creek.

If you show up at a launch/takeout sites during heavy-volume hours, observe the following rules of etiquette:

1. Don't park on the boat ramp and get your gear ready for the day. Taking care of this beforehand will allow a smooth transition from trailer to water and ease congestion.

2. Park in a designated parking spot.
3. Pull your boat or raft upstream after launching. This will allow other boats to put in and keep boat launches running smoothly.
4. When taking your boat out at a ramp, if you see boats ahead of you, wait your turn. Pushing into a crowd of boats furthers the takeout process.
5. After your boat is on the trailer, do not crowd the boat ramp. Pull your trailer away from congestion so other boats can launch or take out.
6. Store the day's trash in a container so that it doesn't blow out on the highway.

Following these simple rules makes outdoor life easy on everyone and makes for a much more enjoyable day.

With the amount of angling pressure the Colorado River receives, I think it's important to discuss proper fish-handling techniques. Using barbless hooks and not playing the fish to exhaustion goes without saying, but during low-water years, parts of the Colorado can get extremely hot. When water temperatures exceed 68 degrees, anglers should halt fishing operations immediately. Playing fish in these temperatures usually results in high mortality rates. Anglers may think that if the trout swam away, it's fine, but it usually will suffer a slow death. On warm-water days, try fishing early in the morning or later in the evening; during the dog days of August, fishing is better during these times anyways.

There are obviously fish photographs in this book, but never were the fish handled to get the shot. Taking photographs is a fun way to remember your trip, but posing with a trout for even 15 seconds is lethal to the fish. When taking photographs, be sure to have your camera ready to go. Leave the fish in the water as long as possible, and try shooting photographs close to the water's surface in an effort to not accidently drop the fish. Following these simple rules will make a better fishery for generations to come.

Taking photos of trout in the net is one way to not harm the fish. Trout that are mishandled have a much lower survival rate. BOB DYE

RESOURCES

Estes Park, CO

Hotels:
Rocky Mountain Park Inn: www
.rockymountainparkinn.com
Campgrounds:
Rocky Mountain National Forest:
www.fs.fed.us/r2/recreation
/camping
Places to Eat and Drink:
Donut Haus: www.donuthaus
-estespark.com
Smokin' Dave's BBQ:
www.smokindavesq.com
Twin Owls Steakhouse:
www.twinowls.net
Fly Shops:
Kirks Fly Shop:
www.kirksflyshop.com
Estes Angler: www.estesangler.com

Grand Lake, CO

Hotels:
Spirit Lake Lodge:
www.spiritlakelodge.com
Americas Best Value:
www.americasbestvalueinn.com
/bestv.cfm?idp=407
Lone Eagle Lodge:
www.loneeaglelodge.com
Campgrounds:
Green Ridge Campground:
www.fs.usda.gov/recarea/arp
/recreation/ohv/recarea
/?recid=28538&actid=29
Places to Eat and Drink:
Roadhouse Bar & Grill: www
.facebook.com/roadhousegl
Cy's Deli: www.cysdeli.com

Granby, CO

Hotels:
Trail Riders Motel: (970) 887-3738
Little Tree Inn:
www.littletreeluxuryinn.com

Places to Eat and Drink:
Ma's Country Cabin and Saloon:
(970) 887-3137
Mustachio's on the Lake:
www.mustachiosonthelake.com
Brickhouse 40: www.brickhouse40
.com

Hot Sulphur Springs, CO

Hotels:
Ute Trail Motel: www.utetrailmotel
.com
Hot Sulphur Springs Resort & Spa:
www.hotsulphursprings.com
The Canyon Motel:
www.canyonmotelcolorado.com
Places to Eat and Drink:
Glory Hole: (970) 725-3237

Kremmling, CO

Hotels:
Allington Inn: www.allingtoninn.com
Places to Eat and Drink:
Moose Cafe: (970) 724-9987
Big Shooter Coffee: (970) 724-3735
Rocky Mountain Bar and Grill:
(970) 724-9219

Eagle, CO

Hotels:
Holiday Inn Express:
www.hiexpress.com
Places to Eat and Drink:
Moe's Original Bar B Que:
www.moesoriginalbbq.com
Red Canyon Cafe:
www.redcanyoncafe.com
Route 6 Cafe: www.routesixcafe.com

Glenwood Springs, CO

Hotels:
Cedar Lodge Motel:
www.cedarlodgemotel.net
Glenwood Suites:
www.ascendcollection.com/hotel
-glenwood_springs-colorado-CO226

Places to Eat and Drink:
Italian Underground:
    www.theitalianunderground.com
Juicy Lucy's Steakhouse:
    www.juicylucyssteakhouse.com
Doc Holliday's:
    www.glenwoodspringsbar.com
Slope & Hatch:
    www.slopeandhatch.net
Fly Shops:
Roaring Fork Anglers:
    www.roaringforkanglers.com
River Shuttles:
Charm Shuttles:
    www.charmcarservice.com/charm
    -shuttles, (970-379 3966)

Winter Park, CO

Hotels:
America's Best Value Sundowner
    Motel: www.americasbestvalueinn
    .com/best
Olympia Lodge:
    www.olympialodge.com
Places to Eat and Drink:
Winter Park Pub: (970) 726-4929
Casa Mexico: (970) 726-9674
Fly Shops:
Mo Henry's Trout Shop:
    www.mohenrys.com

Fraser, CO

Hotels:
Holiday Inn Express: www.ihg.com
    /holidayinnexpress/hotels/us/en/
    fraser/fexco/hoteldetail
Places to Eat and Drink:
Elevation Pizza:
    www.elevationpizzaco.com
Sharky's Eatery:
    www.sharkyseatery.com
El Pacifico Express: (970) 363-7231
Fly Shops:
Winter Park Fly Fisher:
    www.fraserflyshop.com

Minturn, CO

Hotels:
Holiday Inn Vail: www.apexvail.com
Places to Eat and Drink:
Magustos Pizza & Burger Pub:
    www.magustos.com
Minturn Saloon:
    www.minturnsaloon.com
Fly Shops:
Minturn Anglers:
    www.minturnanglers.com
Gore Creek Fly Fisherman:
    www.gorecreekflyfisherman.com

Carbondale, CO

Hotels:
Comfort Inn: www.reservations.com/
    Inn/Carbondale
White House Pizza:
    www.whitehousepizza.com
The Goat: http://thegoatkitchenandbar
    .com
Village Smithy:
    www.villagesmithy.com
Fly Shops:
Crystal Fly Shop:
    www.crystalflyshop.com
Alpine Angling:
    www.roaringforkanglers.com
River Shuttles:
Charm Shuttles:
    www.charmcarservice.com
    /charm-shuttles

Basalt, CO

Hotels:
Basalt Mountain Inn:
    www.basaltmountaininn.com
Aspenalt Lodge: www.aspenalt.com
Places to Eat and Drink:
Sure Thing Burger:
    www.surethingburger.com
Riverside Grill:
    www.riversidegrillbasalt.com
Brick Pony Pub: (970) 279-5021

Fly Shops:
Taylor Creek Fly Shops:
www.taylorcreek.com
Frying Pan Anglers:
www.fryingpananglers.com

Rifle, CO
Hotels:
La Quinta Inn: www.laquintarifle.com
Comfort Inn: www.comfortinn.com
/hotel-rifle-colorado-
Places to Eat and Drink:
Rib City Grill: www.ribcity.com
Base Camp Cafe: (970) 625-0374
Jay's Steakhouse: (970) 625-1435

Breckenridge, CO
Hotels:
The Lodge at Breckenridge:
www.thelodgeatbreckenridge.com
The Wayside Inn:
www.breckwayside.com
Places to Eat and Drink:
Oscar's of Breckenridge:
(970) 453-2167
Briar Rose Chophouse:
www.briarrosechophouse.com
Columbine Cafe: (970) 547-4474
Fly Shops:
Breckenridge Outfitters:
www.breckenridgeoutfitters.com
Mountain Angler:
www.mountainangler.com

Shops and Outfitters
Winter Park-Winter Park Flyfisher:
(970) 726-5231,
jeff@grandflyfishing.com
Mo Henry's Trout Shop:
(970) 531-8213,
mohenrys@hotmail.com
Dillon/Silverthorne-The Colorado
Angler: (970) 513-8055,
contact@thecoloradoangler.com
Cutthroat Anglers: (970) 262-2878,
anglers@fishcolorado.com
Breckenridge-Breckenridge
Outfitters: (970) 453-4135,
info@breckenridgeoutfitters.com
Mountain Angler: (970) 453-4665,
info@mountainangler.com
Vail-Vail Valley Angler:
(970) 926-0900,
info@vailvalleyangler.com
Eagle-Eagle River Angler:
(970) 328-2323
Glenwood Springs-Roaring Fork
Anglers: (970) 945 0180
Alpine Angling: (970) 963-9245
Basalt-Taylor Creek Outfitters:
(970) 927-4374, tcreek@ssv.net
Blue Quill Angler: (303) 674-4700

Index